More Than Conquerors

More Than Conquerors

An Interpretation of the Book of Revelation

William Hendriksen

Published by Baker Books
a division of Baker Publishing Group
P.O. Box 6287, Grand Rapids, MI 49516-6287
www.bakerbooks.com

Paperback edition published 1998

Eighth printing, July 2007

Commemorative cloth edition published 1982 by Baker Book House from the 1962 edition by Tyndale Press, London.

Printed in the United States of America

ISBN 10: 0-8010-5792-2
ISBN 978-0-8010-5792-2

Library of Congress Catalog Card Number: 54-924

CONTENTS

WILLIAM HENDRIKSEN

1900-1982

A commemorative word about William Hendriksen to acknowledge his prodigious writing and profound Christian commitment is a natural response of a grateful publisher. That these comments appear in an edition of *More than Conquerors,* however, is especially appropriate.

Publisher Herman Baker presented the first trade copies of *More than Conquerors* to the author in July 1939. The book has remained in print and is now in its twenty-fifth impression. Its long life parallels William Hendriksen's prolific writing career.

Forty-two years later, William Hendriksen at the age of eighty-one was still writing as intensely and productively as ever—up to within a few months before his death in January, 1982. He was progressing well with his next work, a commentary on First Corinthians, having finished the introduction and first chapter.

The vibrancy of the words "More than Conquerors" was mirrored in William Hendriksen's firm possession of a triumphant biblical faith. The fuller rendering of the apostle's victory cry in Romans 8—"We are more than conquerors through him who loved us"—reverberated in William Hendriksen's tenacious labors to interpret God's Word with clear, rich, and irenic exposition. At his death, it was fitting to see a copy of *More than Conquerors* as the focal point of the floral tribute placed on his casket.

The wide distribution of *More than Conquerors* is evidence of consistent and broadening respect accorded William Hendriksen as a trusted and eminent New Testament scholar. Dr. Hendriksen gained most of his prominence through his commentaries. He began the New Testament Commentary series in 1952 with the first volume of the Gospel of John, and he most recently completed the Book of Romans (1981). As each volume was released, scholars enthusiastically endorsed it. Typical of the statements by reviewers are:

> The volumes in the N.T.C. (New Testament Commentaries) are appealing in style, language, and exposition.

> . . . style is concise, his language clear, and his exposition conservative

> . . . demonstrates his indefatigable energy, his scholarly acumen, and his ardent desire for the proper understanding of the biblical

> revelation of God's sovereign grace in Jesus Christ as understood in the Reformed tradition.
>
> Another noticeable feature of Hendriksen's commentaries is the care he takes to study thoroughly different points of view before drawing his conclusion.
>
> . . . careful exegesis . . .
>
> . . . reflects facility with the grammar and syntax
>
> . . . awareness of the scholarly literature
>
> . . . mature exegetical commentary

Dr. Hendriksen's mastery of languages was a major factor in his incisive exposition. He was fluent in Hebrew as well as Greek (rare among New Testament scholars) and could read in twenty languages. He learned Spanish after he retired from the pastorate. His own Greek translation appears in each of his commentaries, and his familiarity with the theological literature of Germany and Holland added breadth to his expositions.

His linguistic competence prompted involvement as a consultant and translator in the preparation of the *New International Version* of the Bible. During the NIV editorial sessions, Dr. Hendriksen became a close friend of Dr. Edwin H. Palmer, whose high admiration for Hendriksen was published in a 1976 issue of *The Banner,* a magazine of the Christian Reformed Church, the denomination Dr. Hendriksen served. Dr. Palmer seemed to be making certain that William Hendriksen would be a prophet honored "in his own country." The tribute titled "New Testament Giant" began:

> While Dr. William Hendriksen is still hale and hearty, I want to draw the attention of the *Banner* readers to this New Testament Giant. . . . The first thing that comes to my mind when I think of Dr. Hendriksen is his New Testament commentaries. I know of no finer commentaries in the English language. They are so superb that every church ought to buy a complete set for its pastor, if he does not already have one.

Dr. Palmer continued, summarizing the features of the commentaries and asserted that they:

> assume that the Bible is the completely authoritative, inerrant Word of God
>
> presuppose the Reformed faith

have meat without being pedantic

are well organized

exhibit a wholesome emotional piety

Writing verse-by-verse commentaries, some of which have more than a thousand pages, at such a steady pace reveals Dr. Hendriksen's driving will power and unwavering self-discipline. These traits emerged in part out of the fabric of his early family life. William's perfectionistic bent had its parental model in his father, who by trade was a carpenter (and an excellent one), but one who also expressed a highly creative nature as a talented woodcarver. William Hendriksen remembers his father producing beautiful carvings, "working on them for weeks, often for months. When they were finished he would give them away." As far as William knew, his father never accepted money for any of them.

William's penchant for hard work came to him environmentally as well. Of hardy immigrant stock, he came at age ten with his family from the Netherlands to settle in Kalamazoo, Michigan. Family dreams of prosperity by starting fresh in America remained elusive—the family was large (William was the youngest of eight children) and the country was gripped by an economic depression. Older children were expected to work for the family's financial survival. The livelihood of William's father was so precariously small that at times the master woodcarver had no recourse other than to apply his skills doing minor repair work on items such as clocks and sewing machines.

William did his share to help support the family. After passing the eighth grade, he briefly attended a new high school, which folded several months after classes started in the fall. William went to work, finding jobs wherever he could. He began as a produce peddler and later worked in a gold-leaf printing company, in a radiator repair shop, in a grocery store as a clerk, and in a stationery factory.

A desire to become a minister of the gospel came early to William—even before his family emigrated from the Netherlands. Throughout his life, Dr. Hendriksen believed that when he was five or six years old God planted in his heart a resolve to become a minister.

> The story of God's love toward sinners, and of the cross of Christ, as told by excellent Sunday school teachers and, of course, also by my parents, had impressed me deeply. I wanted everybody to know

about it. I loved our minister. So I was entirely sincere in wishing to become a preacher.

The intensity of this feeling for the ministry never faded from William's heart. His father, however, did not encourage this dream of his youngest child. This is surprising since both his mother (who died when William was sixteen) and father taught their eight children to love the gospel. Furthermore, the lives of his parents exemplified loving service as well as believing correct Christian doctrine. The home was hospitable, and in personal ways his parents frequently helped those with special needs. When he was a teenager, William held this conversation with his father:

> "I'm still planning to study for the ministry." My father's response was brief and decisive: *"Daar komp toch niks van"* [Nothing will ever come of that].

Nonetheless William pursued his goal of preparing for the ministry. On the job by day, he studied at night by enrolling in a Carnegie college correspondence course, which covered the first two years of high school. William completed this course in just nine months. At age eighteen he accepted a one-semester appointment to teach fourth-graders at a Christian school in Roseland, Chicago. In January he started in his second teaching position—a one-room, eight-grade school near Hospers, Iowa. He continued with education by correspondence (with state-approved courses) to qualify for permanent certification for teaching. Of this phase of young Hendriksen's education, Dr. Edwin Palmer relates that William studied for these courses in the winter

> . . . wearing an overcoat in an unheated, rented room. Such self-discipline continued even into his state of retirement, where he maintained a regular schedule for work, starting the day at five in the morning.

At the age of twenty, William Hendriksen was accepted at Calvin College where he enjoyed science subjects—especially chemistry—along with his B.A. courses in languages and history. One college science professor attempted to lure William into lecturing on organic chemistry as an assistant professor, advising William against a career in the ministry because of his weak voice. Teaching on the college level was tempting, but William declined the offer and entered Calvin Seminary. With seminary training completed in 1927, William Hendriksen served large pastorates in

Michigan for the next sixteen years. He also used this time for advanced studies, earning his Master of Theology degree at Calvin Seminary and a doctorate at Princeton Seminary. In 1943 he became Professor of New Testament at Calvin Theological Seminary and served in this capacity for nine years. Dr. Hendriksen then reentered the pastoral ministry, continuing until his retirement at age sixty-five.

William Hendriksen was married thirty-five years to Rena Baker, who died in 1960. They were the parents of three children. In 1961 he married again. For the rest of his life, he and his second wife Reta worked together on the commentary ministry.

Reta was a loyal and loving wife, and her proficiency in typing and editorial assistance was also highly valued by Dr. Hendriksen:

> One can well imagine what this qualification of hers meant to me in my work as an author. Never could I have accomplished half as much had it not been for the constant help of Reta. . . . Capability, sympathy, warmth, and wisdom—all these are found in her in a very high degree.

William Hendriksen pursued his course actively up to the final months of his life when his last surgery drained most of his strength. A. A. Koning concluded his tribute with these words:

> Even as his last illness began to lay hold on him, he received a request from England to come and speak. But he had to turn it down—he wanted to finish his writing. Now he is no longer gazing darkly into a mirror but seeing face to face.

Throughout the various stages of his career—whether pastoring, teaching, or writing, William Hendriksen remained in a profound sense a supreme educator. Part of the genius of his work was his unique ability to encase his commanding scholarship in simplicity and warmth that enlightened and inspired both advanced and beginning students of God's Word.

The publications by Dr. William Hendriksen include:

More than Conquerors
Bible Survey
Lectures on the Last Things
Bible on the Life Hereafter
Israel and the Bible
Israel in Prophecy
Survey of the Bible
Beginner's Book of Doctrine
Covenant of Grace
New Testament Commentary
(both separate and combined editions are listed)

Matthew
Mark
Luke
John (Vol. 1)
John (Vol. 2)
Romans (Vol. 1)
Romans (Vol. 2)
Galatians
Ephesians
Philippians
Colossians and Philemon
I & II Thessalonians
I & II Timothy and Titus
John (combined)
Romans (combined)
Galatians and Ephesians (combined)
Philippians, Colossians, and Philemon (combined)
I & II Thessalonians, I & II Timothy and Titus (combined)

CHAPTER ONE

PURPOSE, THEME AND AUTHORSHIP OF REVELATION

IN form, symbolism, purpose and meaning the book of Revelation is beautiful beyond description. Where in all literature do we find anything that excels the majestic description of the Son of man walking in the midst of the seven golden lampstands (Rev. 1: 12–20), or the vivid portrayal of the Christ, Faithful and True, going forth unto victory, seated upon a white horse, arrayed with a garment sprinkled with blood, followed by the armies of heaven (19: 11–16)? Where, again, do we find a sharper contrast than that between the doom of Babylon on the one hand, and the joy of Jerusalem the Golden on the other (18: 19; 21: 22)? And where are the throne set in heaven and the blessedness of heavenly life depicted in a manner more serenely simple, yet beautiful in its very simplicity (4: 2—5:14; 7: 13–17)? What a wealth of comfort; what an insight into the future; above all, what an unveiling of the love of God are contained in the words of the prophecy of this book!

I. THE PURPOSE OF THE BOOK

In the main, the purpose of the book of Revelation is to comfort the militant Church in its struggle against the forces of evil. It is full of help and comfort for persecuted and suffering Christians. To them is given the assurance that God sees their tears (7: 17; 21: 4); their prayers are influential in world affairs (8: 3, 4) and their death is precious in His sight. Their final victory is assured (15: 2); their blood will be avenged (19: 2); their Christ lives and reigns for ever and for ever. He governs the world in the interest of His Church (5: 7, 8). He is coming again to take His people to Himself in 'the marriage supper of the Lamb' and to live with them for ever in a rejuvenated universe (21: 22).

As we think of the glorious hope of the second coming, our hearts are filled with joy; our souls are consumed with a breathless impatience; our eyes attempt to pierce the dark clouds which veil the future, hoping that the glorious descent of the Son of man may burst upon the view. It is a longing which gushes into words: 'And the Spirit and the bride say, Come. And he that hears, let him say, Come' (22: 17).

But as we consider these truths we realize that already He is with us—with us *in the Spirit,* walking in the midst of the seven golden lampstands (1: 12–20). 'And he laid his right hand upon me, saying, Fear not; I am the first and the last, and the living one; and I was dead, and behold, I am alive for evermore, and I have the keys of Death and Hades.' We are, indeed, more than conquerors through Him that loved us!

II. THE THEME OF THE BOOK

The theme is the victory of Christ and of His Church over the dragon (Satan) and his helpers. The Apocalypse is meant to show us that things are not what they *seem.* The beast that comes up out of the abyss *seems* to be victorious. He 'makes war with them, overcomes them, and kills them. And their dead bodies lie in the street of the great city which spiritually is called Sodom and Egypt, where also their Lord was crucified. And from among the peoples and tribes and tongues and nations do men look upon their dead bodies three days and a half, and suffer not their dead bodies to be laid in a tomb. And they that dwell on the earth rejoice over them, and make merry; and they send gifts one to another; because these two prophets tormented them that dwell on the earth' (11: 7–10). But this rejoicing is premature. In reality it is the believer who triumphs. 'And after the three days and a half the breath of life from God entered into them, and they stood upon their feet; and great fear fell upon them that beheld them . . . the dominion over the world became the dominion of our Lord and of his Christ; and he shall reign for ever and ever' (11: 11,15).

Throughout the prophecies of this wonderful book Christ is pictured as the Victor, the Conqueror (1: 18; 2: 8; 5: 9 ff.; 6: 2; 11: 15; 12: 9 ff.; 14: 1,14; 15: 2 ff.; 19: 16; 20: 4; 22: 3). He conquers death, Hades, the dragon, the beast, the false prophet, and the men who worship the beast. *He* is victorious; as a result, so are *we,* even when we seem to be hopelessly defeated.

Let us look, for instance, at the great company of believers who are portrayed in chapter 7. Their garments were filthy, but they are washed and made white in the blood of the Lamb.

They were in 'great tribulation', but have come out of it (7: 14). They were killed, but they stand upon their feet (11: 11). They are persecuted by the dragon, the beast, and the false prophet, but in the end we see them standing victorious on Mount Zion. Rather, we see the Lamb, and with Him a hundred and forty-four thousand, having His name, and the name of His Father written on their foreheads (14: 1). They triumph over the beast (15: 2).

Does it *seem* as if their prayers are not heard (6: 10)? The judgments sent upon the earth are God's answer to their pleading (8: 3–5). These very prayers constitute the key that will unlock the mysteries of any sound philosophy of history.

Do they *seem* to be defeated? In reality they reign! Yes, they reign upon the earth (5: 10), in heaven with Christ a thousand years (20: 4), in the new heaven and earth for ever and ever (22: 5).

And what happens to those who *seem* to be conquerors, the dragon (12: 3), the beast (13: 1), the false prophet (13: 11) and Babylon (14: 8)? They are defeated—and in exactly the reverse order. Babylon falls in 18: 2, the beast and the false prophet are horribly punished in 19: 20 and the dragon is confined to unending torment in 20: 10.

In short, the theme of this book is stated most gloriously and completely in these words: 'These shall war against the Lamb, and the Lamb shall conquer them, for he is Lord of lords, and King of kings; and they also shall conquer that are with him called and chosen and faithful' (17: 14).

III. THE PEOPLE TO WHOM THE BOOK IS ADDRESSED

On my desk lies a recently published commentary on the Apocalypse. It is a very 'interesting' book. It views the Apocalypse as a kind of history written beforehand. It discovers in this last book of the Bible copious and detailed references to Napoleon, wars in the Balkans, the great European War of 1914–1918, the German ex-emperor Wilhelm, Hitler and Mussolini, and so on. But these kinds of explanations, and others like them, must at once be dismissed.[1] For what possible good would the suffering and severely persecuted Christians of John's day have derived from specific and detailed predictions

[1] For a descriptive note on the various theories of interpretation see M. C. Tenney, *New Testament Survey* (I.V.F.), pp. 387 ff.; and L. Morris, art. 'Book of Revelation' in *The New Bible Dictionary* (I.V.F.).

concerning European conditions which would prevail some *two thousand years later*?

A sound interpretation of the Apocalypse must take as its starting-point the position that the book was intended for believers living in John's day and age. The book owes its origin, at least in part, to contemporary conditions. It is God's answer to the prayers and tears of severely persecuted Christians scattered about in the cities of Asia Minor.[1]

Nevertheless, although it is true that we must take as our starting-point the age in which John lived, and must even emphasize the fact that the conditions which actually prevailed during the last decade of the first century AD furnished the immediate occasion for this prophecy, we should give equal prominence to the fact that this book was intended *not only* for those who first read it, but for all believers throughout this entire dispensation.

We submit the following arguments for this position.

First, the affliction to which the Church was subjected in the days of the apostle John is typical of the persecution which true believers must endure throughout this entire dispensation (2 Tim. 3: 12), and especially just before Christ's second coming (Mt. 24: 29,30).

Secondly, many of the predictions in which the book abounds (*e.g.* the 'seals', 'trumpets' and 'bowls') concern principles and happenings which are so broad in their scope that they cannot be confined to one definite year or period of years, but span the centuries, reaching out to the great consummation.

Thirdly, the letters in chapters 2 and 3 are addressed to the seven churches. Seven is the number which symbolizes completeness. Its use here indicates that the Church as a whole is in mind and that the admonitions and consolations of this book were meant for Christian believers throughout the centuries.

Finally, all those who read and study this book in any age are called blessed (1: 3). As at the beginning, so also at the close of the book the author addresses himself, not merely to one group of men living in one decade, but to 'every man that hears the words of the prophecy of this book' (22: 18).

IV. THE AUTHOR OF THE BOOK

The author tells us that his name is *John* (1: 1, 4, 9; 22: 8). But the question is, which John? For some deny that John, the

[1] See chapter 6, pp. 44 f., for a fuller discussion of this point.

beloved disciple, wrote the Apocalypse. This is partly due to the fact that whereas the author of the Fourth Gospel and the three love-Epistles never mentions his own name, the author of the Apocalypse tells us that his name is John.

Again, it is pointed out that there is a striking difference between the style and general tone of the Gospel and Epistles on the one hand, and Revelation on the other. But read the Gospel of John and then read the Apocalypse. Do you notice the difference? In the former the ideas flow smoothly; in the latter they are introduced abruptly—you never know what the author is going to talk about next. The former emphasizes God's love; the latter—so it is said—stresses His stern justice. The former describes the inner condition of the heart; the latter dwells on the external course of events. The former is written in beautiful, idiomatic Greek; the latter is written in what has been called 'rugged, Hebraistic, barbarous' Greek.[1]

It is also claimed that there is a marked difference between the *doctrine* of the Gospel and the Apocalypse. The former is broad-minded, universalistic; it preaches the 'whosoever' gospel and the doctrine of salvation by grace. The latter, it is said, is narrow-minded, particularistic; it is Jewish in its doctrine of salvation and it stresses the necessity of good works.[2]

Finally, it is pointed out that, as early as the third century AD, Dionysius of Alexandria ascribed the book of Revelation to 'another John', a view that was adopted by the ecclesiastical historian Eusebius.

Now some are convinced by these arguments that some John other than the beloved disciple wrote the Apocalypse.[3] They still believe that John, the apostle, was responsible for the Fourth Gospel. Others accept the Johannine authorship of the Apocalypse but claim that some other person—maybe another John, maybe not even a John—wrote the Gospel.[4] And, of course, there are the radicals who deny that the apostle John wrote either the Gospel or the Apocalypse.[5]

But let us examine the arguments for a moment. The first impresses one by its weakness. Surely the very fact that the author of the Apocalypse merely calls himself *John* indicates that he was very well known, not only in one particular locality

[1] Eusebius, *Ecclesiastical History*, vii. 25.
[2] W. Beyschlag, *New Testament Theology*, II, p. 362.
[3] See for example the writings of F. Bleek and J. Neander.
[4] This view is held by the Tübingen school.
[5] Bousset, Harnack, Holtzmann, and Moffatt, are amongst these.

but throughout the churches of Asia. When he simply called himself *John*, without any additional designation, everybody knew just who was meant. Does not the conclusion seem warranted that this person who was so well known must have been the apostle John? Suppose the author of the book which you are now reading simply called himself William; do you think for a minute that everybody would immediately guess who wrote it? We are thoroughly convinced that there was only one John who did not need to add 'the apostle', for the very reason that he was known as the apostle! Besides, the author does not call himself *apostle* for the simple reason that he wrote this book in the capacity of *seer*, to whom visions were revealed (*cf.* Jn. 15: 27; Acts 1: 22–23; 1 Cor. 9: 1).

The difference in grammar, in style and in general tone must be admitted. But does this mean that John, the apostle, cannot have written the Apocalypse? In our opinion it does not. How, then, shall we account for this difference? Some there are who hold that when John wrote the Gospel he had assistants, perhaps the elders in Ephesus; and that the absence of these assistants when John was in Patmos would account for the peculiar grammar and style of the Apocalypse.[1]

Other elements may enter into the explanation. First, we should not exaggerate these differences in style and language. Between the Gospel and the Apocalypse there is also a strong body of *resemblances*—a fact that, of late, many are beginning to emphasize. These similarities are striking. They are to be found even in peculiar grammatical constructions and in characteristic expressions. (*Cf.* Jn. 3: 36 with Rev. 22: 17; Jn. 10: 18 with Rev. 2: 27; Jn. 20: 12 with Rev. 3: 4; Jn. 1: 1 with Rev. 19: 13; and Jn. 1: 29 with Rev. 5: 6[2].)

Again, with reference to the style, should we expect to find the same style in a history of events (the Gospel), a personal letter (the Epistles), and the Apocalypse or unveiling (Revelation)? In this connection, let us not forget that when John wrote the last book of the Bible, his soul was in such a condition of deep, inner emotion, surprise and ecstasy (for he was 'in the Spirit'), that his earlier, Jewish training may have exerted itself more forcibly and may even have influenced his style and language.

[1] An interesting explanation is given in A. Pieters, *The Lamb, the Woman, and the Dragon*, pp. 18 ff. See also A. T. Robertson, *Word Pictures*, VI, p. 274.

[2] For further similarities between the Gospel and the Apocalypse, see J. P. Lange, *The Revelation of John* (*Commentary of the Holy Scriptures*, The New Testament, X), pp. 56 ff.

We feel certain that the transcendent nature of the subject-matter, the deeply emotional state of the author when he received and wrote these visions, and his abundant use of the Old Testament—Hebrew and Greek[1]—are responsible to a large extent for the differences in style which remain after the striking similarities have been taken into account.

We need not dwell at length on the so-called difference in doctrinal emphasis. The simple fact is that the Fourth Gospel and the Apocalypse do not clash on even a single point. In fact, the agreement in doctrine is remarkable.[2] The Gospel calls Jesus 'the Lamb of God' (*amnos*) in John 1: 29; so does the Apocalypse (*arnion*), twenty-nine times. The Epistles and the Gospel use the title 'the Logos' with reference to our Lord (Jn. 1: 1 ff.; 1 Jn. 1: 1); so does the Apocalypse (19: 13). The Gospel represents Christ as the pre-temporal, eternal Being (1: 1 ff.); so does the Apocalypse (22: 13; *cf.* 5: 12,13). The Gospel of John ascribes man's salvation to the sovereign grace of God and to the blood of Jesus Christ (1: 29; 3: 3; 5: 24; 10: 10,11); so does the Apocalypse (7: 14; 12: 11; 21: 6; 22: 17)—most emphatically. And the 'whosoever' doctrine is found in both books (Jn. 3: 36; Rev. 7: 9; 22: 17).

There are no doctrinal differences!

Finally, with reference to the opinion of Dionysius, already quoted, it should be clear that this view rests upon a misreading of a very careful statement of Papias,[3] and was probably influenced by opposition to Chiliasm[4] which sought to justify itself by an appeal to the book of Revelation.[5]

The early Church is almost unanimous in ascribing the Revelation to the apostle John. That was the opinion of Justin Martyr (*c.* AD 140), of Irenaeus (*c.* AD 180), who was a disciple of a disciple of the apostle John, of the Muratorian Canon (*c.* AD 200), of Clement of Alexandria (*c.* AD 200), of Tertullian of Carthage (*c.* AD 220), of Origen of Alexandria (*c.* AD 223) and of Hippolytus (*c.* AD 240).[6]

[1] See A. T. Robertson, *The Minister and His Greek New Testament*, p. 113.

[2] For a survey of this whole subject, see H. Gebhardt, *The Doctrine of the Apocalypse*, especially pp. 304 ff.; and G. B. Stevens, *The Theology of the New Testament*, pp. 536 ff., 547.

[3] See the discussion in R. C. H. Lenski, *Interpretation of St. John's Revelation*, pp. 8 ff.

[4] From Gk. *chilioi*, '1000'; a term used to describe eschatological views which are strongly millennarian in character.

[5] N. B. Stonehouse, *The Apocalypse in the Ancient Church*, p. 151.

[6] *Ante-Nicene Fathers*, I–III. See also N. B. Stonehouse, *op. cit.*, pp. 153 ff.

When we add to all this that according to a very strong tradition the apostle John was banished to the isle of Patmos (*cf.* 1: 9), and that he spent the closing years of his life at Ephesus, to which the first of the seven letters of the Apocalypse was addressed (2: 1), the conclusion that the last book of the Bible was written by 'the disciple whom Jesus loved' is inescapable.

V. THE DATE OF THE BOOK

The question now arises, when did John write the Apocalypse? In the year 69 (or even earlier), or must we reverse the figure and make it 96 (or perhaps 95)? One cannot find a single really cogent argument in support of the earlier date. The arguments produced are based on late and unreliable testimonies, on the wholly imaginary idea that John did not yet know his Greek when he wrote the Apocalypse, and on a very questionable literal interpretation of certain passages which most certainly have a symbolical meaning. Thus, for example, we are told that the Temple at Jerusalem was still standing when the Apocalypse was written, for 11: 1 reads: 'Rise and measure the temple of God.'

The late date has very strong support. Says Irenaeus: 'For that (the apocalyptic vision) was seen not a very long time since, but almost in our own day, toward the end of Domitian's reign.' Again he says: '. . . the church in Ephesus, founded by Paul, and lived in by John until the time of Trajan (AD 98–117), is a true witness of the tradition of the apostles.'[1]

When, in connection with these strong and definite evidences, we remember that the Apocalypse reflects an age in which Ephesus has already lost its first love; Sardis is already 'dead'; Laodicea—which was destroyed by an earthquake during Nero's reign—has been rebuilt and is boasting of its spiritual wealth (3: 17); John has been 'banished'—a very common form of persecution during Domitian's reign; the Church has already endured persecutions in the past (20: 4); and the Roman Empire, as such, has become the great antagonist of the Church (17: 9); when we remember all these facts we are forced to the conclusion that the late date (AD 95 or 96) is correct.[2] The

[1] *Ante-Nicene Fathers*, I, pp. 416, 559.

[2] For the earlier date, however, see H. Cowles, *The Revelation of St. John*, pp. 17 ff. Amongst those who support the late date are Alford, Godet, Moffatt, Ramsay, Swete, Warfield and L. Berkhof in his *New Testament Introduction*, pp. 347 f.

Apocalypse was written toward the end of Domitian's reign by the apostle John.

Yet the real author is not John but the Almighty God Himself. 'The revelation of Jesus Christ, *which God gave him* . . . and he sent and signified it by his angel unto his servant John . . .'(1: 1). To be sure, John, the apostle, wrote the Revelation. But God, through Christ, was the real Author. Therefore what this book predicts is not the product of human fancy, prone to error, but the revelation of the mind and purpose of God concerning the history of the Church.

At Copenhagen, among the many noble sculptures of Thorwaldsen, there is one of the apostle John. His countenance is suffused with the serenity of heaven. He is actually looking up to heaven. His writing-tablet is before him. In his hand is his pen. But the apostle's pen does not touch the tablet. He will not venture on a single word until it is given to him from above.[1]

[1] See A. Plummer, *The Book of Revelation* (*Pulpit Commentary*), p. 150.

CHAPTER TWO

GENERAL ANALYSIS

I. THE SEVEN PARALLEL SECTIONS

1. *Christ in the midst of the lampstands* (1: 1–3: 22)

THE central theme of the first three chapters of Revelation seems to be Christ in the midst of the seven golden lampstands. These lampstands represent the seven churches (1: 20). To each church John is directed to write a letter (see chapters 2 and 3). As this number seven occurs again and again in the Apocalypse and is everywhere symbolical of completeness, we may safely take it for granted that such is the case here, and that it indicates the entire Church throughout the full span of its existence to the very end of the world. Thus interpreted, each individual church is, as it were, a type, *not* indicating one definite period in history, but describing conditions which are constantly repeated in the actual life of the various congregations.[1] Therefore this section appears to span the entire dispensation, from Christ's first coming to save His people (1: 5) to His second coming to judge all nations (1: 7). The last of these seven letters is written to the church at Laodicea. It is evident that chapter 4 introduces a new—though closely related—subject.

2. *The vision of heaven and the seals* (4: 1–7: 17)

Chapters 4–7 constitute the next natural division of the book. Chapter 4 describes the One who is sitting upon the throne and the worship of those who surround Him. In the right hand of the Lord there is a book sealed with seven seals (5: 1). The Lamb takes this book and receives adoration. From chapter 6 we learn that the Lamb opens the seals one by one. Between the sixth and the seventh seals we have the vision of the one hundred and forty-four thousand who were sealed and of the countless multitude standing before the throne.

[1] See W. Milligan, *The Book of Revelation* (*Expositor's Bible*), VI, p. 836; E. H. Plumptre, *The Epistles to the Seven Churches*, p. 9; W. M. Ramsay, *The Letters to the Seven Churches of Asia*, pp. 30, 177 ff.; R. C. Trench, *Commentary on the Epistles to the Seven Churches in Asia*, pp. 59 ff.; C. F. Wishart, *The Book of Day*, p. 22.

It should be carefully noted that this section also covers the entire dispensation, from the first to the second coming of Christ. The very first reference to Christ pictures Him as having been slain and as now ruling from heaven (5: 5,6). Towards the end of this section the final judgment is introduced. Notice the impression of the second coming on unbelievers. 'And they say to the mountains and to the rocks, Fall on us and hide us from the face of the One sitting on the throne, and from the wrath of the Lamb! For it came, the day, the great one, of their wrath; and who is able to stand?' (6: 16,17). Now notice the bliss of believers. 'They shall hunger no more, neither thirst any more; neither shall the sun fall upon them, nor any heat; for the Lamb that is in the midst of the throne shall be their shepherd, and shall lead them to life's springs of water; and God shall wipe away every tear out of their eyes' (7: 16,17). This is a picture of the entire Church triumphant, gathered out of all the nations and thus, in its entirety, standing before the throne and before the Lamb, an ideal which is not realized until the day of the great consummation. We have again spanned the entire gospel age.

3. *The seven trumpets* (8: 1–11: 19)

The next section consists of chapters 8–11. Its central theme is the seven trumpets that affect the world. What happens to the Church is described in chapters 10 and 11 (the angel with the little book, the two witnesses). Also at the close of this section there is a very clear reference to the final judgment. 'The dominion over the world became the dominion of our Lord, and of his Christ: and he shall reign for ever and ever.' '. . . And the nations were wroth, and thy wrath came, and the time of the dead to be judged . . .' (11: 15,18). Having reached the end of the dispensation, the vision ends.

4. *The persecuting dragon* (12: 1–14: 20)

This brings us to chapters 12–14: the woman and the Man-child persecuted by the dragon and his helpers. This section also covers the entire dispensation. It begins with a very clear reference to the birth of the Saviour (12: 5). The dragon threatens to devour the Man-child. The Child is caught up to God and to His throne. The dragon now persecutes the woman (12: 13). As his agents, he employs the beast coming up out of the sea (13: 1) and the beast coming up out of the earth (13: 11,12) and the great harlot, Babylon (14: 8). This section, too, closes with a stirring description of Christ's second coming in judgment. 'And I saw, and behold, a white cloud; and on the cloud I saw one sitting like unto a son of man, having on his head a golden crown, and in his hand a sharp sickle. . . . And he that sat on the cloud cast his sickle upon the earth; and the earth was reaped' (14: 14,16).

5. *The seven bowls* (15:1–16: 21)

The next section comprises chapters 15 and 16 and describes the bowls of wrath. Here, too, we have a very clear reference to the final judgment and events that will take place in connection with it. Thus we read in 16: 20, 'And every island fled away, and the mountains were not found.'

6. *The fall of Babylon* (17: 1–19: 21)

Next comes a very vivid description of the fall of Babylon and the punishment inflicted upon the beast and the false prophet. Notice the picture of Christ's coming unto judgment (19: 11 ff.). 'And I saw the heaven opened; and behold, a white horse, and he that sat thereon called Faithful and True; and in righteousness he judges and does battle. . . .'

7. *The great consummation* (20: 1–22: 21)

This brings us to the final section, chapters 20–22, for Revelation 20: 1 definitely begins a new section and introduces a new subject.[1] This new subject is the devil's doom. A comparison, moreover, with chapter 12 reveals the fact that at the beginning of chapter 20 we are once more standing on the threshold of the new dispensation. While in 12: 9 we are told that in connection with Christ's ascension and coronation the devil is *cast down*, here in 20: 2, 3 we read that he is *bound* for a thousand years after being cast into the abyss. The thousand years are followed by the little season during which Satan is loosed out of his prison (20: 7). This, in turn, is followed by a description of the final overthrow of Satan in connection with Christ's coming in judgment (20: 10,11 ff.). At this coming the present universe, fleeing away, makes room for the new heaven and earth, the new Jerusalem (20: 11 ff.).

A careful reading of the book of Revelation has made it clear that the book consists of seven sections, and that these seven sections run parallel to one another. Each of them spans the

[1] See chapter XIV, p. 184.

entire dispensation from the first to the second coming of Christ. This period is viewed now from one aspect, now from another.[1]

II. OTHER ARGUMENTS FOR PARALLELISM

There is another line of reasoning which confirms our position that each of the seven sections extends from the beginning to the end of the new dispensation and that the seven run parallel to one another.[2] Different sections ascribe the same duration to the period described. According to the third cycle (chapters 8–11) the main period here described is one of forty-two months (11: 2), or twelve hundred and sixty days (11: 3). Now, it is a remarkable fact that we find that same period of time in the next section (chapters 12–14), namely, twelve hundred and sixty days (12: 6), or a time and times and half a time ($3\frac{1}{2}$ years) (12: 14). The three designations—forty-two months, twelve hundred and sixty days, time and times and half a time—are exactly equivalent. So the section on the trumpets (chapters 8–11) must run parallel with that which describes the battle between Christ and the dragon (chapters 12–14).

A careful study of chapter 20 will reveal that this chapter describes a period which is synchronous with that of chapter 12. Therefore by this method of reasoning, parallelism is vindicated.

Each section gives us a description of the entire gospel age, from the first to the second coming of Christ, and is rooted in Israel's history under the old dispensation to which there are frequent references.

We have indicated that the section on the trumpets (chapters 8–11) is parallel with that on the woman and the dragon (chapters 12–14) and with the final section (20–22), which also extends beyond it (in chapters 21, 22). We shall now prove that this same section (chapters 8–11) has every appearance of being parallel with that on the bowls of wrath (chapters 15, 16). Notice, therefore, that the first trumpet (8: 7) affects the earth; so does the first bowl (16: 2). The second trumpet affects the sea; so does the second bowl. The third trumpet refers to the rivers; so does the third bowl. The fourth, in both cases, refers

[1] This view, in one form or another, is adopted by R. C. H. Lenski, *op. cit.*, pp. 216, 240, 350, 358; S. L. Morris, *The Drama of Christianity*, p. 26; M. F. Sadler, *The Revelation of St. John the Divine*, pp. xvi. ff. See further B. B. Warfield, *Biblical Doctrines*, pp. 645, 661.

[2] Although the visions describe the *new* dispensation, they have the *old* dispensation as their starting-point. *Cf.*, *e.g.*, 12: 1–4; 17: 10; 20: 3 ('that he should deceive the nations *no more*').

to the sun. The fifth refers to the pit of the abyss or to the throne of the beast, the sixth to Euphrates, and the seventh to the second coming in judgment.[1]

Again, notice that the fourth section (chapters 12–14) introduces, as the enemies of Christ and His Church, the dragon, the two beasts, and the harlot (Babylon). These four arise together. It is but natural to infer that they go down together. This becomes clear when we realize that the meaning of the beasts and the harlot, Babylon, is as follows: The beast that comes up out of the sea is Satan's persecution of Christians, embodied in world-governments and directed against the *bodies* of believers. In John's day this was the Roman government.

The beast that arises out of the earth is Satan's antichristian religion which aimed to deceive the minds and enslave the wills of believers. At the time when these visions appeared to John, that beast out of the earth was incorporated in the pagan religion and emperor-worship of Rome.

The great harlot, Babylon, is Satan's antichristian seduction, which strove to steal the hearts and pervert the morals of believers. At that time the harlot revealed herself as the city of Rome. So, when Satan falls, the beasts and the harlot also fall. They rise together; they go down together. The sixth section (chapters 17–19) describes the fall of the great harlot, Babylon (chapters 17, 18), and of the beasts (19: 20); while the seventh cycle describes the fall of Satan (20: 10), and his final defeat in the day of judgment. The one final judgment upon these four enemies—the dragon, the beast out of the sea, the beast out of the earth, and the great harlot—is described in two separate sections. Therefore these two must be parallel. Each describes a period which extends to the same final conflict, the same last judgment when all the enemies of Christ and His Church will receive their final and never-ending punishment.[2]

In this very connection there is another strong argument for the position that the sections run parallel, as each ends with the coming of the Lord in judgment. The evidence to which we now refer is somewhat obscured by our English versions. The section on the bowls of wrath (chapters 15, 16) ends with a reference to a battle. (See 16: 14 where this conflict is called the battle of the great day of God, the Almighty.) The next section (chapters 17–19) again ends with a battle scene. (See 19: 19.) According to the original this is the same battle which

[1] S. L. Morris, *op. cit.*, p. 64.
[2] R. C. H. Lenski, *op. cit.*, p. 553.

was mentioned in 16: 14, for we read 'gathered together to make battle against him'. Finally, in the closing section (chapters 20–22), we once more read 'to gather them together to battle'. (See 20: 8.) All three sections, therefore, describe events which lead up to the same great battle of Jehovah. They are parallel.

The seven sections are parallel. Our final argument in support of the parallelistic position is the fact that we find exactly the same thing in the prophecies of Daniel, which has been called the Apocalypse of the Old Testament. Thus the parts of Nebuchadnezzar's dream (chapter 2) correspond exactly with the four beasts of Daniel's dream (chapter 7).[1] The same period of time is covered twice, and is seen from various aspects.

The division of the Apocalypse into seven sections[2] is favoured by many authors, although there is no unanimity with respect to the exact boundaries of each section.[3] We favour the division given, with slight variations, by L. Berkhof, S. L. Morris, B. B. Warfield, and others. It is by far the most natural. It is very clearly provided by the book itself, each section ending, as we have shown, with at least a reference to the coming of Christ in judgment. This is true even with respect to the final section (chapters 20–22; see 22: 20), though this reaches out beyond the final judgment and describes the new heaven and earth. (*Cf.* 7: 9 ff.) Moreover, if interpreted in this way, each section embodies a theme that can be easily distinguished from all the others. Our division is as follows:

1. Christ in the midst of the seven golden lampstands (1–3).
2. The book with seven seals (4–7).
3. The seven trumpets of judgment (8–11).
4. The woman and the Man-child persecuted by the dragon and his helpers (the beast and the harlot) (12–14).
5. The seven bowls of wrath (15, 16).
6. The fall of the great harlot and of the beasts (17–19).
7. The judgment upon the dragon (Satan) followed by the new heaven and earth, new Jerusalem (20–22).

[1] S. L. Morris, *op. cit.*, p. 27; W. M. Taylor, *Daniel the Beloved*, p. 124.

[2] For one of many other systems of division, see H. B. Swete, *The Apocalypse of St. John*, pp. xxxiii and xliv.

[3] The varying systems of division into these seven sections will be found in L. Berkhof, *op. cit.*, p. 339; H. B. Swete (for Ewald's division), *op. cit.*, p. xlv; P. Mauro, *The Patmos Visions*, pp. 11 f.; W. Milligan, *op. cit.*, *passim*; S. L. Morris, *op. cit.*, p. 29; M. F. Sadler, *op. cit.*, pp. xvi ff.; C. F. Wishart, *op. cit.*, p. 30; B. B. Warfield, *op. cit.*, p. 645 note.

We are now ready to formulate the first proposition.

PROPOSITION I. *The book of Revelation consists of seven sections. They are parallel and each spans the entire new dispensation, from the first to the second coming of Christ.*

III. THE TWO MAJOR DIVISIONS

According to the opinion of many commentators, the seven sections fall into two groups.[1] Chapter 12: 1 (or 11: 15) seems to be the point where the first group or series of visions ends and the second begins.[2] In the first group (chapters 1–11) we see the struggle among men, that is, between believers and unbelievers. The world attacks the Church but the Church is avenged, protected, and victorious. In the second group of visions (chapters 12–22) we are shown that this struggle on earth has a deeper background. It is the outward manifestation of the devil's attack upon the Man-child. The dragon attacks the Christ. Repulsed, he directs all his fury against the Church. As his helpers, he employs the two beasts and the great harlot, but all these enemies of the Church are defeated in the end. It is evident that the sections which comprise this second group (chapters 12–22), though synchronous, present a continued story. The dragon, the beasts, the harlot (note the order) assail the Church. The harlot, the beasts, the dragon (again, note the order) are overthrown.

It will be seen that the first of these two major divisions contains three sections: chapters 1–3; 4–7; and 8–11. The second contains four: chapters 12–14; 15, 16; 17–19; and 20–22. In the first of these two major divisions (1–11) we see the surface: the Church persecuted by the world. In the second we see the underlying conflict between the Christ and the dragon (Satan). The book of Revelation therefore reveals a progress in depth or intensity of spiritual conflict.

Some may say this division of the book into two major parts is artificial,[3] but it is very definitely the division suggested by the book itself. Lampstands, seals, trumpets, bowls, *etc.* constitute distinct sections of the book, whether we like it or not. This is the apostle's own grouping.

[1] H. B. Swete, *op. cit.*, p. xxxix.

[2] See J. P. Lange, *op. cit.*, p. 83; A. Pieters, *op. cit.*, p. 159; A. T. Robertson, *Syllabus for New Testament Study*, p. 260; H. B. Swete, *op. cit.*, pp. xl, lxii.

[3] See C. J. Ellicott, *The Revelation* (*Handy Commentary*), p. 19.

In this connection, moreover, there is another fact worthy of special consideration. The author of the Apocalypse is constantly speaking in terms of *seven*. This number occurs fifty-four times. What is even more striking is the fact that he again and again arranges his sevens in groups of three and four or four and three.[1] Our arrangement, instead of being artificial, is exactly in harmony with the genius of the book.

We can now present the following completed outline of the Apocalypse, which has as its theme the victory of Christ and His Church over Satan and his helpers.

a. The struggle on earth. The Church persecuted by the world. The Church is avenged, protected and victorious (Rev. 1–11).

1. Christ in the midst of the seven golden lampstands (1–3).
2. The book with seven seals (4–7).
3. The seven trumpets of judgment (8–11).

b. The deeper spiritual background. The Christ (and the Church) persecuted by the dragon (Satan) and his helpers. Christ and His Church are victorious (Rev. 12–22).

4. The woman and the Man-child persecuted by the dragon and his helpers (the beasts and the harlot) (12–14).
5. The seven bowls of wrath (15, 16).
6. The fall of the great harlot and of the beasts (17–19).
7. The judgment upon the dragon (Satan) followed by the new heaven and earth, new Jerusalem (20–22).

> PROPOSITION II. *The seven sections may be grouped into two major divisions. The first major division (chapters* 1–11*) consists of three sections. The second major division (chapters* 12–22*) consists of four sections. These two major divisions reveal a progress in depth or intensity of spiritual conflict. The first major division (chapters* 1–11*) reveals the Church, indwelt by Christ, persecuted by the world. But the Church is avenged, protected and victorious. The second major division (chapters* 12–22*) reveals the deeper spiritual background of this struggle. It is a conflict between the Christ and the dragon in which the Christ, and therefore His Church, is victorious.*

One more remark in closing. We have concentrated our attention on the *division* of the book. Yet it is not the division but the *unity* of the book, the very close relationship between all the parts, that should be emphasized. This is often forgotten, so we shall devote the next chapter to that subject.

[1] I. T. Beckwith, *The Apocalypse of John*, pp. 254, 523.

CHAPTER THREE

THE UNITY OF THE BOOK

HAVING given our analysis of the book of Revelation, we now proceed to answer those authors who claim that this book is a hotch-potch of baseless phantasies; that, indeed, the Apocalypse is not even one single book, but a compilation of several fragments of other books.[1]

These views are utterly unacceptable. Far from being a hotch-potch, this book reveals a most organic, systematic arrangement. The two main divisions complement one another. They belong together. The seven sections reveal a most glorious unity. There is an easy transition from one vision to the next. To see this is to understand the book. Not to see it is to miss its deepest meaning.

Keeping our Bibles open before us, let us make another survey of Revelation. This time we do not ask the question, how does the book divide itself? That has already been answered. We now ask, what is the meaning of the book, taken as a whole? How are its parts related to each other?

I. CHRIST IN THE MIDST OF HIS CHURCH

With that question in mind let us turn once more to the very first section (chapters 1–3). First, the vision of the Christ in the midst of the seven golden lampstands presents itself to our view (1: 12 ff.). We see the Son of man with eyes flashing fire, with a sharp, two-edged sword proceeding from His mouth, coming to judge those who are fiercely persecuting the Church and those who are trying to lead true believers astray.

In considering chapter 2, care must be taken not to set up a barrier between chapters 1 and 2. They belong together. The Christ-indwelt Church is revealed in this section (chapters 1–3). Christ's constant and abiding presence in His Church is the theme. The exalted Son of man, who was dead yet lives for evermore, is comforting the Church by His presence (1: 13),

[1] This is the view held, for example, by Harnack. J. Moffatt, *Introduction to the Literature of the New Testament*, pp. 489 ff., gives a detailed account of the different views.

revealing hidden things (3: 1), reproving error (2: 4), threatening punishment upon those who oppose truth and righteousness and who try to lead others astray (2: 16), approving whatever is commendable (2: 2,3), promising a reward (2: 7), and earnestly entreating His erring disciples to repent (3: 18,19). We seem to hear Him whisper, as we read this section (chapters 1–3), 'Lo, I am with you alway, even unto the end of the world.'

Notice the very close connection between chapter 1 and the next two chapters. In chapter 1 we see the vision of the Christ. The next two chapters reveal that same Christ and even describe Him in terms almost identical with those found in chapter 1. In order to make this point very clear we place the two descriptions in parallel columns:

DESCRIPTION OF CHRIST IN CHAPTER 1	DESCRIPTION OF CHRIST IN CHAPTERS 2, 3
'And he had in his right hand seven stars . . . in the midst of the lampstands one like unto a son of man.' 1: 16,13.	'. . . he that holds the seven stars in his right hand, he that walks in the midst of the seven golden lampstands.' 2: 1.
'I am the first and the last and the living one, and I was dead, and and behold, I am alive for evermore.' 1: 17,18.	'. . . the first and the last, who became dead, yet lived.' 2: 8.
'And out of his mouth proceeded a sharp, two-edged sword.' 1: 16.	'he that has the sharp two-edged sword.' 2: 12.
'. . . his eyes were as a flame of fire, and his feet like unto burnished brass.' 1: 14,15.	'. . . his eyes like a flame of fire, and his feet are like unto burnished brass.' 2: 18.
'. . . and from the seven spirits that are before his throne . . . and he had in his right hand seven stars.' 1: 4,16.	'he that has the seven spirits of God and the seven stars.' 3: 1.
'the faithful witness . . . I . . . have the keys of death and Hades.' 1: 5,18.	'. . . he that is true, he that has the key of David.' 3: 7.
'. . . Jesus Christ, the faithful witness, the first-born of the dead, and the ruler of the kings of the earth.' 1: 5.	'the Amen, the faithful and true witness, the beginning of the creation of God.' 3: 14.

II. THE CONFLICT BETWEEN THE CHURCH AND THE WORLD

Thus, the first section (chapters 1–3) reveals the Christ-indwelt Church represented by the symbolism of the seven golden lampstands, with the Son of man walking among them. The Church reveals the light of heaven to a world that lies in darkness.

The Church and the world—a conflict is unavoidable. The darkness hates the light. As a result, persecution is in store for the Church. Accordingly, in the vision of the seals (chapters 4–7) we see the Church oppressed by the world. The light shines in the darkness (chapters 1–3) and the darkness hates the light (chapters 4–7)—these always follow each other in that order.

But even before these trials are described we receive the bracing assurance that they are included in God's decree. They constitute part of His plan. The Church needs these afflictions in order that it may be purged. The Church reveals the light of heaven to a world that lies in darkness, but actual study of Revelation 2 and 3 shows that the light shines with different degrees of purity and brilliance. In Smyrna the glory of the ever-living Christ shines forth in all its purity, but Sardis has only a few who did not defile their garments: there the light is just flickering. Again, Philadelphia is radiant with the lustre of its wonderful Saviour and receives an open door; but Laodicea is lukewarm. We repeat, the Church needs these trials in order that it may be cleansed and purified and in order that true believers may be brought closer to God. By means of affliction and cross-bearing God's children make progress in sanctification. The Christ on the throne overrules evil for good. It is for this reason that the section opens with the glorious vision of the throne set in heaven (chapter 4), and the scroll in the right hand of the Lord (chapter 5). It is the Christ who takes this scroll and opens the seals (5: 7 ff.). The Son of man, exalted in glory, governs the world in the interest of the Church. We are more than conquerors! Let the trials then come!

In chapter 6 these trials are described—persecution and tribulation of every variety. Christ always brings the sword. Notice the striking connection between chapters 5 and 6:

5: 5. 'the Root of David has conquered.'	6: 2. 'And I saw, and behold, a white horse, and he that sat thereon had a bow; and there was given unto him a crown: and he came forth conquering and to conquer.'

The rider on the white horse is Christ.[1]

[1] See chapter IX, p. 93. This identification is made by Irenaeus, the disciple of a disciple of the apostle John, in his work *Against Heresies*. S. L. Morris, *op. cit.*, p. 52, says, 'The church . . . in all the ages has been practically unanimous in interpreting it as the conquering Christ entering upon His militant world career.' Amongst other modern scholars who support it are J. P. Lange, R. C. H. Lenski, W. Milligan and A. Plummer, in the works cited above.

The trials are in evidence during this entire era, from the first to the second coming of Christ. Wherever and whenever the Christ enters upon the scene of history in the fullness of His saving power, there and then the sword is bound to appear. Christ's disciples become cross-bearers. Peace is taken from the earth. The earth is drenched with the blood of the followers of the Lamb.[1] Observe the close connection between Revelation 6: 2,4 and Matthew 10: 34 ff.:

Rev. 6: 2,4. '. . . a white horse, and he that sat thereon . . . came forth conquering and to conquer . . . And another horse came forth, a red horse; and to him that sat thereon it was given to take peace from the earth, and that they should slaughter one another: and there was given unto him a great sword.'	Mt. 10: 34 ff. 'Think not that I came to send peace on the earth: I came not to send peace but a sword . . . And he that does not take up his cross and follow after me, is not worthy of me.'

This passage from Matthew 10: 34 ff. is constantly in the mind of the seer.[2] Not only here, in Revelation 6: 2,4, does he definitely refer to it, but also in 3: 5, which is a striking parallel to Matthew 10: 32.

Yet the section on the seals describes not only persecutions. It is far more comprehensive. *All* the woes and trials of the Church are included in the vision and also those which the Church suffers together with the world. The main question, however, is, how do these trials affect the Church? (*Cf.* Ezk. 14: 21 ff.; 16: 20 ff.; Mt. 24: 13.)

In complete harmony with this interpretation and with the unity of the whole book the fifth seal reveals the souls of them that had been slaughtered for the Word of God and for the testimony which they held (6: 9). Many commentators imagine that 'an entirely new vision' begins here, having little if any connection with the foregoing. On our interpretation—which rests upon the solid basis of a comparison of pertinent parallels—

[1] The preterists offer a more consistent explanation here than others. They see the unity of Rev. 6: 3–11. See, for example, H. Cowles, *op. cit.*, pp. 98 ff.; P. Mauro, *op. cit.*, p. 202; A. Plummer, *op. cit.*, p. 184. R. C. H. Lenski, on the other hand, holds that what happens to believers is not even included in the symbolism of the horsemen (*op. cit.*, p. 223). His reason for this position is, however, that he takes the 'Hades' of verse 8 to mean hell, whereas it is in fact the state of death, always following death. See art. 'Hades' in *ISBE* (1929 edn.).

[2] See R. H. Charles, *The Revelation of St. John* (*International Critical Commentary*), I, p. 165; P. Mauro, *op. cit.*, p. 200; H. B. Swete, *op. cit.*, p. clvi; F. C. Thompson, *The New Chain Reference Bible*, on this passage.

there is no difficulty whatever. The preceding seals symbolized trial and persecution affecting the Church. Among other things, believers were persecuted and slaughtered. What is more natural than that the souls of those who had been slaughtered should now be seen underneath the altar? With the opening of the sixth seal we have reached the end, the day of the final judgment.

These seals of trial and persecution are in evidence throughout this entire dispensation; in a sense, throughout the history of the world. The saints, however, need have no fear. The judgments which are about to fall upon the world will not really harm the true believers here on earth (7: 1–8). Moreover, by and by the Church will come 'out of the tribulation, the great one', the sum total of all tribulations. In heaven the Church triumphant, the countless palm-bearing multitude, drawn out of every nation and representative of all tribes and peoples and tongues will celebrate its victory in the great day of the consummation of all things (7: 9–17). *We are more than conquerors!*

III. THE JUDGMENTS UPON THE PERSECUTORS

But what about the persecutors? Do they go free? Will the Church not be avenged? Our Lord sees the tears of His persecuted children. Their prayers, made fragrant by the intercession of Christ, ascend to heaven. The Lord answers. The censer is filled with the altar fire which is cast upon the earth (8: 5). 'And there occurred peals of thunder, loud blasts, flashes of lightning, and quaking.' In other words, God is constantly sending His judgments upon the world in answer to the prayers of His persecuted children. It is for this reason that the seventh seal immediately introduces the trumpets of judgment; the seals of trial and persecution render necessary the trumpets of judgment.[1] Wrong must be avenged.

Thus this section on the trumpets of judgment teaches us that by means of plagues upon the land (8: 7), the sea (8: 8),

[1] A. T. Robertson, in *Syllabus for New Testament Study*, p. 265, mentions as an objection to the synchronous (parallelistic) view that in 8: 1 the trumpets seem to grow out of the seals. This is indeed true, and yet the two series—seals and trumpets—run parallel. Throughout history seals of persecution always give rise to trumpets of judgment. Hence, both series span the same long period of time, and the trumpets always grow out of the seals. Thus the seventh seal is not given a content of its own but immediately introduces the trumpets. The whole difficulty arises from the fact that parallelists have neglected the *unity* of the entire book.

the rivers (8: 10), the sun, moon and stars (8: 12), the evil influences of demons (9: 3,11), the battle-field (9: 16), and the dreadful expectation of the final judgment (11: 15), our risen and exalted Redeemer is constantly avenging the Church and sending judgments upon the persecutors. Yet these judgments, though severe, are charged with warning. They are not final. They destroy a third part. By means of them God is still calling men to repentance. The function of the trumpet is to warn.

But do they actually result in repentance? On the whole, and apart from the saving operation of the Holy Spirit, they do not. 'They repented not of their murders, nor of their sorceries, nor of their fornication, nor of their thefts' (9: 21). This, too, was true in John's day, has been true ever since, and always will be true. The Apocalypse is a book for every age. It is always up to date.

While these judgments are falling upon the world, what is happening to the Church? Its safety, witness to others, power, cross-bearing, and final victory are described in chapters 10 and 11.

IV. VICTORY THROUGH CHRIST

The section closes with a paean of victory, a song of triumph. 'The dominion over the world became the dominion of our Lord and of his Christ; and he shall reign for ever and ever.' The saints receive their reward. God destroys the destroyer (11: 18). More than conquerors are we!

Here the first division of the book (chapters 1–11) ends.[1] But the book does not end here. Nor is it true that it might as well have ended here. There are two questions which cry out for an answer. 1. What is the underlying cause of this persecution of the Church by the world? In other words, why do unbelievers hate believers so vehemently? What is behind this? 2. What is going to happen to these impenitent individuals (9: 21) who do not heed God's warning voice revealed in the trumpets of judgment?

These two questions are answered in the second division (chapters 12–22). Chapters 1–11 show the surface: the Christ-filled Church shines in the darkness of this world (chapters 1–3). The world hates the light and persecutes the Church so that the souls of the slaughtered saints appear underneath the altar

[1] See chapter II, pp. 22f.

(chapters 4–7). The blood of the saints is avenged; their prayers are answered; judgments, of every description, fall upon the world while the Church triumphs (chapters 8–11). Chapters 12–14 teach us that this struggle between the Church and the world is but the outward manifestation of the conflict between Christ and Satan. Christ is here called the Man-child.[1] Satan is called the dragon.[2] The dragon's purpose is to devour the Child (12: 4). Failing in this, he persecutes the woman, that is, the Church (12: 13). As his helpers, the dragon employs the beast out of the sea (13: 1–10), that is, antichristian persecution (in John's day concentrated in the empire and government of Rome); the beast out of the earth, that is, antichristian religious propaganda (in John's day centred in the pagan religion and emperor-worship of Rome); and the great harlot, Babylon, that is, antichristian seduction (in John's day spreading from the city of Rome, which tried to satisfy the lust of the flesh).[3] Their purpose is to destroy the Church. But do these forces of evil succeed? Who is victorious, the dragon or the Lamb? Chapter 14 furnishes the answer; the Lamb stands as victor upon Mount Zion, and with Him 144,000 saints! The twofold harvest, of believers and of unbelievers (14: 14 ff.), brings us again to the final judgment.

To read about this victory of the Christ and of His Church fills us with comfort. But we naturally ask, what happens to the foe? Chapters 12–14 introduce five enemies of the Church. They are the following: 1. the dragon himself; 2. the beast out of the sea; 3. the beast out of the earth, also called the false prophet; 4. the great harlot, Babylon; 5. 'the men that have the mark of the beast' (13: 16; 16: 2). All these are defeated together. When Satan is cast into the lake of fire and brimstone, his allies also are cast into it. This is on the day of final judgment. Yet the end of each of these five is described separately, except that the two beasts are taken together (19: 20).

First, the seer shows us what happens to those who have the mark of the beast (chapters 15, 16, but see especially 16: 2). These are the impenitents of 9: 21. (For proof of this, see chapter 16: 9,11).

You will recall that the second question which the first

[1] This, of course, cannot be open to doubt. The Man-child can be none other than the Christ. Abundant evidence for this is given in chapter XI.

[2] Notice that the Man-child is here represented as the Seed of the woman, while the dragon opposes Him. The entire passage is rooted in Gn. 3: 15.

[3] *Cf.* R. C. H. Lenski, *op. cit.*, p. 412; A. Pieters, *op. cit.*, p. 412.

division of the book leaves unanswered is this. What is going to happen to these impenitent individuals? We have already noticed a very close connection between this section on the bowls of wrath (chapters 15 and 16) and that on the trumpets of judgment (chapters 8–11). The two sections are exactly parallel, as we showed in chapter II.[1] At the same time, this section on the bowls of wrath (chapters 15 and 16) is a direct continuation of the one which immediately precedes it; the men who have the mark of the beast are introduced, as such, in 13: 16; while in 16: 2 we are told what happens to them.

This raises the question of what happens when Christ's trumpets of judgment do not result in penitence and conversion. Does the Ruler of the universe permit such impenitence and such hardness of heart to remain unpunished? The answer, according to chapters 15 and 16, is that whenever, in the entire history of the world, any individual remains impenitent, and hardens himself against the initial manifestation of God's displeasure in judgments, the final outpouring of divine wrath will follow sooner or later. When the ten plagues did not bring about Pharaoh's willing and cheerful obedience, but revealed a hardened heart, the entire host of Egypt was drowned in the Red Sea (*cf.* 15: 2,3). Because those of the new dispensation hardened themselves in spite of their greater privileges and opportunities, this principle of divine moral government is evident today more than ever before, and will become increasingly evident until its culminating manifestation is reached in the day of the final judgment. This, briefly, is the meaning of the bowls of wrath (chapters 15, 16). Bear in mind always that trumpets warn and bowls are poured out.

What about the other enemies of Christ and His Church? The dragon, the two beasts, and the great harlot were introduced in that order (chapters 12–14). The great harlot, the two beasts, and the dragon meet their doom in that order. Remember, however, what has been said before; they are all overthrown at one and the same time. Throughout the history of the world whenever one falls they necessarily all fall. Their final discomfiture takes place on the day of judgment. The subject, however, is so vast, the concepts are so mighty and comprehensive, that the seer, in his description of what happens, first shows us the downfall of the great harlot, then that of the two beasts, and finally that of the dragon.

[1] See pp. 19f.

Thus Revelation 17–19 describes the fall of Babylon, the great harlot. We are shown the inevitable, complete, and terrible character of Babylon's fall, the rejoicing in heaven which results, and finally the Author of this victory over the world in its rôle as the centre of seduction. The Christ has conquered (19: 11 ff.).

This same section also shows us the ruin of the two beasts (19: 20). Now there remains only one enemy whose final overthrow has not yet been described, namely, the dragon, the greatest of them all, their leader and commander, who was introduced first of all. The final section of the book (chapters 20–22) describes his utter defeat. Already the dragon is bound (20: 2). By and by, on the day of judgment, he will be cast into the lake of fire and brimstone to be tormented for ever and ever.

And what of the saints? Already the souls of the martyrs live and reign with Christ, the Victor, on heavenly thrones. After the final judgment (20: 11–15) these saints will reign for ever and ever (22: 5) in the new heaven and earth (21: 1). The Lamb occupies the throne (22: 1,3). He is victorious. We ourselves are more than conquerors.

V. THE BOOK AN ORGANIC WHOLE

We have seen that this book is one single, beautiful, gradually developing whole. Every section of the book is exactly where it should be. The book, moreover, describes principles of human conduct and divine moral government which are always operative, and in that very order. The Church always functions as a light-bearer, shining in the midst of the darkness of this world (chapters 1–3). It shines because Christ dwells in it, and consequently the world persecutes the Church (chapters 4–7) with the inevitable result that divine judgments, of every description, always fall upon the world, while the Church is victorious (chapters 8–11). This struggle between the Church and the world always reveals a deeper conflict between Christ and Satan. Satan always employs just those allies mentioned in chapters 12–14. They always—and especially on the day of judgment—go down in defeat. The victory is always ours! There is, of course, nothing mechanical about these seven sections. They are not seven 'blocks of thought'. They do not constitute seven water-tight compartments. The book is an organism, every part of which is vitally related to all the others. Thus. for example, the fall of Babylon is already announced in

14: 8. Yet it is not described until we reach chapters 17–19. Similarly, the persecution of the Church by the world and even the judgment upon the world are presupposed and introduced in the very first section (1: 9,13 ff.). But the main theme of that section is the Christ-indwelt Church shining in the midst of the world.

The teachings of these seven sections, which reveal such a glorious unity and gradual blossoming of thought, agree with the whole Bible.

1. Chapters 1–3. *Cf.* Matthew 28: 20. '. . . lo, I am with you alway, even unto the end of the world.' Matthew 5: 14. 'Ye are the light of the world.'

2. Chapters 4–7. *Cf.* John 16: 33. 'In the world ye have tribulation: but be of good cheer; I have overcome the world.'

3. Chapters 8–11. *Cf.* Luke 18: 7. 'And shall not God avenge his elect, that cry to him day and night . . .?'

4. Chapters 12–14. *Cf.* Genesis 3: 15. 'And I will put enmity between thee and the woman, and between thy seed and her seed: he shall bruise thy head, and thou shalt bruise his heel.'

5. Chapters 15, 16. *Cf.* Romans 2: 5. '. . . but after thy hardness and impenitent heart treasurest up for thyself wrath . . .' *Cf.* Exodus 14: 15.

6. Chapters 17–19. *Cf.* 1 John 2: 17. 'And the world passes away, and the lust thereof . . .'

7. Chapters 20–22. *Cf.* Romans 8: 37. '. . . we are more than conquerors through him that loved us.' *Cf.* Jude 6.

PROPOSITION III. *The book is one. The principles of human conduct and divine moral government are progressively revealed; the lampstands give rise to the seals, the seals to the trumpets, etc.*

CHAPTER FOUR

PROGRESSIVE TEACHING CONCERNING FINAL JUDGMENT

THE book of Revelation reveals an inner, organic unity. It acquaints us with the principles of human conduct and divine moral government. These principles are always and everywhere in evidence. This book is as fully up to date today as it was in AD 1000. Fifty or a hundred years from now it will still be up to date. It is applicable to conditions in the churches of Europe, of America, of Asia, of every continent.

Wherever there is a church, it is a lampstand or light-bearer so that we see the light of Christ shining in the midst of the darkness (chapters 1–3). Wherever this happens, the world hates the Church; the darkness refuses to be conquered by the light. Persecution follows; also trials of every description (chapters 4–7). These trials, however, are overruled for the good of the Church. The throne is always in heaven, not on earth. Believers are always victorious. They come out of the tribulation, the great one.

Wherever and whenever the Church is persecuted, the Lord hears and answers the prayers of His persecuted children. He sees the blood of the martyred saints, and trumpets of judgment warn the wicked (chapters 8–11).

This struggle on the surface—between Church and world—always indicates a deeper struggle between Christ and the dragon (chapters 12–14). For the impenitent, bowls of final wrath always follow trumpets of judgment (chapters 15, 16). That is true today; it was true yesterday; it will be true to-morrow, whether you live in Africa, Europe, or America. Satan and all his helpers always seem to be victorious, but in reality are always defeated (chapters 17–19; also 20–22).

Thus interpreted—and we are convinced that this is the only tenable explanation—the Apocalypse is really very simple. It is simple and yet most profound. It gives us the real philosophy of history. It shows us the principles of human and satanic conduct and of divine moral government as they are constantly revealing themselves. It indicates how we should interpret the news contained in our newspapers and the events which we study in history books.

We have seen that throughout the history of the world bowls of final wrath always follow trumpets of judgment whenever the latter are unheeded. The order is never reversed.[1] Trumpets warn. Bowls are poured out. In the final judgment, moreover, these bowls of wrath will be completely emptied upon impenitent, hardened sinners. Similarly, 'Babylon' falls whenever the kingdoms of the world—whether Babylonia, Assyria or Rome—collapse. The great and final fall of Babylon occurs in connection with the second coming of our Lord to judge the world.

Thus conceived, we notice that the final sections of the Apocalypse, though synchronous with the other sections and applicable to the entire course of history, describe especially what will happen in connection with the final judgment.

So although all the sections of the Apocalypse run parallel and span the period between the first and second comings of Christ and are rooted in the soil of the old dispensation, yet there is also a degree of progress. The closer we approach the end of the book the more our attention is directed to the final judgment and that which lies beyond it. The seven sections are arranged, as it were, in an ascending, climactic order. The book reveals a gradual progress in eschatological emphasis.[2]

A careful examination of the Apocalypse will make this clear. In the first series—Christ in the midst of the seven golden lampstands—we have no more than a mere announcement of Christ's coming unto judgment (1: 7). There is no description of the judgment. In the second section (chapters 4–7), the final judgment is not merely announced but definitely introduced; we catch a glimpse of the horror which fills the wicked when they see the Judge coming to them (6: 12 ff.). But that is all. There is no description. A few verses are devoted to a description of the Church triumphant after the final judgment (7: 9 ff.). The next vision, similarly (chapters 8–11), introduces the final judgment and the joy of the redeemed (11: 15 ff.).

In these three sections which comprise the first main division of the book (chapters 1–11), we do not come across anything more than a mere announcement of or introduction to the final judgment. But as soon as we enter the second main division of the book there is a change. In the very first section of this main

[1] R. C. H. Lenski, *op. cit.*, p. 267.

[2] J .P. Lange, *op. cit.*, p. 81; see also p. 5; B. B. Warfield, *Biblical Doctrines*, p. 645.

division we have a real description of the final judgment (14: 14 ff.). It is, however, a symbolic representation. Under the symbolism of a double harvest the final judgment is pictured to us. The next vision (chapters 15, 16) describes the pouring out of God's final wrath, so that this section, though synchronous with the others, is in a special sense descriptive of the final judgment. In the next minor division, the fall of Babylon (chapters 17–19), this emphasis upon Christ's second coming in judgment and its meaning for the world and for the Church, both militant and triumphant, is even greater. (See especially 19: 11,12.) The seventh or final section (chapters 20–22) not only describes the final judgment, but in this description drops much of the symbolism of the earlier visions. Nothing is vague or indefinite and little is clothed with symbolism (20: 12 ff.). The joy of the redeemed in the new heaven and earth is described much more circumstantially than, for example, in 7: 9 ff. The book has reached its glorious climax.

> PROPOSITION IV. *The seven sections of the Apocalypse are arranged in an ascending, climactic order. There is progress in eschatological emphasis. The final judgment is first* announced, *then* introduced *and finally* described. *Similarly, the new heaven and earth are described more fully in the final section than in those which precede it.*

To this conception of the book we give the name 'progressive parallelism'.

CHAPTER FIVE

SYMBOLISM IN THE BOOK

THE book of Revelation is a series of pictures. The pictures move. They are full of action. Everything is constantly astir. One picture makes place for another; and then another, and another. Let us watch these constantly-changing scenes.

Here we have seven golden lampstands with someone walking among them. He is wearing a long robe with a gold belt around his breast. His hair is white as snow, and his eyes blaze like fire. In his right hand he is holding seven stars, and from his mouth issues a sharp double-edged sword. The scene changes. We see a halo-encircled throne. Out of the throne come flashes of lightning, rumblings, and peals of thunder. In the right hand of the Lord on the throne there is a scroll, sealed with seven seals. Now someone approaches the throne who is introduced as the Lion of the tribe of Judah. He takes the scroll. Immediately the four living ones round the throne and also twenty-four elders fall down before the Lamb. Each has a harp and gold bowls full of incense, and they are singing the new song. As this music dies, we see four horses, white, red, black, and pale in colour. As the horses and riders go out, we see people slaughter one another. Some seem to be hungry; indeed, starving. Others are being thrown before the wild beasts. We now see the souls of the slaughtered individuals. In a loud voice they are crying underneath the altar. But now the sun becomes black as sackcloth. The full moon takes on the colour of blood. The stars of the sky are falling on the earth. The sky is being rolled up just like a scroll. Every mountain and island is being dislodged from its place. People—including kings, nobles, officers, the rich and the poor alike—are hiding themselves in caves and rocks. Four angels are holding back the four winds so that they do not immediately damage anything on earth or sea. Now 144,000 people are marked with a seal, and a great crowd which no-one could possibly count, people of every nationality and region on earth, with palm-branches in their hands, appear and cry with a loud voice, 'Our salvation is the work of our God who is seated upon the throne, and of the Lamb.'

Seven angels with seven trumpets now appear. Another angel is busily engaged offering incense. Now the censer is being filled with fire. It is emptied upon the earth. This is followed by peals of thunder, rumblings, flashes of lightning and an earthquake.

The entire book consists of changing scenes like these, of moving pictures and active symbols.[1] Moreover, there are sounds, voices, songs, responses, choruses. (*Cf.* 4: 8,11; 5: 9,10, 12,13,14; 11: 15–18; 12: 10; 15: 3,4; 19: 1–8; 22: 17.)[2] It is rather like a magnificent sound-film.

I. THE NEED TO CONCENTRATE ON THE CENTRAL THEME

But the question arises, what do these pictures mean? How shall we interpret them? In order to answer that question, let us make a little detour.

You remember, of course, the parable of the good Samaritan in Luke 10. Now, there are some who would interpret this beautiful story in the following manner: 'The man who is on his way from Jerusalem to Jericho represents Adam, the head of the human race. He left the heavenly city and is travelling down to the city of earth, the profane city. But, having turned his desires towards the earth, he falls into the hands of robbers; that is, he is overpowered by Satan and his evil angels. These robbers strip him of the garment of original righteousness. They also beat him, leaving him full of wounds, half-dead (*half-dead* in sins and trespasses!). The priest and the levite represent the law and the sacrifices. They cannot save the sinner. They are powerless to help. But the good Samaritan, namely, Jesus Christ, is travelling that way and helps the poor sinner. This good Samaritan dresses his wounds with the oil of the Holy Spirit and with wine, namely, the blood of His passion. He then puts the poor man on His own mule, that is, on the merits of His own righteousness. He takes the poor man to an inn, that is, to church. The next day, the good Samaritan gives the host two shillings, that is, the Word and the Sacraments, in order that with these he may provide for the spiritual needs of the poor sinner. Then this good Samaritan departs but promises to return later.'

Now, if the reader has the type of mentality that enjoys such

[1] *N.B.* the first verse of the book 'and he made it known by means of signs (or symbols)'.

[2] S. L. Morris, *op. cit.*, pp. 32, 46, *etc.*

spiritualizing explanations, he might as well close this book. He will never really understand the parables of our Lord. Neither will he ever be able to understand the book of Revelation. Let us emphasize the fact that the explanation just given is wrong from start to finish. It is altogether wrong to ask what is meant by the poor man who fell among the robbers, what is meant by the robbers, the priest, the levite, the good Samaritan, the wine, the oil, the mule, the inn, and the two shillings. Not one of these things has any 'deeper' spiritual meaning whatever! If the mule must be spiritualized, who is going to determine exactly what is its meaning? And what about the two shillings? Do they represent the two sacraments, the Word and the Sacraments, or the two testaments? Who is going to determine this? The context in which the parable occurs says nothing about it, and because the context says nothing, we should say nothing.

Surely all these elements of the parable, the wine, oil, priest, levite, inn, two shillings, *etc.*, have their value, for without them the parable would not be complete and would convey no meaning. But you should not ascribe a separate, spiritual meaning to each of these features. They simply serve to make the parable complete. Then, once you have read the entire parable, you should ask, What is the meaning of this parable, taken as a whole?[1] Each parable teaches one central lesson. A little study of the context usually makes this one central lesson perfectly clear. In the light of Luke 10: 25–29, and also verses 36 and 37, we see that the meaning of this beautiful story is that instead of asking, 'Who is my neighbour?' we should be neighbour to whoever the Lord happens to place in our path.

II. THE NEED TO DISTINGUISH BETWEEN PRINCIPLE AND DETAIL

Something similar holds good with respect to the interpretation of the symbols of the Apocalypse. One must not begin to press the details. One must not ask, in the symbol of the locusts that came out of the abyss (9: 1–11), what is the *separate* meaning of their hair, teeth, breast-plates, *etc.*? We must not pluck the symbol apart and lose the unity. These details belong to the picture, just as the mule, wine, oil, *etc.*, belong to the parable of the good Samaritan. One should ask, first, what is the picture taken as a whole? Second, what is the one central meaning of this picture?[2]

[1] See W. M. Taylor, *The Parables of Our Saviour*, p. 14.
[2] A. Pieters, *op. cit.*, p. 71.

As a rule[1] the details belong to the picture, to the symbol. We must not try to give a 'deeper' interpretation to the details, unless the interpretation of these details is necessary in order to bring out the full meaning of the central idea of the symbol. Thus, in the symbol of the new Jerusalem (chapters 21, 22), the central idea is perfect fellowship with God. The details—wall, foundations, gates, river, *etc.*—describe the glorious character of this fellowship. What we are after is the total impression, the central idea, of each complete symbol. As in the parables, so here, the context helps to explain the meaning of the picture, and a thorough study of all the details is also necessary in order to determine what is the central thought.

This brings us to our next proposition.

> PROPOSITION V. *The fabric of the book consists of moving pictures. The details that pertain to the picture should be interpreted in harmony with its central thought. We should ask two questions. First, what is the entire picture? Second, what is its predominant idea?*

III. WHAT DO THE SYMBOLS MEAN?

This having been established, another question immediately arises. Granted that we should interpret the symbol as a whole and its details in harmony with the whole, what does the symbol mean? Does it refer to a specific event in history, a particular happening, a detail of chronology, an important date, or what?

In this connection, it is well to distinguish between two kinds of symbols. There are symbols which describe the beginning or the end of the course of the new dispensation. These symbols, as is very evident from the context, generally refer to a specific event. Thus, for example, the radiant woman who is delivered of a Son, a Man-child, refers to the Church bringing forth the Christ, His human nature (12: 1–5). Again, the twofold harvest (14: 15 ff.) refers to the final judgment, to that one great event.

But there are also other symbols, namely, those that seem to intervene between Christ's first and second comings. We are thinking of such symbols as the lampstands, the seals, the trumpets, the bowls, *etc.* Do these symbols refer to specific events, single happenings, dates or persons in history? For if they do, then we may as well admit that we cannot interpret them.[2]

[1] B. B. Warfield, *op. cit.*, p. 646.
[2] A. Pieters, *op. cit.*, pp. 132 ff.

Because among the thousands of dates and events and persons of history that show certain traits of resemblance to the symbol in question, who is able to select the one and only date, event, or person that was forecast by this particular symbol? Confusion results. We get thousands of 'interpretations', but no certainty. And the Apocalypse remains a closed book.

Yet we do not believe that this is a closed book. We fully believe that it is a *revelation*, an *unveiling*. So we must look for some other rule of interpretation.

We hold that this rule, far from being superimposed on the symbols, is derived from them. It is on the basis of the symbols themselves, as described in the Apocalypse, that we arrive at this very significant conclusion, namely, that the seals, trumpets, bowls, and similar pictures, refer not to specific events or details of history, but to principles that are operating throughout the history of the world, especially throughout the new dispensation.

Let us submit evidence in favour of this important rule of interpretation. Notice, first of all, that the sphere in which these seals, trumpets, and bowls operate is very extensive. These symbols affect, respectively, the fourth part of the earth; the third part of the earth, sea, trees; the whole earth, sea, *etc.* (See chapters 6, 8 and 9, 16.) This could hardly be true if each seal, trumpet or bowl had reference to just one single event in history, an event that takes place at a certain specific date in a definite locality. But if, on the other hand, we regard the symbol as indicating a whole series of happenings from the beginning to the end of the dispensation these descriptions of the sphere in which the symbols operate begin to have meaning. Thus, for example, we can understand the expression 'a huge mountain all ablaze' that was 'hurled into the sea' if it represents all maritime disasters throughout the dispensation.

Again, these symbols affect not just one very limited group of people, but a multitude that cannot be counted. The trumpets, for example, affect mankind. They do not refer merely to some people living in Europe who happen to have a quarrel with the Pope. Read 9: 20. 'And the rest of mankind, who were not killed by these plagues . . .' The description is even more general than this, for these symbols seem to affect not only all the unregenerate in one age, but also former generations. Notice, 16: 6. '. . . for they poured out the blood of saints and prophets.' We cannot escape the impression, therefore, that the symbols refer to *series* of happenings, to principles of human and satanic conduct and of divine moral government. They refer to things that happen again and again and again, so that the book of Revelation is always up to date. The symbols describe principles of conduct and of divine moral government that are in evidence today as well as during the first century AD.

In this connection, let us not forget that each of these series—whether lampstands, seals, trumpets, or bowls—appears to span the long period beginning with the first and ending with the second coming of our Saviour.[1] This also would seem to harmonize better with the idea that the symbols indicate ever-operative principles than with the theory that they signify single, isolated happenings in Europe.

Nor must we fail to observe that the symbols usually come in groups of seven. The number seven occurs fifty-four times. The book is addressed to seven churches, represented by seven lampstands. There are seven stars symbolizing seven angels of the churches. There are seven spirits of God represented by seven lamps. Further, there are seven seals and a Lamb with seven eyes and seven horns. Seven angels blow seven trumpet-blasts. Seven other angels pour out the contents of seven bowls full of the final seven plagues. Seven thunders utter voices. The beast out of the sea has seven heads. There are seven mountains, seven kings, and so on.[2] This number seven indicates completeness. It harmonizes very well with the idea that the symbols refer to principles of human conduct and of divine government that are always operative, especially throughout this entire dispensation.

Our final line of evidence is, perhaps, the most conclusive. We should constantly bear in mind that the purpose of God and of the seer is to make men wise unto salvation. The book has an ethical and a spiritual purpose. For if these symbols merely indicate and predict isolated, future events, it may satisfy some people's curiosity but it can hardly be said that people, in general, are edified. On the other hand, if we believe that the book reveals the principles of divine moral government which are constantly operating, so that, whatever age we happen to live in, we can see God's hand in history, and His mighty arm protecting us and giving us the victory through our

[1] See chapter II, pp. 16–19.

[2] Other numbers found in the Apocalypse are: ½; 1; 2; 3; 3½; 4; 5; 6; 10; 12; 24; 144; 666; 1000; 1260; 1600; 7000; 12000; 144000; 100,000,000; 200,000,000. See C. F. Wishart, *op. cit.*, pp. 19 ff., for a very fine treatise on the significance of numbers in the Apocalypse.

Lord Jesus Christ, then, and only then, are we edified and comforted.[1]

All this can be summed up in our sixth proposition:

> PROPOSITION VI. *The seals, trumpets, bowls of wrath and similar symbols refer not to specific events, particular happenings, or details of history, but to principles—of human conduct and of divine moral government—that are operating throughout the history of the world, especially throughout the new dispensation.*[2]

[1] See B. B. Warfield, *op. cit.*, p. 646.

[2] See further, W. Milligan, *op. cit.*, VI, pp. 860, 867; S. L. Morris, *op. cit.*, p. 65; H. B. Swete, *op. cit.*, p. ccxvi; C. F. Wishart, *op. cit.*, p. 42.

CHAPTER SIX

BACKGROUND AND BASIS FOR INTERPRETATION

THE Apocalypse is rooted in contemporary happenings in the sacred Scriptures which John and his readers knew well and in direct, special revelation of the mind and purposes of God. All these must be carefully considered if the book is to be rightly interpreted.

I. THE NEED TO NOTE THE CONTEMPORARY BACKGROUND

We shall never be able to understand the book of Revelation unless we interpret it in the light of contemporaneous events. We should always ask, how did the first readers understand this book? We should make an earnest attempt to appreciate the conditions and circumstances out of which this prophecy arose. The Apocalypse has as its immediate purpose the strengthening of the wavering hearts of the persecuted believers of the first century AD.[1] Therefore every paragraph of this glorious prophecy is filled with significance, instruction and comfort for the seven churches of proconsular Asia. This book is an answer to the crying need of that particular day, and we must permit contemporaneous circumstances to shed their light on its symbols and predictions. True, this book has a message for today, but we shall never be able to understand 'what the Spirit is saying to the churches' of today unless we first of all study the specific needs and circumstances of the seven churches of 'Asia' as they existed in the first century AD.

We find, then, that the Apocalypse is replete with references to contemporaneous events and circumstances. Believers were being severely and bitterly persecuted. Their blood was being poured out (6: 10; 7: 14; 16: 6; 17: 6; 19: 2). Some were pining away in dingy dungeons or were about to be imprisoned (2: 10). They were suffering from hunger, thirst or famine (6: 8; 7: 16). Some had been cast before the wild beasts (6: 8). Many had been beheaded (20: 4). At Pergamum, Antipas had been killed (2: 13). John had been banished to the isle of Patmos (1: 9). The Roman government encouraged persecu-

[1] See chapter 1, pp. 7–10.

tion; its emperor-worship inspired false religion; its capital was the centre of lust (13: 7,15; 17: 18). False teachers and sects were troubling the churches (2: 2,14,20,24). Nevertheless, true believers were causing the light of Christ to shine in the darkness of superstition and unbelief. Philadelphia had 'an open door' (3: 8).

All these things were real; they were facts—many of them *hard* facts—for the Church of that day and age. These believers were not primarily interested in the great events of future centuries so much as in the struggle between light and darkness, the Church and the world, Christ and the dragon, truth and error, which was being waged in their own time. The Apocalypse is an answer to the crying needs of these persecuted, sorely afflicted believers.[1]

This does not mean that the seer was limited to matters within his own historical horizon. We must remember that the real Author of the book is not the apostle John but God Omniscient Himself. As we have proved abundantly, this book spans the entire dispensation and is intended for us as well as for believers in the first century AD. But it was occasioned by the need and suffering of Christians in the first century AD. It is definitely rooted in contemporaneous events and circumstances and must be interpreted in harmony with them. True, it speaks of forces that are constantly operative in the history of the world—for example, the beast—but it discusses these in terms that are expressive of the contemporaneous form in which these forces manifested themselves—for example, Rome. We can sum this up as follows:

> PROPOSITION VII. *The Apocalypse is rooted in contemporaneous events and circumstances. Its symbols should be interpreted in the light of conditions which prevailed when the book was written.*

II. THE NEED TO HAVE REGARD TO THE WHOLE CONTEXT OF SCRIPTURE

We should interpret this book in the light of its background. It is rather strange, however, that the very interpreters who strongly insist upon this fail to do full justice to this principle.[2] They, as it were, see only the surface-soil: contemporaneous

[1] See H. Cowles, *op. cit.*, p. 43; A. Pieters, *op. cit.*, pp. 67 ff.; H. B. Swete, *op. cit.*, p. ccxiii.

[2] This is where the preterists (see chapter 1, note 1) often fall down.

circumstances and events. But there is also a subsoil. The Apocalypse is firmly rooted in this subsoil! We refer to the sacred Scriptures. The mind of the seer was, as it were, immersed in these Scriptures. He was thoroughly acquainted with them. He *lived* them. They were hidden away in his heart. We maintain, therefore, that the Apocalypse is rooted not only in the surface-soil of contemporaneous events but also, and especially, in the subsoil of the sacred Scriptures. To be sure, the events of the particular day and age in which the apostle was living determined, to a certain extent, the mould in which this prophecy was cast. Nevertheless, they cannot begin to compare with the ages of history and prophecy with which the seer was so thoroughly familiar. We must explain this book in the light not only of external events but also of the entire religious heritage held in reverence by believers who lived when these visions were seen and recorded.

Let us give a very striking example. When we study Revelation 13: 1–10, we immediately notice that its symbolism is rooted in Daniel 7: 2–8. In both cases the same animals are referred to, though in Daniel they occur singly, one by one, while in the Apocalypse they are combined. Thus, the latter gives us the picture of a composite beast. It was 'like a leopard, and its feet were as the feet of a bear, and its mouth as the mouth of a lion . . .'. Now in Daniel these beasts—lion, bear, leopard, and 'anonymous'—indicate not kings but kingdoms, empires that arise in opposition to God's people. They refer to the world-power in four successive phases of manifestation. So what is more logical than to infer that the composite beast of the Apocalypse also has this same meaning and refers to an antichristian power, the antichristian persecution movement, in successive phases and embodiments? Concerning this beast we read that five of its heads were fallen when the apostle saw the vision. One raised itself at that very time, namely, the sixth. The other had not yet arrived (17: 10). Now, on the basis of a comparison with the book of Daniel, is it not very evident that the heads of this composite beast of the Apocalypse must indicate empires in which the world's persecuting power is successively embodied? For example, ancient Babylonia, Assyria, New Babylonia, Medo-Persia, Greco-Macedonia, and Rome. Yet many interpreters, who insist on explaining the Apocalypse in the light of its contemporaneous background, regard these heads as representing individual rulers, namely, Julius Caesar, Augustus, Tiberius, Caligula, Claudius, and Nero. These inter preters do not take sufficient account of the Old Testament basis of the Apocalypse. They see the surface-soil of contemporaneous history. They forget that there is such a thing as a subsoil, namely, the sacred Scriptures.

Let us permit Scripture to interpret Scripture.

First and foremost, we should do justice to the immediate context in which a passage occurs. This is often forgotten. But unless we interpret the various symbols in harmony with the context in which they occur, we shall never see the wonderful organic unity that characterizes the book. We shall miss the 'thread' of the discussion.

Once the context has been definitely determined and has received its full due, parallel passages should be consulted. First, and most important, parallels occur in the Apocalypse itself. When, for example, we interpret Revelation 20 in the light of what is in some respects its parallel, Revelation 12, the meaning becomes much clearer. The question concerning the devil's captivity will not be so difficult to answer.[1]

There are also parallel passages occurring in other books of the New Testament. Some of those which are found in the Gospel of John have already been indicated.[2] There are others in the Synoptics. Among the most striking New Testament parallel passages are the following:

Rev. 1: 3.	Mt. 24: 6; Lk. 21: 9.	Rev. 12: 9.	Lk. 10: 18.
Rev. 1: 5.	Col. 1: 18.	Rev. 13: 8.	1 Pet. 1: 19,20.
Rev. 1: 7.	Mt. 24: 30.	Rev. 16: 19.	1 Pet. 5: 13.
Rev. 1: 16.	Mt. 17: 2.	Rev. 17: 14.	1 Tim. 6: 15.
Rev. 2: 10.	Jas. 1: 12.	Rev. 18: 4.	2 Cor. 6: 17;
Rev. 2: 20–24.	Acts 15: 28.		Eph. 5: 11.
Rev. 3: 3.	Mt. 24: 42.	Rev. 18: 24.	Lk. 11: 50.
Rev. 3: 5.	Mt. 10: 32.	Rev. 21: 4,5.	2 Cor. 5: 17.
Rev. 6.	Mt. 24; Lk. 21.	Rev. 22: 21.	Eph. 6: 24.

Finally, the Apocalypse is steeped in the thoughts and images of the Old Testament.[3] Let us mention just a few passages which, at least as far as their form is concerned, are patterned after and based on what is found in the Old Testament.

[1] See pp. 184–186.

[2] See chapter 1, pp. 12 f.

[3] J. B. Lightfoot, *St. Paul's Epistle to the Galatians*, p. 361; A. Pieters, *op. cit.*, p. 72; A. T. Robertson, *Syllabus for New Testament Study*, p. 254; H. B. Swete, *op. cit.*, pp. cxxxix ff.; B. F. Westcott and F. J. A. Hort, *The New Testament in the Original Greek*, pp. 612 ff.; C. F. Wishart, *op. cit.*, pp. 14 ff.

	REVELATION	OLD TESTAMENT
Chapter 1.	The description of the Son of man.	Dn. 7: 9 ff.; 10: 5,6; Ezk. 1: 7, 26 ff.; 43: 2.
Chapter 2.		Observe such Old Testament expressions as: 'tree of life', 'paradise of God', 'Balaam' and 'Balak', 'Jezebel', 'rod of iron'.
Chapter 3.	The book of life.	Ex. 32: 33; Ps. 69: 28; Mal. 3: 16.
	The key of David.	Is. 22: 22.
Chapter 4.	A throne set in heaven.	Is. 6: 1; Ezk. 1: 26,28.
	The four living creatures.	Ezk. 1: 10; 10: 14.
Chapter 5.	The scroll.	Ezk. 2: 9; Zc. 5: 1–3.
	The Lion that is of the tribe of Judah.	Gn. 49: 9; Is. 11: 10.
Chapter 6.	The horses and their riders.	Ps. 45: 3,4; Zc. 1: 8; 6: 3.
Chapter 7.	Sealing the servants of God upon the forehead.	Ezk. 9: 4.
	The blessedness of the redeemed.	Is. 49: 10; 25: 8; Je. 20: 13; 31: 16; Ezk. 34: 23.
Chapters 8, 9.	The trumpets of judgment.	Ex. 7 ff.; the plagues.
Chapter 10.	The angel's sworn testimony.	Dn. 12: 7.
	The little book.	Ezk. 2: 9; 3: 3.
Chapter 11.	The measuring reed.	Ezk. 40: 3; Zc. 2: 1 ff.
	The two witnesses.	Zc. 4: 2 ff.
Chapter 12.	The woman, the child, and the dragon.	Gn. 3: 15.
	The angel Michael.	Dn. 10: 13,21; 12: 1.
Chapter 13.	The beast out of the sea.	Dn. 2: 31; 7: 3.
Chapter 14.	The white cloud; One like unto a Son of man.	Dn. 7: 13; 10: 16.
	The wine-press.	Is. 63: 3.
Chapter 15.	The song of Moses.	Ex. 15.
Chapter 16.	Har-Magedon.	Jdg. 5; 2 Ch. 35.
Chapters 17-19.	The fall of Babylon.	Is. 13; 14; 21; 46; 47; 48; Je. 25; 50; 51; Dn. 2; 7; Hab. 3. Compare also Ezk. 27; the fall of Tyre.
	The invitation to the birds.	Ezk. 39: 17–20.
Chapter 20.	Gog and Magog.	Gn. 10: 2; Ezk. 38; 39.
	The books of judgment.	Dn. 7: 10; 12: 1; Ps. 69: 28.
Chapter 21.	The new heaven and earth.	Is. 65: 17 ff.; 66: 22 ff.
	The new Jerusalem.	Ezk. 48: 30 ff.
Chapter 22.	The river of water of life; the tree of life.	Gn. 2; Ezk. 47: 1–12.

This is just a beginning. Westcott and Hort[1] give nearly four hundred references or allusions to the Old Testament, and an intensive study of any chapter of the Apocalypse soon reveals that this list of four hundred references is itself incomplete.

It is on the basis of these sacred Scriptures that we must interpret the Apocalypse. Nevertheless, we must be very careful: the seer is not a copyist. He receives visions. To be sure, these visions are of such a character that they can be received by an apostle of Jesus Christ whose mind and moral consciousness are saturated with the teachings of the Old Testament. John, however, is writing down what he sees and hears. The Old Testament teachings, moreover, are often poured into new moulds and acquire a slightly modified meaning in the Apocalypse. Whether or not this is true in any given case is determined by the immediate context.[2]

In emphasizing this basis of the Apocalyptic visions in the subsoil of the sacred Scriptures we must always bear in mind that it is wise to proceed from the clearer to the more obscure and never *vice versa*.[3] This has often been forgotten. A passage which by itself is rather obscure is seized on; for example, Revelation 20: 2. It is given a most literal interpretation. Then—to cap the climax—all the clear passages in the more didactic portions of Scripture are distorted in such a fashion that they will agree with the meaning which the 'interpreter' has poured into the obscure passage.

The result is that we get a good many novelties, that is, items of information which are not clearly derived from the plain teachings of Scripture elsewhere. A sound method of interpretation will endeavour to steer clear of novelties. The historical method of interpretation furnishes thousands of warning examples. Even parallelists who have written excellent commentaries have not always avoided them.[4]

This leads us to our eighth proposition which we formulate as follows:

> PROPOSITION VIII. *The Apocalypse is rooted in the sacred Scriptures. It should be interpreted in harmony with the teachings of the entire Bible.*

[1] *Op. cit.*, pp. 612 ff.

[2] F. Bleek, *Lectures on the Apocalypse*, p. 643; H. B. Swete, *op. cit.*, p. cliii.

[3] See B. B. Warfield, *op. cit.*, p. 643.

[4] R. C. H. Lenski (*op. cit.*, p. 600), who has made a very successful attempt to avoid them in his commentary, refers to a few of these novelties found in the commentaries of others.

III. THE ORIGIN OF THE BOOK IN THE MIND OF GOD

The Apocalypse is rooted in contemporaneous circumstances and in the sacred Scriptures. In the final analysis it is rooted in direct, special revelation. It has its origin in the mind of God. It was God who prepared and formed the soul of the apostle John so that he was able to receive this glorious prophecy. It was God who gave this vision. The God who inspired all the sacred writings so that they are all God-breathed is also the Author of the Apocalypse.

> PROPOSITION IX. *The Apocalypse is rooted in the mind and revelation of God. God in Christ is the real Author, and this book contains the purpose of God concerning the history of the Church.*[1]

[1] See chapter 1, p. 15.

CHAPTER SEVEN

REVELATION 1: THE SON OF MAN

1. *The Introduction* (verses 1–3)

THE first chapter of the Apocalypse consists of seven easily recognized parts. The introduction covers the first three verses. It contains the title of the book, a statement of its origin, and the first beatitude. The title of the book is 'The Revelation of Jesus Christ'. It is a revelation or unveiling of the plan of God for the history of the world, especially of the Church. It is, therefore, a direct communication from God and is not derived from any human source.[1] It is called the Revelation of Jesus Christ because Jesus Christ showed it to John and through him to the Church.

Notice the various links in the chain of origin and communication. First, there is God. We read: 'which God gave to him'.[2] It was God who highly exalted the Mediator and committed to Him the government of the world in the interest of the Church (1 Cor. 15: 24–28; Phil. 2: 9). God also gave the Mediator the plan for the history of the world and the Church (Rev. 5: 1,7). God gave Him this plan in order that He should make it known, in its general principles, to His servants. This plan pertains to things which must soon occur. They begin to happen at once.[3]

[1] *Cf.* C. A. Auberlen, *The Prophecies of Daniel and the Revelations of St. John*, pp. 81 ff. He points out that while both prophecy and apocalypse are products of divine, special revelation, the predominance of the divine act of unveiling over the human act of mediation is more clearly evident in apocalypse than in prophecy. The very term 'prophecy' emphasizes the human factor, whereas the word 'apocalypse' ('unveiling') stresses the divine act.

[2] A remarkable agreement with the Christology of John's Gospel. See Jn. 5: 20; 7: 16; 12: 49; 14: 10; 17: 7,8: 'for the words which thou gavest me I have given unto them'.

[3] We do not believe that the term 'shortly', as used here, indicates that the events are to follow one another in rapid succession. After all, a reference to Jas. 1:19; Acts 22: 18 is not decisive. The question is: what does the term mean *here*, in Rev. 1: 1? The context ought to decide. Verse 3 gives us an excellent commentary: the time is at hand: the symbols begin to be realized immediately. This view is confirmed by the parallel passage, Rev. 22: 10: 'And he saith unto me, Seal not up the words of the prophecy of this book;

Secondly, there is Jesus Christ. This is not the Revelation of John. It is the Revelation of Jesus Christ. He both reveals this plan to His Church, and as Mediator enthroned in glory causes it to be realized in history. He reigns on high.

Thirdly, there is His angel. Jesus, in turn, commissions an angel to guide John and to exhibit to him, by means of visions, the elements of the plan which are to be revealed. This angelic guide shows John a vision of heaven; then, of earth, of the wilderness, and of the new heaven and earth.

Fourthly, there is His servant John. The apostle John is meant.[1] John did not conceal these visions. He 'bare witness of the word of God and of the testimony of Jesus Christ, even of all things that he saw'.[2]

Fifthly, there is the reader or lector: 'blessed is he that reads'. Books had to be copied by hand, so they were few in number and very expensive. Besides, many Christians were not able to read. So a lector was appointed to read to the people assembled for worship. The lector who reads with a believing heart is pronounced blessed. This is the first of seven beatitudes.[3]

Sixthly, there are those that hear and keep the words of the prophecy. All believers who read and study this book with the proper attitude of heart are pronounced blessed. Remember, the time is at hand; the predictions begin to be fulfilled immediately.

2. *The salutation and adoration* (verses 4–6)

The book is addressed to 'the seven churches that are in Asia'. These churches are mentioned in verse 11. They were located in the Roman proconsular province of Asia, that is, the western part of Asia Minor. The seven, beginning with Ephesus, which was nearest—and perhaps dearest—to John in Patmos, then proceeding north to Smyrna and Pergamum, then south-east to Thyatira, Sardis, Philadelphia and Laodicea, formed a kind of irregular circle. It is helpful to consult a Bible map here. These seven churches represent the entire Church throughout this dispensation.[4]

for the time is at hand.' (*Cf.* 20: 7,12.) Thus interpreted—and we are confident that this is the correct interpretation—the very first verse of the Apocalypse deals the death-blow to any futuristic view.

[1] See chapter I, pp. 10ff.

[2] The term 'to bear witness' is characteristic of John's writings.

[3] The seven are found in the following passages: Rev. 1: 3; 14: 13; 16: 15; 19: 9; 20: 6; 22: 7; 22: 14. This is one more strong argument in favour of the unity of the entire book.

[4] See chapter I, p. 10; and chapter VIII, pp.60, 79f.

Notice the peculiar and very beautiful form of the salutation: 'Grace to you and peace from him who is and who was and who is to come.' Grace is God's favour given to those who do not deserve it, pardoning their sins and bestowing upon them the gift of eternal life. Peace, the reflection of the smile of God in the heart of the believer who has been reconciled to God through Jesus Christ, is the result of grace. This grace and this peace are provided by the Father, dispensed by the Holy Spirit, and merited for us by the Son. Therefore all three are mentioned in the salutation. Literally we read: 'Grace to you and peace from "He who is and was and is coming".' This is both good Greek and good English.[1] It very beautifully indicates the unchangeable God of the covenant (*cf.* Ex. 3: 14 ff.). The expression 'the seven spirits' refers to the Holy Spirit in the fullness of His operations and influences in the world and in the Church. With respect to Christ we notice He is described first with reference to His ministry on earth as the faithful witness; then in connection with His death and resurrection as the firstborn of the dead; and finally, in terms that express His present exaltation, as the ruler of the kings of the earth.

In this salutation we have the order of Father, Spirit, Son. The reason for this order, probably, is that God is viewed as dwelling in His heavenly tabernacle or temple (7: 15). Grace and peace are represented as coming from the Father, who dwelt above the ark in the holy of holies; and from the Spirit, indicated by the candlestick with its seven lamps in the holy place; and from Jesus Christ, whose atonement was symbolized by the blood under the altar of burnt-offering in the court.

The mention of Jesus Christ in the salutation results in this spontaneous adoration: 'Unto him that loves us . . . be the glory and the dominion for ever and ever. Amen.' Notice that believers are said to be loosed, not merely washed, from their sins. In that one observation, properly understood, there is material for a whole sermon. Observe also that the characterization 'kingdom . . . priests', which was formerly applied to Israel (Ex. 19: 6), is now applicable to believers collectively, that is, to the Church. In the Church Israel lives on. Can anyone read these words and still maintain that Christ is not the King of the Church?

Throughout this book the glory is ascribed not to the creature but to God in Christ (1: 6; 4: 8,11; 5: 9,13; 7: 10,12, *etc.*).

[1] We should not be too ready to condemn John's grammar. See Moffatt's translation, and *cf.* A. Pieters, *op. cit.*, p. 83.

3. *The announcement of Christ's second coming* (verse 7)

This is not the central theme of the book.[1] Yet it constitutes a real source of comfort for afflicted believers. It is the hope of believers and the consternation of the enemies of the Church. He comes 'with the clouds', that is, with glory (Dn. 7: 13; Mk. 14: 62; Ezk. 1: 4–28; Rev. 14: 14), and with anguish, wrath, judgment (Zp. 1: 15; Ps. 97: 2). The Bible knows nothing about an invisible or secret second coming. Nowhere is this taught. On the contrary, 'every eye shall see him'. Those who pierced His side shall also see Him. It is possible that the expression 'and they that pierced him' also indicates all others who have pierced the Christ by means of their disobedient lives. The expression is taken from Zechariah 12: 10 ff. (*Cf.* Jn. 19: 34, 37; 20: 25,27.)[2] The Jews who rejected Him are then going to see that Jesus of Nazareth, whom they crucified, is, indeed, the Christ!

'And all the tribes of the earth shall mourn for him.' This is not the mourning of repentance but that of hopelessness: 'as one that is in bitterness for his first-born'. (See Zc. 12: 10.) The expression refers to beating the breast in mourning and despair. Unbelievers will hide themselves in the caves and in the rocks of the mountains and will say, 'Fall on us and hide us from the face of him that sits on the throne, and from the wrath of the lamb . . .' (6: 16).

4. *Christ's self-designation* (verse 8)

That this glorious title refers to Christ should not be open to doubt. Both the immediately preceding and the immediately succeeding contexts have reference to Christ (see verses 7,13). The expression 'I am the Alpha and the Omega' is found in a slightly modified form in verse 17—'I am the first and the last'—where it refers to Him who was dead and is alive for evermore. Observe also the parallel passages, 21: 6–8 and 22: 13.

John hears the Lord Jesus Christ Himself speaking to him and saying, 'I myself am the Alpha and the Omega.' Alpha and Omega are the first and the last letters of the Greek alphabet. Thus Christ here describes Himself as being the complete

[1] In stating that the second coming is not the dominant note nor the main theme of the book we disagree with many excellent commentaries. See chapter 1, pp. 8 f; and D. S. Clark, *The Message from Patmos*, p. 25.

[2] This is yet another link between the Fourth Gospel and the Apocalypse. Both the author of the Fourth Gospel (Jn. 19: 37) and the author of the Apocalypse (Rev. 1: 7) follow the Massoretic Hebrew text of Zc. 12: 10, and desert the LXX, which adds weight to the evidence for common authorship.

and perfect and eternal revelation of God. He says, as it were, 'I am from the very beginning to the very end, that is, the Eternal One. Take courage; your enemy cannot destroy your Christ.' He Himself tells us that He is fully equal with the Father, for He adds: 'declares the Lord God, who is and who was, and who is to come, the Almighty.' Notice that the same phrase which in verse 4 described the Father here designates the Son. 'I and the Father are one' (Jn. 10: 30). Was this, perhaps, the voice which caused John to be 'in the Spirit'?

5. *John's commission to write the Apocalypse* (verses 9–11)

In verse 8 it was Christ who was speaking. Here, in verse 9, John himself again begins to speak. Observe the amiable way in which the apostle addresses his fellow Christians in order to gain their full confidence and to make them feel that he is standing on common ground with them: 'I John, your brother and partaker with you in the tribulation and kingdom and patience which are in Jesus.' He tells us that he was in the isle that is called Patmos for the Word of God and the testimony of Jesus. Does this mean that the apostle had been sentenced to hard labour because he refused to drop incense upon the altar of a pagan priest as a token of worshipping the emperor.[1] We are not sure. We do know that in some way or other his loyalty to Christ and His gospel had resulted in cruel exile.

It is the Lord's day, that is the first day of the week, the day on which we commemorate the Lord's resurrection.[2] John is probably thinking about Ephesus and the other churches in Asia Minor. Suddenly the earth seems to sink away under his feet, and his soul seems to be liberated from the shackles of time and space. He is taken out of contact with the physical world round about him; he is 'in the Spirit'. He sees, indeed, but not with physical eyes. He hears, but not with physical ears. He is in direct spiritual contact with his Saviour. He is alone . . . with God! (*Cf.* Dn. 8: 2; Is. 6: 1; Ezk. 1: 4; Acts 10: 10;

[1] W. M. Ramsay, *op. cit.*, pp. 85, 98.

[2] There is no reason for identifying 'the Lord's Day' with 'the Day of the Lord'. The Lord's Day is the day which we observe in commemoration of the Lord's resurrection; just as the Lord's Supper, 1 Cor. 11: 20, is the supper which we observe in remembrance of the Lord's death on the cross. The term 'the Day of the Lord' is a translation of the Hebrew 'the Day of Jehovah' and has a completely different meaning (see I. T. Beckwith, *op. cit.*, pp. 20 ff.). To identify these two terms in support of the notion that John in the Spirit was transported to the day of Christ's second coming is quite without foundation.

11: 5.) He is wide awake and every avenue of his soul is wide open to the direct communication coming from God.

In this condition John hears behind him a great voice as of a trumpet. Whenever God had anything to impart to His people during the Old Testament dispensation, He gathered them by means of a trumpet-sound (Ex. 19: 16,19; Lv. 25: 9; Jos. 6: 5; Is. 58: 1; *etc.*). Yet notice: '*as of* a trumpet'.

The voice said, 'What thou seest write in a book and send it to the seven churches', *etc.* The voice was that of Jesus Christ Himself. He ordered John to write what he saw and to send to the churches what he had written. We believe that John wrote down these visions while he received them (10: 4) or shortly afterward (1: 19).

6. *The vision of the Son of Man* (verses 12–16)

'And having turned I saw seven golden lampstands . . .' And among these lampstands John sees—with what a rush of memories and what a rapture of surprise!—the very Saviour on whose bosom he had once reclined. He is the same Saviour, yet different from the days of His humiliation. John describes this vision of the Son of man (verses 12–16).[1] Do not destroy the unity of the symbol. For example, do not interpret the sharp two-edged sword that proceeds out of Christ's mouth as indicating the sweet and tender influences of the gospel in its mission of conversion. Notice that in 2: 16 we read: 'and I will do battle against them with the great sword of my mouth'. This is addressed to those who refuse to repent. The entire description must be taken as one whole and interpreted as such.[2]

Let us try to see it thus. Notice that the Son of man is here pictured as clothed with power and majesty and with awe and terror. That long royal robe; that golden belt buckled at the breast; that hair so glistening white that like snow on which the sun is shining it hurts the eye; those eyes flashing fire, eyes which read every heart and penetrate every hidden corner; those feet glowing in order to trample down the wicked; that loud, reverberating voice, like the mighty breakers booming against the rocky shore of Patmos; that sharp, long, heavy great-sword with two biting edges; that entire appearance 'as the sun shines in its power', too intense for human eyes to stare at—the entire picture, taken as a whole, is symbolical of Christ, the Holy One,

[1] We use the definite article advisedly here. The term 'Son of man' is to be regarded as a proper noun which does not need the definite article in the original.

[2] See chapter v, pp. 38ff.

coming to purge His churches (2: 16,18, 23), and to punish those who are persecuting His elect (8: 5 ff.).

7. *The effect of the vision on John* (verses 17–20)
'When I saw him, I fell at his feet as one dead.' (*Cf.* Gn. 3: 8; 17: 3; Ex. 3: 6; Nu. 22: 31; Jos. 5: 14; Is. 6: 5; Dn. 7: 15; *etc.*) Yet the real purpose of the vision was not to terrify but to comfort John. We have something very similar in Habakkuk 3. After a very vivid description of the awe-inspiring march of Jehovah we read: 'Thou wentest forth for the salvation of thy people.' That also is the point here. 'Fear not, I am with thee, O persecuted flock.' The Son of man tenderly lays His right hand on John, an expression of love and an imparting of strength, so that the apostle's drooping and exhausted frame revives and he arises. Then the Saviour utters these words of comfort, 'Fear not; I am the first and the last, and the living one; and I was dead, and behold, I am alive for evermore, and I have the keys of death and Hades.'

Christ, too, had been put to death. But He had risen from the dead; glorious comfort for all those who were being persecuted unto death. Their living souls would join the ever-living Christ. He has the 'keys' of death, that is, authority and power over death, so that death cannot injure the believer but is to be considered gain for the kingdom; and so, also, for the believer. Not only has the Son of man the keys of death but also of Hades. Had He not Himself been in Hades? (See Acts 2: 27,31.)

It is evident that the term 'Hades' as used here cannot mean hell or the grave. It signifies the state of disembodied existence.[1] It refers to the state of death which results when life ceases and when body and soul separate. Thus Hades always follows death (Rev. 6: 8). But Hades was not able to hold the Son of man. He arose gloriously and now has authority over death and Hades, and from their terrors He is able to deliver believers, through the power of His resurrection (*cf.* 20: 13,14). Does not the Son of man reveal that He has the keys of death whenever He welcomes the soul of a believer into heaven? And does He not prove that He has the keys of Hades when at His second coming He reunites the soul and body of the believer, a body now gloriously transformed? What a wonderful comfort for persecuted believers, some of whom were soon to lay down their lives for the cause of the gospel.

[1] See art. 'Hades' in *ISBE* (1929 ed.). For Lenski's view see chapter III, p. 27, note 1.

Christ instructs John to write the things which he saw, that is, this vision of the Son of man; and 'the things which are', that is, the condition at that very time, of the seven churches in Asia Minor; and 'the things which shall come to pass hereafter', that is, the events that would happen throughout the entire future, according to their leading principles.

In harmony with the central meaning of the entire vision, there were two details needing additional comment. Christ here gives us His own explanation. He tells John that the seven stars which he had seen in the right hand of the Son of man indicate the angels of the seven churches. Angels must be taken in the sense of pastors, ministers.[1] The Lord holds them in His right hand; He exercises absolute authority over them; they are His ambassadors. He protects them; they are safe when they obey Him and are faithful in His service. '. . . And the seven lampstands are seven churches.' The churches are lampstands, that is, light-bearers. See Matthew 5: 14: 'Ye are the light of the world.' (*Cf.* Ex. 25: 31; Zc. 4: 2.) It is interesting to observe that the very word 'lampstand' is used in Matthew 5: 15. Notice the context: 'Neither do men light a lamp, and put it under a bushel, but on the lampstand (*lychnia*, the same word as in Revelation); and it shines to all that are in the house. Even so let your light shine before men; that they may see your good works, and glorify your Father who is in heaven.' (*Cf.* also Mk. 4: 21; Lk. 8: 16; 11: 33; Heb. 9: 2.)

In the Tabernacle there was one lampstand with seven lamps; here in Revelation we have seven lampstands. The reason for the difference is that during the old dispensation there was a visible unity, the Jewish church-state, whereas the churches of the new dispensation find their spiritual unity in Christ who is present and active among them in and through His Spirit. Therefore they need not fear. 'For where two or three are gathered together in my name, there am I in the midst of them' (Mt. 18: 20).

[1] If these 'angels' in fact indicated the messengers of the churches sent to visit John, as the Scofield Bible holds, the expression 'To the angel of the church at . . . write' would be meaningless. Nor can real angels, heavenly beings, be meant, for it would have been rather difficult to deliver the book or its epistles to them. Neither do we believe that the expression 'angels' can mean the churches as personified or as in the expression 'the *Spirit* of Ephesus'. We seriously doubt whether the expression, thus interpreted, would have been understood by those who first read or heard the book. For an excellent defence of the view that these angels refer to the bishops, pastors, or ministers of the churches, see R. C. Trench, *op. cit.*, pp. 53–58.

CHAPTER EIGHT

REVELATION 2, 3: THE SEVEN LAMPSTANDS

THE Apocalypse is a work of art, marvellous art, divine art. By subtle bands its various parts are tied together. One is unable to understand chapters 2 and 3 unless he has read chapter 1. And chapters 2 and 3, in turn, form the setting, as it were, for the later portions of the book. The promises found in these two chapters return and are explained more fully in later passages.

Do you wish to know what is meant by the words: 'To him that overcomes, to him will I give to eat of the tree of life, which is in the paradise of God'? Then turn to Revelation 22: 2,14. Again, are you looking for a definition of 'the second death' in view of the glorious promise: 'he that overcomes (or conquers) shall not be hurt of the second death'? Revelation 20: 14 offers you just what you are seeking. The 'new name' which is promised to the 'conquerors', 2: 17, reappears again and again: 3: 12; 14: 1; 22: 4; *cf.* 19: 12,13,16. The authority over the nations of 2: 26 receives its commentary in 12: 5; 20: 4. The morning star of 2: 28 re-occurs at 22: 16; and so it is with all the other promises.[1] The seven epistles belong to the very essence of the book. The book is one.

These seven epistles, moreover, reveal—with slight modifications—one pattern. This pattern appears most clearly in the epistles to Ephesus, Pergamum, Thyatira and Sardis. The seven parts are as follows:

1. The *salutation* or *address*; *e.g.*, 'To the angel of the church in Ephesus . . .'
2. Christ's *self-designation*; *e.g.*, 'he that holds the seven stars in his right hand . . .'
3. Christ's *commendation*; *e.g.*, 'I know thy works, and thy toil, and thy patience . . .'
4. Christ's *condemnation*; *e.g.*, 'But I have this against thee . . .'
5. Christ's *warning* and *threat*; *e.g.*, 'Remember therefore . . . or else . . .'

[1] R. C. Trench, *op. cit.*, p. 97; W. Milligan, *op. cit.*, p. 841.

6. Christ's *exhortation*; *e.g.*, 'He that has an ear, let him hear what the Spirit is saying to the churches.'

7. Christ's *promise*; *e.g.*, 'to him that overcomes . . . I will give to eat of the tree of life.'

In each church—with the single exception of Laodicea—Christ finds something to commend. In five of the seven He finds something to condemn. The laudable exceptions are Smyrna and Philadelphia.

These seven epistles are divided into two groups: one of three and one of four.[1] In the first three letters the exhortation is followed by the promise. In the last four this order is reversed.

The notion that these seven churches describe seven successive periods of Church history hardly needs refutation.[2] To say nothing about the almost humorous—if it were not so deplorable—exegesis which, for example, makes the church at Sardis, which was dead, refer to the glorious age of the Reformation; it should be clear to every student of the Bible that there is not one atom of evidence in all the sacred writings which in any way corroborates this thoroughly arbitrary method of cutting up the history of the Church and assigning the resulting pieces to the respective epistles of Revelation 2 and 3.

The epistles describe conditions which occur not in one particular age of Church history, but again and again.

1. *The letter to Ephesus* (2: 1–7)

Ephesus was wealthy, prosperous, magnificent, and famous for its shrine of Diana. The city was located near the western coast of Asia Minor, on the Aegean Sea and near the mouth of the Cayster River. Its harbour—in the days of its glory—accommodated the largest ships. Moreover, it was easily accessible by land, for Ephesus was connected by highways with the most important cities of Asia Minor. Ephesus was for a long time the commercial centre of Asia. The temple of Diana was at the same time a treasure house, a museum, and a place of refuge for criminals. It furnished employment for many, including the silversmiths who made miniature shrines of Diana.[3]

Paul visited this city (Acts 18: 19–21) on his way from Corinth

[1] See chapter II, pp. 22f. and R. C. Trench, *op. cit.*, p. 90.

[2] W. J. McKnight, 'The Letter to the Laodiceans', *Biblical Review*, XVI, p. 519; A. Pieters, *op. cit.*, pp. 100 ff. (an excellent discussion). The contrary view is defended by the Scofield Reference Bible.

[3] W. M. Ramsay, *op. cit.*, pp. 210–236.

to Jerusalem. This was during his second missionary journey, about AD 52. Here it was that he left Priscilla and Aquila (18: 19); and that Apollos taught with burning zeal (18: 25). On his third missionary journey Paul spent three years here (Acts 20: 31). His work was greatly blessed, not only in Ephesus proper but also in the surrounding region. The sale of silver shrines began to fall off, and when the temple of Diana was burned in AD 262 it was never rebuilt. Homeward bound from his third missionary journey, Paul bade farewell to the elders of the church at Ephesus in a very touching manner (Acts 20: 17–38). This was about the year AD 57. During his first imprisonment, AD 60–63, Paul sent his letter to the Ephesians from Rome.[1] After his release, the apostle in all likelihood made some more brief visits to Ephesus and left Timothy in charge of this church (1 Tim. 1 : 3). A few years later, in all probability very soon after the beginning of the Jewish war, say in AD 66, we find the apostle John in Ephesus.[2]

It was during the reign of Domitian (AD 81–96) that John was banished to Patmos. He was released and died during the reign of Trajan. Tradition relates that at a very old age John, too feeble to walk, would be carried into the church and would admonish the members, saying, 'Little children, love one another.'

Thus it will be evident that the church at Ephesus was more than forty years old when Christ dictated this epistle. Another generation had arisen. The children did not experience that intense enthusiasm, that spontaneity and ardour which had been revealed by their parents when the latter first came into contact with the gospel. Not only this, but they lacked their former devotion to Christ. A similar condition occurred in Israel after the days of Joshua and the elders (Jdg. 2: 7,10,11).[3] The church had departed from its first love.

Notice Christ's self-designation: 'He that holds the seven stars in his right hand, he that walks in the midst of the seven golden lampstands.' What is the reason for this designation? It is given because the seven stars indicate the ministers of the churches, Christ's true ambassadors, and the church at Ephesus had been troubled by 'false apostles' (2: 2), who had tried to

[1] This is not affected by whether or not we regard this Epistle as a circular letter. R. C. H. Lenski ably defends the genuineness of the words 'that are at Ephesus' (Eph. 1: 1) in his *Interpretation of St. Paul's Epistles to the Galatians, to the Ephesians, and to the Philippians*, pp. 329 ff.

[2] See F. Godet, *Commentary on the Gospel of John*, pp. 43 ff.

[3] See R. C. Trench, *op. cit.*, p. 80.

counteract the work of the true ministers. So to this church is given the assurance that the Son of man, exalted in glory, rules the ministers and knows what happens in the churches: He holds the stars and walks in the midst of the lampstands. Thus we find that in each separate instance Christ's self-designation has its bearing on the church to which the epistle is addressed.[1]

The church at Ephesus is praised for its work, toil, and endurance. With respect to these things it was a lampstand, causing the light of the Saviour to shine in the midst of the darkness of the world. It is worth special note that this church is also praised for its 'intolerance'. It had examined the would-be apostles, and, upon finding them false, had rejected them. In all these trials this church had been loyal to the true doctrine and had not become weary. It had heeded Paul's warning (Acts 20: 28, 29; *cf.* 1 Jn. 4: 1).

Then, suddenly, we read the accusation: 'But I have this against thee, that thou didst leave thy first love.' We have already explained the meaning of this serious reproach. To be sure, there were works, toil, and endurance in Ephesus; but all these may be present even though there has been a decay in love. A wife, for example, may be very faithful to her husband and may give evidence of bustling assiduity in all matters pertaining to him—and yet there may be a lessening of love. Her sense of duty alone may cause her to remain faithful in all the details of attention which she bestows upon him. Similarly, a church member may be very regular in his attendance at the services but, in spite of that, may not be as devoted to the Lord as he formerly was.

The church is urged to reflect on its fall, to come to a 'change of mind', so that it may again perform the first works. The threat 'or else I come to thee, and will move thy lampstand out of its place', was fulfilled. There is today no church in Ephesus. The place itself is a ruin.[2]

Then, very tenderly, the Lord resumes His praise: 'But this thou hast, that thou hatest the works of the Nicolaitans which I also hate.' It is probable that these Nicolaitans and 'those that hold the teaching of Balaam' (2: 14), and the followers of the woman Jezebel (2: 20), represent in general the same group or school of heretics. We shall meet them again. It would seem

[1] All commentators note this fact.

[2] See E. L. Harris's article, 'Some Ruined Cities of Asia Minor', in *The National Geographic Magazine*, Dec. 1908.

that they were individuals who not only refused to stay away from the immoral and idolatrous banquets of the heathen, but also tried to justify their sinful practices.[1] The Lord hates any compromise with the world. He praises the church at Ephesus for its firm stand against the works of the Nicolaitans.

Then follows the exhortation 'he that has an ear, let him hear what the Spirit is saying to the churches'. Note the plural. Each epistle must be read by all the churches and not merely by the one for which it is primarily intended.[2]

The expression 'to him that overcomes' means 'to the conqueror'. It is the same word used in 6: 2: 'and he came forth conquering and to conquer'. The conqueror is the man who fights against sin, the devil, and his whole dominion and in his love for Christ perseveres to the very end. To such a conqueror is promised something better than the food offered to idols, with which the heathen at their licentious festivals probably tried to tempt church members. The conqueror would be given to eat of the tree of life (Gn. 3: 22; Rev. 22: 2,14); that is, he would inherit eternal life in the paradise of heaven. Thus the promise is adapted to the general character of the epistle, as is true with respect to each of these seven messages.

2. *The letter to Smyrna* (2: 8–11)

This city, located on an arm of the Aegean Sea, was a rival of Ephesus. It claimed to be the 'First City of Asia in beauty and size'. A gloriously picturesque city, it sloped up from the sea, and its splendid public buildings on the rounded top of the hill Pagos formed what was known as 'the crown of Smyrna'. The westerly breeze, the zephyr, comes from the sea and blows through every part of the city rendering it fresh and cool even during the summer. From the very beginning of Rome's rise to power, even before its days of greatness, Smyrna was its loyal ally and was recognized as such by Rome. The faithfulness and loyalty of the Smyrnians became proverbial.[3]

In all probability the church at Smyrna was founded by Paul during his third journey, AD 53–56. We are not sure of this, but it would seem to be a safe conclusion from what we read in Acts 19: 10, '. . . so that all they that dwelt in Asia heard the word of the Lord, both Jews and Greeks'.

[1] See our explanation of the epistle to Pergamum and of that to Thyatira, especially pp. 67, 71 f.

[2] This fact is likewise stressed by almost all commentators.

[3] W. M. Ramsay, *op. cit.*, pp. 251–267.

It is possible that Polycarp was bishop of the church at Smyrna at this time. He was a pupil of John. Faithful to death, this venerable leader was burned at the stake in the year AD 155. He had been asked to say, 'Caesar is Lord', but refused. Brought to the stadium, the proconsul urged him, saying, 'Swear, and I will set thee at liberty, reproach Christ.' Polycarp answered, 'Eighty and six years have I served him, and he never did me any injury: how then can I blaspheme my King and my Saviour?' When the proconsul again pressed him, the old man answered, 'Since thou art vainly urgent that . . . I should swear by the fortune of Caesar, and pretendest not to know who and what I am, hear me declare with boldness, I am a Christian . . .' A little later the proconsul answered, 'I have wild beasts at hand; to these will I cast thee, except thou repent. I will cause thee to be consumed by fire, seeing thou despisest the wild beasts, if thou wilt not repent.' But Polycarp said, 'Thou threatenest me with fire which burneth for an hour, and after a little is extinguished, but art ignorant of the fire of the coming judgment and of eternal punishment, reserved for the ungodly. But why tarriest thou? Bring forth what thou wilt.' Soon afterwards the people began to gather wood and faggots; the Jews especially, according to custom, eagerly assisting them. Thus Polycarp was burned at the stake.[1]

We have purposely included this brief account of Polycarp's martyrdom so that the reader may become better acquainted with actual conditions which existed in the church during the first and second centuries AD.

It is to this church that Christ addresses Himself as follows: 'These things declares the first and the last, who became dead, yet lived',[2] that is, the One who was alive even while He was dead: the ever-living One. As in all the other epistles, so here: Christ's self-designation is in beautiful harmony with the general character of the message. Christ, the conqueror of death, the ever-living One, was able to say, as He does in this letter, 'Be thou faithful unto death, and I will give thee the crown of life' (2: 10).

'I know thy tribulation and thy poverty.' Extreme poverty is meant. These people were often thrown out of employment as a result of the very fact of their conversion. Besides this, they were usually poor in earthly goods to begin with. Becoming a Christ-

[1] *Ante-Nicene Fathers*, I, pp. 37 ff.

[2] See W. M. Ramsay, *op. cit.*, p. 269. He seems to prove his point with respect to the meaning of the aorist here.

ian was, from an earthly point of view, a real sacrifice. It meant poverty, hunger, imprisonment, often death by means of the wild beasts or the stake.[1]

The Lord tells these believers at Smyrna that they must not begin to pity themselves. They may seem to be poor but in reality they are rich, namely, in spiritual possessions, in grace and its glorious fruits (Mt. 6: 20; 19: 21; Lk. 12: 21). What a comfort for these persecuted believers to realize that their Lord 'knows' all this.

'. . . And the blasphemy of them that say they are Jews and they are not, but are a synagogue of Satan.' These Jews had very likely chosen Smyrna as their place of residence because it was a city of commerce. They not only vilified the Messiah but eagerly accused the Christians before the Roman tribunals. As always, they were filled with malign antagonism against Christians. (*Cf.* Acts 13: 50; 14: 2,5,19; 17: 5; 24: 1.) These so-called Jews might consider themselves to be 'the synagogue of God'; in reality they constituted 'the synagogue of Satan', the chief accuser of the brethren. How anyone can say that the Jews of today are still, in a very special and glorious and pre-eminent sense, God's people, is more than we can understand. God Himself calls those who reject the Saviour and persecute true believers 'the synagogue of Satan'. They are no longer His people.

'The devil is about to cast some of you into imprisonment, that ye may be tried.' Behind the Roman persecutors we see the Jews, filled with malign envy and hatred against believers and accusing them before the Roman tribunals. And these Jews in turn, are the instruments used by the devil himself. The devil would cast some into imprisonment, which very often meant death. But while Satan would be tempting the believers, God, by this selfsame affliction, would be proving, testing, or trying them: 'that ye may be tried'. This tribulation would last 'ten days', that is, a definite, full, but brief period.[2] The fact that the trial is but for a 'short season' is often given as an encouragement to endurance (Is. 26: 20; 54: 8; Mt. 24: 22; 2 Cor. 4: 17; 1 Pet. 1: 6).

'Be thou faithful unto death', does not merely mean 'be loyal until you die, but 'be faithful even though it costs your life'. Said the pilot, sailing his boat on a tempestuous sea, 'Father Neptune, you may sink me if you will; you may save

[1] E. H. Plumptre, *op. cit.*, p. 91.
[2] See W. Milligan, *op. cit.*, p. 845.

me if you will. But, whatever happens, I'll keep my rudder true.' A similar attitude is urged here—whatever happens, keep the rudder true; be faithful unto death. To those who are faithful is promised the wreath of victory, namely, the life of glory in heaven.[1] Even though believers may be put to death, namely, the *first* death, they are not going to be hurt by the *second* death, that is, they will not be cast, body and soul, into the lake of fire at Christ's second coming (Rev. 20: 14).

Smyrna was true to its calling to be a light-bearer. The testimony of Polycarp, given in the presence of Jews and heathen, was emulated by others.[2]

3. *The letter to Pergamum* (2: 12–17)

This city was located upon a huge rocky hill which, as it were, plants its foot upon the great surrounding valley. The Romans made it the capital of the province of Asia. Here Aesculapius, the god of healing, was worshipped under the emblem of a serpent, which to believers in Christ was the very symbol of Satan. Here were to be seen the many pagan altars and the great altar of Zeus.[3] All these things may have been in the mind of Christ when He called Pergamum the place 'where Satan dwells'. Yet, it seems to us that the obvious purpose of the Author is to direct our attention to the fact that Pergamum was the capital of the province and, as such, also the centre of emperor-worship. Here the government was carried on and here were the temples dedicated to the worship of Caesar. Here believers were asked to offer incense to the image of the emperors and to say 'Caesar is Lord'. Here Satan has his throne; here he has free rein. 'These things declares he that has the sharp two-edged sword.' Again the self-description is in harmony with the general tone of the letter. Christ is here said to have the sharp two-edged sword because He is going to war against the Nicolaitans, unless they repent (verse 16).

But in spite of the fact that Satan's throne was located here and the fact that Antipas had been put to death here because he refused to become unfaithful to his Lord, believers at Pergamum still clung tenaciously to their confession, to their Christ.

They made one big mistake, however, probably owing to the fact that they emphasized individual salvation at the expense

[1] See E. H. Plumptre, *op. cit.*, note on p. 97. This is not the royal diadem (Trench) but the wreath of victory.

[2] On the present condition of Smyrna see E. L. Harris, article cited above.

[3] W. M. Ramsay, *op. cit.*, pp. 281–290.

of a Christian's duty to be concerned about the welfare of the church as a whole: they neglected discipline.[1] Some of the members of the church had attended heathen festivals, and had, in all probability, even participated in the immoralities that characterized these feasts. Similar practices had occurred among the children of Israel in the days of Balaam (Nu. 25: 1,2; 31: 16). Like Israel, too, Pergamum had its Nicolaitans. Let us not think too lightly of this temptation. Refusing to partake of idol-meats, and especially refusal to attend the heathen feasts, meant withdrawal from a great part of the whole social life of that time. For one thing, the trades had their tutelary deities which would be worshipped at the feasts. Refusal to join in these feasts often meant that a man would lose his job, his trade; he would become an outcast.[2] Hence, some people began to argue that, after all, one might attend the feasts and partake of meats offered to idols, and perhaps even offer incense to the gods of the heathen, provided that he constantly bear in mind—a kind of mental reservation—that an idol is nothing! Others might carry this line of reasoning even farther and say, 'How can you condemn and defeat Satan unless you have become thoroughly acquainted with him?'

The church at Pergamum was not fully awake to the dangers of this compromising attitude, this half-way covenanting with the world. It should have disciplined these erring members. If it fails to do so, Christ is going to war against them with the sword of His mouth. We do not believe that this refers to a merely verbal condemnation. The verbal condemnation is contained in this epistle. It signifies destruction: Christ is going to destroy those who persist in their worldly practices: He will carry out His sentence of condemnation.

The conqueror, on the other hand, will receive 'the hidden manna', that is, Christ in all His fullness (Jn. 6: 33,35), hidden from the world, but revealed to believers even here on earth and especially in the life hereafter. In other words, those conquerors who overcome the temptation to participate in the heathen festivals and to eat food sacrificed to idols shall be fed by the Lord Himself; the grace of Christ and all its glorious fruits will be their food, invisible, spiritual, and hidden, indeed, but nevertheless very real and very blessed. They receive the bread from heaven.[3]

'And I will give him a white stone, and upon the stone a new

[1] See W. Milligan, *op. cit.*, p. 846.

[2] See pp. 71f.

[3] See W. Milligan, *op. cit.*, p. 846.

name written, which no one knows, but he that receives it.' Commentators are greatly divided in their opinions with respect to the meaning of these words. After lengthy study we have come to the conclusion that there are only two interpretations which are worthy of serious consideration. All others are objectionable on the surface.[1]

Each of the two remaining theories has so much in its favour that we have not been able to make a definite decision. We shall, therefore, state the theories and the arguments in support of each and then leave the reader to make his own choice, or to remain undecided.

According to the first interpretation the stone represents the person who receives it, just as in Israel the twelve tribes were represented by twelve precious stones in the breastplate of the high priest (Ex. 28: 15–21). Now this stone is white. This indicates holiness, beauty, glory (Rev. 3: 4; 6: 2). The stone itself symbolizes durability, imperishability. The white stone, therefore, indicates a being, free from guilt and cleansed of all sin, and abiding in this state for ever and ever. The new name written upon the stone indicates the person who receives the stone. It expresses the real, inner character of the person; his distinct, individual personality. Every one of the blessed is to have a particular and unique consciousness of that personality: a knowledge given to none but the recipient himself.[2]

[1] The following are among the views which we cannot accept:

a. That the white stone of the Apocalypse is the *tessera* or ticket which the visitor receives, admitting him to the feast of the Great King. See E. H. Plumptre, *op. cit.*, pp. 127 ff. for a very able defence of this view. An excellent refutation of this theory is found in an article by M. Stuart, 'The White Stone of the Apocalypse', in *Bibliotheca Sacra*, O, pp. 461–477.

b. That the white stone represents the pebble of acquittal used in courts of justice. M. Stuart, in the article just mentioned, likewise refutes this view.

c. That the white stone with the name inscribed upon it refers to the Old Testament Urim and Thummim. This is very ably argued by R. C. Trench, *op. cit.*, pp. 132 ff. and A. Plummer (*op. cit.*, p. 64) finds it a very attractive theory. It cannot, however, be correct. The arguments of Plumptre (*op. cit.*, pp. 126 ff.) against this view are decisive.

d. R. H. Charles, *Revelation* (*International Critical Commentary*), pp. 66 ff., argues that the true source of the symbol is to be found in the sphere of popular superstition. This needs no answer. A variety of other explanations may be found in *The Speaker's Commentary;* art. 'Stones' in Smith's *Dictionary of the Bible*, and elsewhere.

[2] This view (which is the popular one), with variations, is defended by J. P. Lange, *op. cit.*, p. 120, who, however, views the white stone itself as indicating acquittal; by R. C. H. Lenski, *op. cit.*, p. 113, and a host of others.

The following arguments may be presented in favour of this view:

a. The words 'which no one knows but he that receives it' must mean 'which no one knows but he that receives the name', not the stone. The believer himself receives this name and it must be his own new name. This is entirely in harmony with Revelation 19: 12, where we read this concerning the Christ: 'and he has a name written which no one knows but he himself'. The name, then, indicates the person who receives it.

b. If this new name had indicated the name of God or of Christ, this would have been plainly stated as in other cases (*e.g.* 3: 12; 14: 1; 22: 4).

c. This explanation rests upon the firm foundation of Old Testament parallel passages, for example:

> 'And thou shalt be called by a new name, which the mouth of Jehovah shall name' (Is. 62: 2);
>
> 'And he will call his servants by another name' (Is. 65: 15).

d. According to Scripture the name indicates the character or position of the bearer. On that account, very often, a person whose character is changed is given a new name to correspond with it. In glory we shall receive a new holiness, a new vision, *etc.* Therefore we shall receive a new name.

According to the second interpretation the pellucid, precious stone—a diamond?—is inscribed with the name of *Christ.* Receiving this stone with its new name means that in glory the conqueror receives a revelation of the sweetness of fellowship with Christ—in His new character, as newly crowned Mediator—a fellowship which only those who receive it can appreciate.[1]

In favour of this explanation the following arguments have been offered:

a. In all other passages of the Apocalypse, without a single exception, the new name refers to God or to Christ. This name is said to be written on the forehead of believers (3: 12; 14: 1; 22: 4).

b. The view that this name refers to Christ is supported by both the preceding and following contexts: the hidden manna refers to what Christ is for the believer; moreover, in this very series of epistles we find a parallel passage (3: 12) in which the name, though written on the believer, is definitely said to belong to Christ.

[1] For a defence of this interpretation see M. Stuart, 'The White Stone of the Apocalypse', *Bibliotheca Sacra,* O, pp. 461–477.

c. Granting that the expression 'which no one knows but he that receives it' means 'he that receives the name', this does not prove that the name is the believer's own new designation. The believer may be said to receive Christ's name inasmuch as Christ's name is written upon his (the believer's) forehead. In this connection it is interesting to observe that unbelievers receive the devil's imitation of the new name. They are said to 'receive a mark upon their foreheads' (20: 4) just as believers receive the name of Christ upon their foreheads (14: 1). Yet this 'mark' indicates 'another', namely, the beast. It is the mark of the beast, which unbelievers are said to receive. Similarly, in our present language (2: 17), believers receive the name of Christ, that is, His name is written on their foreheads, in the sense explained under *d.*

d. This view is in harmony with Old Testament symbolism which is embedded in several passages of the Apocalypse. On the forehead of the high priest—to be exact, on the front of the mitre—a name was written. It was the name not of the high priest himself but of Jehovah. This name designated the high priest as being the consecrated servant of Jehovah, as belonging to him. We read: 'And thou shalt make a plate of pure gold, and grave upon it, like the engravings of a signet, HOLY TO JEHOVAH. And thou shalt put it on a lace of blue, and it shall be upon the mitre; upon the forefront of the mitre it shall be. And it shall be on Aaron's forehead . . .' (Ex. 28: 36 ff.).

The meaning, then, is as follows. Just as during the old dispensation the name of Jehovah was written on the forehead of the high priest to indicate that he was the specially consecrated servant of Jehovah; so believers—who are constantly called priests in the Apocalypse—shall have a new name written on their foreheads, namely, the name of Christ, His new name. This name is not written on a plate of pure gold, but, even better, upon a precious, pellucid stone. It indicates that the conqueror belongs to Christ, is His servant, rejoices in His fellowship, in His new glory and dominion. Moreover, just as in the old dispensation only the high priest knew how to pronounce, and had learned the secrets connected with the name Jehovah, so in the new, only believers know the blessed meaning of the name of the Lord Jesus Christ. They—and they alone—know the meaning of fellowship with Him. In principle, they know it even here on earth; but a further revelation of the meaning of this name is reserved for them in heaven where for evermore those who here on earth were sealed with the seal of the living God on their forehead shall be designated as Christ's very own. They receive His name, that is, His new name is on their forehead.

Let us not exaggerate the difference between these two views. On the basis of the first, the believer receives a new name, that is, a new relation to his Saviour revealed in a gloriously transformed character. On the basis of the second interpretation, Christ reveals His new name to the believer, especially in the hereafter. We should like to ask, therefore, 'Does not Christ's new name—which He certainly has received—imply the believer's new name—which, again, he most assuredly shall receive?'

4. *The letter to Thyatira* (2: 18–29)

This place was situated in a valley connecting two other valleys. Lacking natural fortifications and being wide open to attack and invasion, a garrison was generally stationed here in order not only to defend the town but also to obstruct the path of the enemy to Pergamum, the capital. Being a centre of communication, with many people passing through it, Thyatira became a trading city. Here were to be found the trade-guilds: wool-workers, linen-workers, makers of outer garments, dyers, leather-workers, tanners, potters, *etc.*[1] These trade-guilds were associated with the worship of tutelary deities: each guild had its guardian god. The situation, therefore, was somewhat as follows: if you wish to get ahead in this world, you must belong to a guild; if you belong to a guild, your very membership implies that you worship its god. You will be expected to attend the guild-festivals and to eat food part of which is offered to the tutelary deity and which you receive on your table as a gift from the god. And then, when the feast ends, and the real—grossly immoral—fun begins, you must not walk out unless you desire to become the object of ridicule and persecution!

In this difficult situation what must a Christian do? If he quits the union, he loses his position and his standing in society. He may have to suffer want, hunger, persecution. On the other hand, if he remains in the guild and attends the immoral feasts, eating things sacrificed to idols and committing fornications, he denies his Lord.

In this difficult situation the prophetess Jezebel pretended to know the real solution of the problem, the way out of the difficulty. She, apparently, argued thus: in order to conquer

[1] W. M. Ramsay, *op. cit.*, pp. 316–326.

Satan, you must know him. You will never be able to conquer sin unless you have become thoroughly acquainted with it by experience. In brief, a Christian should learn to know 'the deep things of Satan'. By all means attend the guild-feasts and commit fornication . . . and still remain a Christian; nay rather, become a better Christian!

But if church members can persuade themselves that this course is right, they cannot deceive the One who has eyes 'like a flame of fire' and feet that are ready to trample upon the wicked. The Lord praises whatever is worthy of commendation: works, love, faith, ministry—loving service rendered to the brethren—and endurance. He also praises them for this, 'that thy last works are more than the first'. With respect to all of these Thyatira was, indeed, a lampstand, a light-bearer. But this does not constitute an excuse for failure to exercise discipline with respect to members who make a compromise with the world. Hence, we read: 'But I have this against thee, that thou sufferest the woman—not "thy wife"—Jezebel'. Her name is a synonym for seduction to idolatry and immorality (1 Ki. 16: 31; 18: 4,13,19; 19: 1,2). If this Jezebel of a woman remains impenitent—how gracious of the Lord that He gave her time to repent!—she is going to be cast upon a bed, that is, stricken with sickness; her natural children are going to die a violent death and her spiritual followers will also suffer punishment. Thus all the church shall know that Christ is He who searches the reins and hearts. His penetrating eyes see the hidden motive that makes people follow Jezebel, namely, unwillingness to suffer persecution for the sake of Christ.

On those who remain faithful Christ will impose no fresh burden (*cf.* Acts 15: 28,29). In their relation to the world they must take care not to commit fornication and not to eat things sacrificed to idols.

By and by the tables are going to be turned. At present the world oppresses the church member who desires to keep a clear conscience. By and by the church member who has remained loyal to his Lord is going to rule over the world and, being associated with Christ in the final judgment, is going to condemn the sinner. He is going to share in Christ's dominion over the nations—which Christ, in turn, had received from the Father (Ps. 2: 8,9); and on the day of the final judgment the wicked will be 'broken to shivers'. The potters of Thyatira were able to grasp the meaning of this symbol.

'And I will give him the morning star.' Here again the primary reference is to Christ Himself (Rev. 22: 16). As the morning star rules the heavens, so believers will rule with Christ; they will share in His royal splendour and dominion. The star is always the symbol of royalty, being linked with the sceptre (Nu. 24: 17; *cf.* Mt. 2: 2).

5. *The letter to Sardis* (3: 1–6)

Sardis, the impregnable, was situated upon a nearly inaccessible hill, overseer of the Hermus Valley, and in ancient times the proud capital of Lydia. Its people were arrogant, over-confident. They were sure—too sure, alas!—that no-one could scale this hill with its perpendicular sides. There was only one point of access: a very narrow neck of land toward the south and this could easily be fortified. But the enemy came, in 549 BC and again in 218 BC, and . . . took Sardis. One unobserved, unguarded weak point, an oblique crack in the rockwall, the one chance in a thousand for a night attack by skilful mountain-climbers, was all that was necessary to deal a crushing blow to the arrogance of the over-confident citizens of this proud capital. The hill upon which Sardis stood was too small for a growing city. Therefore the ancient Sardis, the acropolis, began to be deserted and a new city arose in its vicinity. When the Apocalypse was written, Sardis was facing decay, a slow but sure death.[1] In the year AD 17 the city was partly destroyed by an earthquake. Thus, again and again, the self-satisfied and boastful inhabitants of Sardis had seen destruction coming upon them 'as a thief in the night', most suddenly and unexpectedly.

Sardis was sinking into spiritual stupor. This explains Christ's self-description: 'the One who has the seven—life-giving—spirits.' He also has in His right hand the seven stars. By means of the ministers of the Word and their message the life-giving spirits are able to revive a dead church.

'I know thy works, that thou hast a name that thou livest, and thou art dead.' Sardis *enjoyed* a good reputation but it did not *deserve* this reputation. Whereas in Pergamum and in Thyatira a small element of the congregation had fallen into the temptation of the world, in Sardis the congregation as a whole had 'defiled its garments'. Sardis, too, was in the world. It should have been a light-bearer. It failed in its duty. Neither the Jews nor the Gentiles seem greatly to have troubled the people of Sardis. Sardis was a very 'peaceful' church. It enjoyed peace, but it was the peace of the cemetery! Christ tells these dead

[1] *Ibid.*, pp. 354–368.

church members that they must wake up and remain awake and must make firm the rest of the things that are on the verge of death. The lamp on the stand is beginning to burn more and more dimly. Soon the tiny flame will have been completely extinguished.

'I have found no works of thine filled full before my God.' The forms were there, the ceremonies, the religious customs, the traditions, the services; but the real essence was lacking. The forms were empty. They were not filled full of essence. Faith, hope, and love, genuine and sincere, were lacking. The reality was gone. In the sight of men, Sardis may seem to be a splendid church. 'Before my God' this church is dead. Therefore the people of Sardis should recall the past. With ardour and sincerity they had received the gospel; let them return to a life of obedience to the gospel as it was preached to them and as they—their parents—had received it.[1]

'If therefore thou wilt not watch, I will come as a thief, and thou shalt not know what hour I will come upon thee' (Mt. 24: 43). Sardis certainly would know what this meant.

'But thou hast a few names in Sardis that did not defile their garments; and they shall walk with me in white; for they are worthy.' 'A few names'—these individuals were known by name to the Father in heaven. They were known individually, each separately. God knew exactly who and what they were. He knows His own. They are as shining lights in the midst of the darkness of this world. These few who kept unspotted the garment of grace here would by and by wear the white garment of glory. White indicates holiness, purity, perfection, festivity (Is. 61: 10; Rev. 19: 8).

When earthly citizens die, their names are erased from the records; the names of the spiritual conquerors would never be blotted out; their glorious life would endure. Christ Himself would publicly acknowledge them as His very own. He would do this before the Father and before His angels. (*Cf.* Mt. 10: 32; Lk. 12: 8,9.)

6. *The letter to Philadelphia* (3: 7–13)

This city was situated in a valley, on an important road. It derived its name from Attalus II, 159–138 BC, whose loyalty to his brother Eumenes won him the epithet 'brother-lover'. It was founded with the intention of being a centre for the spread of the Greek language and manners in Lydia and in Phrygia

[1] *Cf.* especially the letter to Ephesus, pp. 61f.

and so from the very beginning it was a missionary city and very successful in its purpose.[1]

To this church Christ addresses Himself as the holy and true One. The pretensions of the false or non-genuine—that is, unbelieving—Jews are not pleasing to Him. Christ *alone* has 'the key of David', that is, the highest power and authority in the kingdom of God. (*Cf.* Is. 22: 22; Mt. 16: 19; 28: 18; Rev. 5: 5.) Christ knows that although this church has but little power, being small in number and in wealth, it has remained loyal to the gospel and has not denied the name of its Lord.

'Behold, I have set before thee a door opened, which none can shut.' The open door means, first, a wonderful opportunity to preach the gospel, and secondly, the operation of God's grace creating willing ears to listen and eager hearts to receive it. (*Cf.* 2 Cor. 2: 12; Col. 4: 3; Acts 14: 27.) Philadelphia's church, though of small account in human eyes, was great in God's eyes. Over against Jewish scoffers and accusers it had 'kept the word of Christ's patience', which probably means the gospel of the cross in which the Lord's patient suffering is set forth. Already it had obtained a wreath of victory in trial, which it is urged to hold fast. Notice that divine protection—'I will also keep thee'—and human exertion—'hold fast that which thou hast'—go hand in hand. A fourfold glorious reward is promised to this church which exhibits in such an adequate manner what it means to be a light-bearer.

First, over against the Jewish accusers and scoffers it will not only prevail—like Smyrna—but will gain the victory, a victory in which the vanquished, through their conversion, will share! Secondly, it will be kept safe through the hour of trial. (*Cf.* Is. 43: 2; Mk. 13: 20.) Thirdly, the conquerors will be made 'pillars' in God's temple. A pillar is something permanent. They will obtain the *one thing* which David desired (Ps. 27: 4). No earthquake will ever fill them with fear or drive them out of the heavenly city. They will abide there. Finally, Christ will write upon the conqueror the name of His God, and the name of the city of His God, the new Jerusalem . . . and His own new name. In other words, to the conqueror will be given the assurance that he belongs to God and to the new Jerusalem and to Christ, and that he will everlastingly share in all the blessings and privileges of all three. For an explanation of the phrase 'which comes down out of heaven from my God', see p. 199.

[1] See W. M. Ramsay, *op. cit.*, pp. 391–400.

7. The letter to Laodicea (3: 14–22)

Laodicea was situated in the neighbourhood of hot springs. Emitting lukewarm water from the mouth was a figure which its citizens could easily understand. A famous school of medicine grew up here, producing, among other things, a remedy for weak eyes. In this city the soft black wool from the sheep of the valley was woven into garments. But Laodicea was especially famous for its wealth. Located at the confluence of three great highways—be sure to consult a map—it grew rapidly into a great commercial and financial centre. It was the home of the millionaires. There were, of course, theatres, a stadium, and a gymnasium equipped with baths. It was a city of bankers and finance. So wealthy was this city that its inhabitants declined to receive aid from the government after the place had been partly wrecked by an earthquake.[1]

The citizens of Laodicea were rich—and they knew it! They were unbearable. Even the church people manifested this same proud, defiant, conceited attitude. Perhaps they imagined that their wealth was a sign of God's special favour. At any rate they began to think that they were 'all it'. They had imbibed the spirit that characterized the city as a whole. They boasted of their spiritual riches.[2] If the inhabitants of Laodicea would have said what they were thinking, their speech would have been as follows; listen carefully to one of these unbearable boasters, one who represents the rest: 'Rich am I—in spiritual goods—and all along I have been getting richer and richer, and whatever I have gained I still possess, and not one single need have I' (verse 17).

It is easy to see that these people were not troubled with any consciousness of sin. They would never even think of standing afar off with downcast eyes and drooping head, smiting their breast, saying, 'O God, be merciful to me, the sinner'. *They* had 'arrived'! Hence, to their own way of thinking, they were not in need of any admonition and they could afford to be lukewarm with respect to any exhortation. 'Lukewarm', that is the word. The people of Laodicea knew exactly what that meant. Lukewarm, tepid, flabby, half-hearted, limp, always ready to compromise, indifferent, listless: that 'we're-all-good-people-here-in-Laodicea' attitude. The author of this book has become

[1] *Ibid.*, pp. 413–423. See also W. J. McKnight, art. cited above, pp. 519 ff.

[2] That they boasted of their spiritual wealth, and not primarily of their material possessions is the view supported by nearly all commentators. W. Milligan, however, defends the opposite view.

personally acquainted with this attitude on the part of some church members. You cannot do anything with such people. With the heathen, that is with those who have never come into contact with the gospel and who are therefore 'cold' with respect to it, you can do something. With sincere, humble Christians you can work with joy. But with these 'we're-all-such-very-good-folks-here-in-Laodicea' people you can do nothing. Even Christ Himself cannot stand them. An emotion, a feeling is here ascribed to the Lord which is not predicated of Him anywhere else in the Good Book. We do not read that He is grieved with them. Neither do we read that He is angry with them. No, He is *disgusted* with these straddlers. And not just slightly disgusted but thoroughly nauseated. 'So because thou art lukewarm, and neither hot nor cold, I will spew thee out of my mouth.' Knowing very well that their entire religion is just so much sham and pretence, so much hypocrisy, the Lord introduces Himself to them as their very opposite: 'These things saith the Amen, the faithful and genuine witness.' In other words, the Lord reveals Himself here as the One whose eyes not only see exactly what is going on in the hearts of these people of Laodicea but whose lips also declare the exact truth as seen. He states, moreover, that He is the 'beginning of the creation of God', that is, the source of the entire creation (*cf.* 21: 6; 22: 13; Jn. 1: 1; Col. 1: 15–18). 'People of Laodicea, you need to become new creatures: you need new hearts. Turn to me, therefore, that ye may be saved.'

Even though the Lord is thoroughly disgusted with this church because it fails in its duty as light-bearer, nevertheless, there is grace here: wonderful, tender love and admonition. Christ does not really say: 'I *will* spew thee out of my mouth', but 'I *am about to* spew thee out of my mouth'. The Lord is still waiting. He sends this epistle in order to drive out that lukewarm spirit. He is very severe in His condemnation because He is very tender and kind, loving and gracious.

To this congregation, and therefore to its typical member, the Lord says, 'You say that you are rich and have become richer right along, and have kept whatever you have gained, and that you have need of nothing whatsoever; but you do not know that *you*, yes *you yourself*, are the one who is wretched and pitiable and beggarly and blind and naked.' Notice, it is not 'miserable' but 'pitiable'. Who is more to be pitied than an individual who imagines that he is a fine Christian, whereas in reality the Christ Himself is utterly disgusted with him? Read those words very slowly and try to see the picture of an individual who has all these five characteristics combined—wretched, pitiable, a cringing beggar, blind, and naked!

'I counsel thee.' How tenderly He speaks—not 'I command' but 'I counsel'. Christ counsels this church to buy of Him—'of me' is very emphatic—gold refined by fire, white garments, and eyesalve. In brief: 'buy of me salvation', for salvation is gold because it makes rich (2 Cor. 8: 9); it is white robes because it covers the nakedness of our guilt and clothes us with righteousness, holiness, and joy in the Lord; it is eyesalve because when we possess it we are no longer spiritually blind. Salvation must be bought, that is, we must obtain rightful possession of it. But how can those who are poor, and so on, buy anything? Read Isaiah 55: 1 ff. and you have the glorious answer!

Is there anything more wonderful in the entire Bible than this, that to these lukewarm people, with whom the Lord is so thoroughly disgusted that He is about to spew them out of His mouth, He now addresses Himself in these words: 'As many as I love, I reprove and chasten: be zealous therefore and repent . . . be zealous, therefore; and once for all repent . . . Behold, I am standing against the door and I am knocking.'

Notice that the Lord, as it were, is pressing against the door that it may be opened. Not only that but—as is evident from the next clause—He not only knocks again and again but He also calls the sinner. Notice the phrase 'if any man hear my voice'. It is not the person who is inside who takes the initiative. No, this text is in complete harmony with the entire Bible in its teaching concerning sovereign grace. It is the Lord who is standing at, or rather, against, the door—no-one has called Him—it is He who is knocking, not once but again and again: it is He who is calling, and this voice of the Lord in the gospel as applied to the heart by the Spirit is the power of God unto salvation. In this way we find that this passage does full justice both to divine, sovereign grace and to human responsibility.[1]

'If any man hear my voice and open the door, I will come in to him, and will sup with him, and he with me.' Notice it is 'if any one . . .' The Lord addresses Himself to individuals. Salvation is a very personal matter. '. . . Hear my voice and open the door'; when the heart has been opened by the voice of the Lord,

[1] It is clear, of course, that man, not God, is here represented as opening the door. Man repents. The opening of the door, accordingly, refers to conversion, and cannot refer to regeneration, which is entirely God's work. In conversion man takes an active part.

this principle of regeneration becomes active so that, by the power of the Holy Spirit, the regenerated individual opens the door and receives the Christ. This opening of the door is what is generally called conversion. Do not confuse regeneration (Jn. 3: 3 ff.; Acts 16: 14) and conversion. Here, in the expression, 'if any man opens the door,' the reference is to conversion, to repentance and faith in Christ, as the context clearly indicates. The Lord enters (Jn. 14: 23). How wonderful! He, as it were, descends from the throne of His glory in order to dine with this individual who in himself is so poor and pitiable. Christ and the believer dine together, which in the East was an indication of special friendship and of covenant relationship. In other words, the believer has blessed fellowship with his Saviour and Lord (Jn. 14: 23; 15: 5; 1 Jn. 2: 24). That fellowship begins even in this present life. It is perfected in the hereafter when the conqueror shall sit with Christ on His throne, just as Christ, the Conqueror, sat down with His Father on His throne. Not only will the conqueror reign by and by; he will reign with Christ (Rev. 20: 4), in the closest possible fellowship with Him.

'He that has an ear, let him hear what the Spirit is saying to the churches.'

The sevenfold condition of these churches actually existed at that time. It exists today. It has existed during the entire intervening period. These seven churches represent the entire Church during the entire dispensation. It has become abundantly evident that the one great question is this, are these churches faithful to their charge? Do they hold fast the name of the Lord in the midst of the darkness of this world (Rev. 1: 20)? In other words, are they lampstands, light-bearers? In Sardis and in Laodicea the world seems to have triumphed. We see but a tiny flicker of light; the light has nearly—yet not entirely—gone out. In Ephesus the light is still shining but the flame is diminishing. In Pergamum and in Thyatira, where the temptation coming from the side of the world was very real, the light is shining but not as brightly as it should be. In Smyrna and in Philadelphia the true character of the church as light-bearer is revealed and here one finds loyalty to Christ; therefore real influence for good is being exerted upon the world. Is this church a real light-bearer? That is the one, main question in all these epistles. Is it true to its Lord in the midst of the world?

The temptation to become worldly and to deny the Christ came from three directions.[1] First, from the side of anti-

[1] See pp. 144ff., 167ff.

christian persecution, the sword, the wild beasts, the stake, imprisonment (2: 10,13; 2: 9 and 3: 9), and the Jews who were constantly accusing the Christians before the Roman courts. Secondly, and very closely related to the first, from the side of the Roman religion, emperor-worship (2: 13). The first source of temptation cannot be separated from the second; yet the two can, and should, be distinguished. Thirdly, there was the temptation of the flesh: the constant invitation to join in the immoral feasts of the heathen in order to make one's social position secure and to enjoy the pleasures of the world. And this form of temptation, as we have seen, was very closely related to the second, religious, form. The church is in the world. That was true then. It is still true today. The church should shine in the midst of darkness.

'Ye are the light of the world—and the seven lampstands are seven churches.'

CHAPTER NINE

REVELATION 4–7: THE SEVEN SEALS

WHENEVER in history the Church is faithful to its calling and bears testimony concerning the truth, tribulation is bound to follow. Apart even from this fact, the Church is *in* the world. Accordingly it suffers along with the world. Children of God do not escape the horrors of war, famine, and pestilence. The Church needs these tribulations. It needs both the direct antagonism of the world and participation in the common woes that pertain to this earthly life as a result of sin. The Church, too, is sinful. It is in constant need of purification and sanctification.

These tribulations, therefore, are employed by our Lord as an instrument for our own spiritual advancement. We see God's footstool. Let us not forget His throne! To be sure, we say that to them that love God all things work together for good; but do we really believe it? Sometimes we speak and act as if the control of events and the destiny of the world rested in the hands of *men* instead of in the hands of God. Chapters 4 and 5, however, supply the needed correction and bring us a vision of the throne which rules the universe.

In the midst of trial and tribulation may our gaze be towards the One who is King of kings and Lord of lords.

1. *The vision of the throne* (4: 1–6)

'After these things I saw, and behold, a door standing open in heaven' (4: 1). Having heard the epistles to the churches, John returned for a while to his ordinary state of mind. How long this interval lasted we do not know. Afterwards he had a vision. He is not yet 'in the Spirit'. When a person has a vision, he may still be sensible to his surroundings. Thus, for example, Stephen is fully aware of the presence of those evil men who are stoning him. In fact, he is addressing them while he has the vision of the heavens opened and the Son of man standing at the right hand of God (Acts 7: 54–60; see also Mt. 3: 16). Similarly, the apostle John now has a vision. With wide-eyed wonder he beholds a door standing open in heaven. (*Cf.* Ezk. 1: 1.) While he is looking, the same voice that spoke to him before (1: 10) addresses him. It is the voice of Christ, bidding him: 'Come up here'. The seer's spirit receives the invitation to ascend to the throne above. We mean, of course, to the throne as it appears in the vision. Only when we view all things, including our tribulations (chapter 6), from the aspect of the throne, shall we gain a true insight into history.

'. . . And I will show you the things which must come to pass hereafter.' This, of course, cannot mean: 'I will show you the things which must come to pass after this dispensation'.[1] As in 1: 19 so here 'hereafter' means 'in the future'.

'Immediately I was in the Spirit.' Was this the result of the voice which the apostle heard? From the condition of merely seeing a vision, the soul of John now enters the higher ecstatic state of 'being in the Spirit'. Certainly what the apostle is about to see is also a vision. If it is not a vision, it is necessary for us to imagine that in heaven there is a material throne surrounded by twenty-four literal, physical thrones, and that the literal Lamb has seven horns and seven eyes. This, of course, is absurd. John receives a *vision*. It is a continuation of 'the door standing open in heaven'. Yet, this is more than a vision, that is, the seer now enters a higher ecstatic state, namely, that of 'being in the Spirit'. One can have a vision without being in the Spirit, as we have already indicated with respect to Stephen. When a person is 'in the Spirit' and being in that state has a vision, there is a suspension of conscious contact with the physical environment. John no longer sees with his physical eyes; he no longer hears with his physical ears. His soul is drawn away from all surrounding objects and wholly fixed on the things which are shown to him in the vision. It is 'carried away' to the region of the throne (*cf.* 17: 3), to the region of the throne as it appears to him in the vision.[2]

But though the various objects which John beholds do not exist in that physical, material form, they express an important spiritual truth. They teach one main lesson. Let us not lose ourselves in our interpretation of details; let us not try to find a 'deeper meaning' when there is none. We repeat: chapters 4 and 5 teach one main lesson. The picture is one; the lesson is one.

[1] This representation is, however, favoured by many pre-millennialists. See the introductory note to the book of Revelation in the Scofield Reference Bible.

[2] *Cf.* C. A. Auberlen, *The Prophecies of Daniel and the Revelations of St. John*, pp. 76 ff.

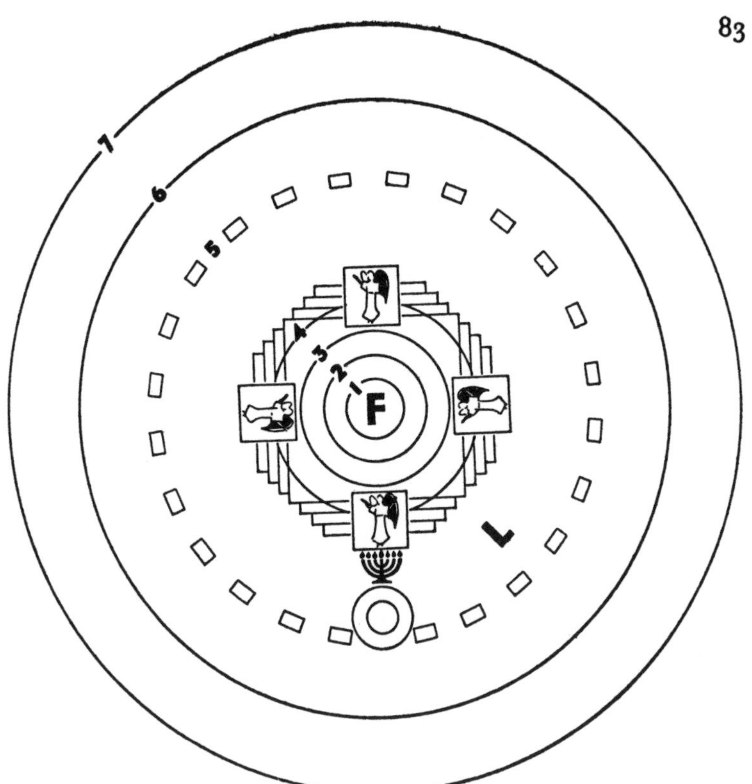

Diagram of the vision described in Revelation 4 and 5:

THE UNIVERSE GOVERNED BY THE THRONE

The vision consists of one single picture and teaches one main lesson. The square at the centre represents the throne with steps leading up to it. In the centre of the throne sits the Father (Rev. 4: 2).

The innermost circle 1 represents the sparkling white diamond (4: 3); circle 2 the sardius (4: 3); circle 3 the emerald rainbow (4: 3); circle 4 the four living ones or cherubim (4: 6); circle 5 the twenty-four thrones with their elders (4: 4); circle 6 the many angels (5: 11); and circle 7 all other creatures in the entire universe (5: 13).

The seven lamps and the sea of glass are also before the throne (4: 5,6). The Lamb (L) *stands between the throne and the living ones on the one side, and the twenty-four elders on the other (5: 6). But the Lamb later advances to the throne (5: 7), and is now seated on it with the Father (22: 1).*

The throne rules over all. Take this lesson to heart!

These chapters, moreover, do not give us a picture of heaven. They describe the entire universe from the aspect of heaven. The purpose of this vision is to show us, in beautiful symbolism, that all things are governed by the Lord on the throne. 'All things' must include our trials and tribulations. That is the point. That is why the description of the throne precedes the symbolic prediction of the trials and tribulations which the Church must experience here on earth. These are described in chapter 6. Study carefully the diagram of this vision in connection with Revelation 4,5, and our explanation.

Chapters 4 and 5 teach one main lesson. Unless we clearly grasp this point, we shall never see the glorious unity of the Apocalypse. We shall lose ourselves in allegorization. That one main lesson may be expressed in the words of the Psalmist: 'Jehovah reigns; let the peoples tremble! He sits above the cherubim; let the earth be moved.' The assurance of this truth should impart comfort to believers in the midst of fiery trials. That is why this vision of the universe governed by the throne precedes the symbolic description of the trials through which the Church must pass, chapter 6. This is a very beautiful arrangement.

With the aid of our diagram let us now study this vision.

'Behold, *a throne*!' The throne is the very centre of the universe, not the physiographical but the spiritual centre. Here is the true foundation for astronomy. The universe of the Bible is neither geocentric nor heliocentric nor sagittario-centric but coelocentric, that is, theocentric.[1] See the diagram. Here, too, is the true philosophy of history. The newspapers and radio announcements give you the headlines and news-flashes. The magazines add the explanations. But these explanations are, after all, in terms of secondary causes. The real mind, the real will which—while fully maintaining the responsibility and freedom of the individual instruments—controls this universe is the mind, the will of the Almighty God! Nothing is excluded from His dominion.

The term 'throne' occurs seventeen times in these two chapters. That throne is not on earth but in heaven. It stands in the Holy of holies of the heavenly temple just as the ark of the covenant stood in the Holy of holies of the earthly Tabernacle or Temple (Ex. 25: 22). In this vision we very definitely have a

[1] At various times in the history of cosmography the earth, the sun and the stars have been placed at the centre of the universe.

tabernacle or temple scene.[1] God is king and as such dwells in the temple. The representation that His throne is in the temple is clearly based upon biblical symbolism (Is. 6: 1; Je. 3: 17; 14: 21; Ezk. 1: 26; 8: 4; 43: 7).

'. . . And one sitting upon the throne.' Upon the throne sits —in majesty—God the Father. What the apostle describes is not God Himself, for He cannot be described (Ex. 20: 4), but His effulgence, His radiance. In the vision He is represented as surrounded with the flashing lustre of the diamond, crystal-clear (21: 11), white, consuming,[2] symbolizing God's holiness; and with the bloody red of the sardius, indicating that this holy character of Jehovah expresses itself in judgments. It cannot tolerate sin, and this explains these seven lamps of fire, and these flashes of lightning, rumblings, and peals of thunder that proceed from the throne (4: 5). Such is God, the Holy One. Such is His throne of majesty. Tremble before Him, O earth and its inhabitants!

Yet, around the throne there is a rainbow translucent green in appearance, signifying that for God's children the storm is over. Christ stood in the poor sinner's place. The sun, long hidden, is shining into the clouds. Even though God's holiness cannot brook sin and must be expressed in judgments, yet these very woes have as their purpose the salvation of the sinner and his furtherance in sanctification. All things—including slaughter and poverty, war, famine, and pestilence—work together for good to them that love God, that are called according to His purpose (see Rom. 8: 28).

'And from what looked like his loins downward I saw something that resembled fire, with a radiance round about it resembling the bow that appears in the clouds on a rainy day.'

2. *The elders and the living ones* (4: 7–11)

Around the central throne John sees twenty-four thrones, and upon these thrones twenty-four elders, probably representing the entire Church of the old and the new dispensation. Think of the twelve patriarchs and the twelve apostles. (*Cf.* Rev. 21: 12–14.) They wear the garments of holiness and upon their heads there are golden crowns of victory. These twenty-four elders are mentioned first for the simple reason that they *are* first in importance and in glory of all creatures in heaven (Gn. 1: 26;

[1] For the opposite view, see R. C. H. Lenski, *Interpretation of St. John's Revelation*, p. 171.

[2] The translation 'jasper' does not fit Rev. 21: 11.

Heb. 2: 8). We must not lose sight of the fact, however, that the real reason why these twenty-four thrones with their occupants are mentioned here is to enhance the glory of the throne that stands in the centre. That throne represents God's sovereignty. The twenty-four elders are constantly rendering homage to the Being upon the throne. So great is the throne!

Whom do these elders worship? Only the Father? No, the triune God. As in 1: 4,5, so also here we have a description of the Trinity in terms of temple symbolism. *The Father* is seated upon the throne out of which issues flashes of lightning and rumblings and peals of thunder. He is pictured here as dwelling in the heavenly Holy of holies.[1] Further, just as in the Holy place of the earthly Tabernacle, so here, John sees seven lamps of fire. Here he sees them as burning before the throne. (See diagram.) They symbolize the ever-active, superlatively wise, and all-seeing *Holy Spirit*, full of fire for the wicked; full of sanctifying power for the godly. Furthermore, as the court of the earthly Tabernacle had its laver or 'sea', so here John beholds a sea. This sea is before the throne. It is of glass, like crystal, indicating sanctifying power. We should think of it as containing, symbolically, the cleansing blood of Christ, *the Son*, in which the saints have 'washed their robes and made them white' (7: 14).

'And in the midst of the throne and around the throne four living ones studded with eyes before and behind' (4: 6). Each of these 'living ones' stands on one side of the throne in the middle of the steps leading up to it so that there is one 'living one' for each side of the throne, and the four encircle the throne. (See the diagram.) These four 'living ones' standing ready to render service to God in any of the four directions, that is, in any part of the universe, represent all the 'living ones', just as the twenty-four redeemed elders represent the entire army of the redeemed. But who are these 'living ones'?

In order to answer this question we should bear in mind that there is a very close connection between this entire throne vision and the first and tenth chapters of Ezekiel. We urge the reader to study Ezekiel 1 and 10 very carefully. Notice the following striking resemblances.[2] In both cases these beings are called 'living ones'. (*Cf.* Ezk. 1: 5 with Rev. 4: 6.) In both cases the symbolic number is the same, namely, four. (*Cf.* Ezk. 1: 5 with Rev. 4: 6.) In both cases the appearance of their

[1] See p. 85, note 1.

[2] *Cf.* R. H. Charles (*op. cit.*, I, pp. 118 ff.) who enumerates various items of contrast.

faces is compared to that of man, lion, ox, and eagle. (*Cf.* Ezk. 1: 10 with Rev. 4: 7.) In both cases they are closely associated with the throne. (*Cf.* Ezk. 1: 26 with Rev. 4: 6.) In both cases fire moves to and fro among the 'living ones'. (*Cf.* Ezk. 1: 13 with Rev. 4: 5: 'Out of the fire went lightning.') In both cases these 'living ones' are said to be studded all over with eyes. (*Cf.* Ezk. 1: 18; 10: 12 with Rev. 4: 8.) In both cases a rainbow encircles the throne with which the 'living ones' are associated. (*Cf.* Ezk. 1: 28 with Rev. 4: 3.) The few minor differences in the description of the 'living ones' need not surprise us. In fact, we should expect them. They are entirely in harmony with the distinct purpose which each author has in mind.[1]

But Ezekiel 10: 20 tells us in so many words that the 'living ones' are the cherubim. We, therefore, fully believe that here in Revelation also these 'living ones' are the cherubim.[2] They are a very high order of angels, one of the highest orders. This conclusion is altogether reasonable. The cherubim guard the holy things of God (Gn. 3: 24; Ex. 25: 20), so it is altogether normal and natural that we find them here in this vision in close proximity to the throne. Besides, we find them here in the heavenly Holy of holies, exactly where one expects to find them (Ex. 25: 20).

Observe also that the song of these 'living ones' is the song of angels. In Isaiah the seraphim sing it (Is. 6: 1–4). Then why should not the cherubim sing it?

This conclusion receives added confirmation from the consideration that the 'living ones' are described as being in strength like the lion, in ability to render service like the ox, in intelligence like man—notice also their many eyes, indicating intellectual penetration—and in swiftness like the eagle, ever ready to obey God's commandments and to render service. Surely it is worthy of attention that the characteristics of strength, service, intelligence, and swiftness are everywhere ascribed to angels. (*Cf.* Ps. 103: 20,21; Dn. 9: 21; Lk. 12: 8; 15: 10; Heb. 1: 14; *etc.*)

When in 5: 11 we read that 'many' angels surrounded the twenty-four elders, this does not in any way conflict with the conclusion which we have reached, namely, that the 'living

[1] So, for example, the fact that each of the cherubim in Ezekiel has *four* faces, so as to be facing in all four directions simultaneously, is thoroughly in harmony with their mission, namely to carry the throne in whichever direction its Occupant wills. In Revelation the cherubim do not carry the throne.

[2] A. Pieters, *op. cit.*, p. 112.

ones' on the steps of the throne are the cherubim.[1] And when in 7: 11 we read that 'all' the angels were standing round about the twenty-four elders, this 'all' refers, of course, to the 'many' of 5: 11: all the 'many' angels were standing around the twenty-four elders.

We do not believe that these cherubim have any deeper significance. We do not believe that they represent all creatures. When the seer wishes to refer to all creatures, he does so in clear language (5: 13).

The question arises, why these cherubim? The answer is that they are introduced for the same reason as the twenty-four elders, that is, to enhance the significance of the throne.[2] So great is the throne that even the all-glorious and holy cherubim arrange themselves around it in reverence, humility, and awe, ever ready to carry out the will of the Sovereign of the universe. They ascribe glory and honour and thanksgiving to the ever-living One who sits upon the throne. (See 7: 12.) They do this not once but again and again. They are constantly saying, 'Holy, holy, holy, Lord God the Almighty, who was and who is and who is coming.' Thus these cherubim glorify God, the Father, who represents the Trinity. (*Cf.* Is. 6: 3.) No wonder, for they dwell in His immediate presence. They see His glory. They take notice of His wisdom and they see better than we do in this sinful world that history is the realization of His will. So they prostrate themselves in the act of worship (5: 8).

Now, on every occasion, their 'Holy, holy, holy', is immediately followed by the song of the elders. It is the song of praise to the Father Creator. These elders, symbolizing the entire host of the redeemed, fall down, in deep humility rendering divine homage (5: 14; 7: 11); they worship, do obeisance, and cast their crowns of victory before the throne, fully realizing that they owe their victory to the Lord on the throne, while they say, 'Worthy art thou, our Lord and God, to receive the glory and the honour and the power: for thou hast created all things and due to thy will they were and were created.' (See Rev. 7: 12.) It is the song of creation. The sovereign will of God is the real and ultimate reason for the existence of all things. All creatures 'were', that is, they existed ideally in the mind of God from eternity. They 'were created', that is, their real existence followed their ideal existence in the mind of God.

[1] For the contrary view, see R. C. H. Lenski, *op. cit.*, p. 182.

[2] The throne (God's sovereignty) controlling and directing all things is the heart and centre of this vision.

3. *The sealed scroll taken by the Lamb* (5: 1–7)

'And I saw on the right hand of the one who was sitting on the throne a scroll written on the inside and on the outside, entirely sealed with seven seals.'

On the right hand of the Father lies a scroll (*cf.* 6: 14). It represents God's eternal plan, His decree which is all-comprehensive. It symbolizes God's purpose with respect to the entire universe throughout history, and concerning all creatures in all ages and to all eternity. It is full of writing on both sides.

This scroll is pictured as being entirely sealed with seven seals. These seals were probably arranged in a row on the outside of the scroll. Thus viewed, they sealed the scroll's enclosure.[1] The meaning is this: the closed scroll indicates the plan of God unrevealed and unexecuted. If that scroll remains sealed God's purposes are not realized; His plan is not carried out. To open that scroll by breaking the seals means not merely to reveal but to carry out God's plan. Because of this, a strong angel proclaims with a loud voice, 'Who is worthy to open the scroll or to break its seals?' The voice is loud and strong so that every creature in the entire universe may hear.

No-one in the entire universe—heaven, earth, under the earth—was able to open the scroll or even to look inside. As a result John weeps audibly.[2] You will understand the meaning of these tears if you constantly bear in mind that in this beautiful vision the opening of the scroll by breaking the seals indicates the execution of God's plan. When the scroll is opened and the seals are broken, then the universe is governed in the interest of the Church. Then, God's glorious, redemptive purpose is being realized; His plan is being carried out and the contents of the scroll come to pass in the history of the universe. But if the scroll is not opened it means that there will be no protection for God's children in the hours of bitter trial; no judgments upon a persecuting world; no ultimate triumph for believers; no new heaven and earth; no future inheritance.

'And one of the elders said to me: "Stop weeping; behold, he has conquered, namely, the Lion, the one out of the tribe of Judah, the Root of David, to open the scroll and the seven seals thereof." '

It was now an elder's turn to speak. Not a strong and mighty angel now but an elder, that is, one who himself had experienced

[1] *Cf.* R. C. H. Lenski, *op. cit.*, p. 194.

[2] *Cf.* the synonyms in J. H. Thayer's *Greek-English Lexicon*, under *klaio*.

the effects of redemption in his own soul; it is his turn to convey to John the wonderful message of cheer.

'He has conquered.' Christ has conquered sin on the cross. The great obstacle had been removed. The blood had been shed. The victory over sin, Satan, death, *etc.*, had been achieved. Notice carefully the names given to the Christ. He is called 'the Lion, the one out of the tribe of Judah', a very clear reference to Genesis 49: 9,10. In conquering Satan and bearing the full burden of the wrath of God to the uttermost he had proved Himself to be, indeed, the Lion. Yet He was also David's Lord, the very Root to which David owed his origin (Mt. 22: 41–45).[1] On the cross this Lion of Judah, this Root of David, had conquered and had thereby earned the right to open the book and to break the seals, that is, to rule the universe in accordance with God's plan.

'And I saw in the midst of the throne and of the four living ones, and in the midst of the elders, a Lamb standing, as having been slaughtered, having seven horns and seven eyes, which are the seven spirits of God, sent forth into all the earth. And he came, and has taken it out of the hand of him who was seated upon the throne.'

In the vision John sees . . . what? You expect 'the Lion'. Instead, you read: 'a Lamb'. Christ in His suffering and death showed the characteristics of both lion and lamb. He is the real Lion, the real Lamb. As a lamb He was led to the slaughter, sacrificed. The apostle sees this Lamb standing between the cherubim-encircled throne and the twenty-four elders. (See the diagram.) The Lamb (*cf.* Jn. 1: 29; Acts 8: 32; 1 Pet. 1: 19; Ex. 12: 3; Is. 53) stands 'as having been slaughtered'. His death has abiding value. This Lamb, namely, our Lord Jesus Christ, has seven horns, indicating His power and authority; and seven eyes, for He is filled with the Holy Spirit.

The Lamb came and took the scroll out of the hand of Him who was seated upon the throne. This very clearly refers to the fact that Christ, as Mediator, at His ascension received authority to rule the universe according to God's eternal decree.[2] It refers to the coronation of the ascended Christ (Heb. 2: 8,9); we see Jesus crowned with glory and honour. As a reward for His redemptive work, Christ, on ascending to heaven, received for

[1] This is not entirely explained by a reference to Is. 11: 1,10. The Messiah is David's *Lord* (Mt. 22: 41–55). The Unincarnate Son forms His father (David) according-to-the-flesh.

[2] *Cf.* C. Hodge, *Systematic Theology*, II, pp. 635 ff.

Himself the kingdom (Lk. 19: 12; Heb. 2: 8,9; Phil. 2: 6–11), as predicted and promised during the old dispensation (Pss. 2; 110; Dn. 7: 9–14).

This does not mean that God, the Father, leaves the throne. But it does mean that Christ, the Mediator, is seated upon the throne together with the Father. From this moment on it is the throne of God and of the Lamb (22: 1). God governs the universe through the Lamb. That is Christ's reward and our comfort. It means that there is the beginning of a new era in heaven (20: 4); and also on earth (20: 2,3).[1] A most significant moment in history is this coronation; the Mediator's investiture with the office of King over the universe.

4. *The adoration of the Lamb* (5: 8–14)

No sooner has the Lamb taken the scroll, and thus accepted the office of King of the universe, than there is a great burst of triumph and exuberant joy in three doxologies.[2] Those nearest the throne lead off, namely, the cherubim and the twenty-four elders. They fall down before the Lamb, rendering divine worship. Each of the elders has a harp, an instrument of joyful music (18: 22), and golden bowls filled with incense, symbolizing prayer and thanksgiving in its most comprehensive sense. They sing a new song. It is new because never before had such a great and glorious deliverance been accomplished and never before had the Lamb received this great honour. The words of the song are these: 'Worthy art thou to take the scroll, and to open the seals thereof; for thou wast slaughtered, and didst purchase for God with thy blood men out of every tribe, and tongue, and people, and nation, and didst make them for our God a kingdom and priests; and they reign upon the earth.'[3] It is the song of redemption.

Here very definitely the Mediator's present rule or dominion over the universe is described as being a reward for His suffering and death. Both the particular and universal aspects of the atonement are beautifully combined. The Lamb did not purchase the salvation of every single individual. No, He paid the price for His elect, that is, for men out of every tribe and tongue,

[1] In *heaven* the souls now reign with the risen and exalted Christ—which, of course, was not possible under the old dispensation; with respect to the *earth* Satan is now bound. (See chapter XIV.) Scripture constantly speaks of the life hereafter in terms of time. (*Cf.* also Eph. 2: 7 and an explanation of Rev. 10: 6.)

[2] See A. Pieters, *op. cit.*, p. 117.

[3] AV reading 'Thou wast slain, and hast redeemed us' is incorrect.

etc. Yet, on the other hand, there is nothing narrow or national about this redemption. It is world-wide in its scope and embraces every group; ethnic (tribe), linguistic (tongue), political (people), and social (nation).[1] Together all the redeemed constitute a kingdom and priests. (See 1: 6.) By means of the incense of their prayers the saints even now reign upon the earth.

Just as the twenty-four elders form a circle around the four living ones, so in turn the angels surround the elders. (See the diagram.[2]) The term 'angel' does not include the cherubim here, nor in Revelation 7: 11. All other angels are meant. The apostle sees them as a very large host: myriads of myriads and thousands of thousands. With a great voice they say, 'Worthy is the Lamb, the slaughtered one, to receive the power and riches and wisdom and strength and honour and glory and blessing': seven excellences representing all virtues and excellences in heaven and on earth. (See 7: 11.) First the elders sing, for they have experienced salvation. Then the angels sing, for they have been instructed in the mysteries of redemption by the elders. (*Cf*. Eph. 3: 10.)

Finally (verse 13), the entire universe in all its parts and with all its creatures joins the chorus of praise. (See the diagram.) We have in this verse the climax of what is found in chapters 4 and 5. Chapter 4 relates to God and creation; chapter 5: 1–12, has reference to the Lamb and redemption. Hence, these last two verses, 5: 13,14, relate to the conjoined glory and adoration of God and the Lamb.[3] All the universe praises God and the Lamb because of their work in creation and redemption.

The four cherubim were constantly saying 'Amen'. After every ascription of praise by the rest of the universe, these four living ones say 'Amen'. They place the seal of their, and God's, approval upon this universal adoration. Also the elders fell down and worshipped, rendering divine homage not only to the triune God but also specifically to the Lamb. Most glorious antiphony!

Thus the entire universe is governed by the throne, that is, by God through the Lamb. When the Lamb ascended to heaven, He sat down at the right hand of God, 'far above all

[1] For the particular and universal character of Christ's redemptive work see L. Berkhof, *Vicarious Atonement Through Christ*, pp. 165 ff.

[2] See not only the outermost circle, but circles 4, 5, 6, 7. The entire universe offers praise.

[3] See R. H. Charles, *op. cit.*, I, p. 151.

rule, and authority, and power, and dominion, and every name that is named, not only in this world, but also in that which is to come: and he (God, the Father) put all things in subjection under his (Christ's) feet, and gave him to be head over all things to the church, which is his body, the fulness of him that fills all in all' (Eph. 1: 22,23). All things ultimately must glorify God: His will is carried out in the universe. The throne rules. The Lamb reigns. As a result, believers need not fear in times of tribulation, persecution, and anguish.

5. *The four riders and their horses* (6: 1–8)

The seals described in chapter 6 are symbolic of such times of trouble and persecution. The Lamb has taken the scroll and immediately begins to open the seals. And each seal, when opened, releases its symbolism. The first four seals give rise to the symbolism of horses and their riders, just as in Zechariah 1: 8 ff.; 6: 1 ff. In Scripture the horse is generally mentioned in connection with the concepts of strength, terror, warfare, and conquest (see Is. 30: 16; 31: 1; Job 39: 22–28). In the Apocalypse we have the same association of ideas (9: 7; 14: 20; 19: 11).

Each of the four 'living ones' takes his turn in introducing a horseman. As with a voice of thunder he says, 'Be going.' The call, in each case, is addressed to the rider.

a. The white horse. 'And I saw, and behold, a white horse, and the one sitting upon it having a bow; and there was given to him a crown: and he went out conquering and to conquer.' We agree with the view of many eminent interpreters who regard the rider upon the white horse as symbolizing the Christ. We have arrived at this conclusion after very careful study and on the basis of the following considerations.

First of all, this view is in harmony with the context. Remember that in the first three chapters we saw the Christ-indwelt Church shining in the midst of the world. You recall, no doubt, the very vivid portrayal of the Son of man revealing His presence among the lampstands (1: 13 ff.). Whenever Christ appears, Satan becomes busy: trials are in store for God's children. In the section which we are studying, chapters 4–7, we have already seen this same Christ pictured as the Lamb who takes the scroll of God's decree and opens the seals. Concerning this Lamb we read: 'Behold, he has conquered, namely, the Lion, the one out of the tribe of Judah . . .'

This was stated in 5: 5. The rest of that chapter contains the description of the adoration of the Lamb. Now chapter 6 opens with the symbolism of the rider who went out 'conquering and to conquer'. Does not the conclusion seem warranted that in both chapters the 'Conqueror' is the same person?

Secondly, this view is in harmony with a careful word-study.

(i) This horse is 'white'. The colour 'white' is always associated with that which is holy and heavenly. Think of the white garments, white cloud, white throne, white stone, *etc.* It is certain, therefore, that the rider upon the white horse cannot be the devil or the antichrist.[1]

(ii) The rider receives a crown. This harmonizes well with 14: 14, where we read that Christ was wearing a crown of gold.

(iii) Finally, wherever in this book the word 'conquer' occurs —with two exceptions[2]—it refers either to Christ or to believers. The two nearest passages to the one which we are now considering are Revelation 3: 21b and 5: 5. In both of these cases this conquering is predicated of Christ. Then in his Gospel the apostle John uses the word just once (16: 33), and here again it refers to Christ. Let us quote these four passages under each other:

John 16: 33: 'In the world you have tribulation; but be of good cheer; I have *conquered* the world.'

Revelation 3: 21b: 'as I also *conquered*, and sat down with my Father in his throne.'

Revelation 5: 5: 'Behold, he *has conquered*, the Lion, the one out of the tribe of Judah.'

Revelation 6: 2: 'and he went forth *conquering and to conquer*.' Meditate on this exalted phrase. We feel sure that, had you never heard another interpretation, you would at once have said: ' This is the conquering Christ.'

Thirdly, this interpretation is demanded by the parallel passage in the book of Revelation itself. In Revelation 19: 11 we have another instance of a rider upon a white horse. In that passage we are definitely told that rider is the Christ, the Word of God, Faithful and True. His name is 'King of kings and Lord of lords'. Excellent commentators have felt that it is entirely impossible to escape the strength of this argument.[3] To say that the rider on the white horse in 19: 11 ff. must be another than the rider on the white horse in 6: 2 because the

[1] See the Scofield Reference Bible, marginal note *f*, on Rev. 6: 2.
[2] Rev. 11: 7; 13: 7.
[3] W. Milligan, *op. cit.*, VI, p. 855.

details in the two descriptions differ misses the point! We expect the details to differ somewhat. That does not argue against our view but corroborates our position. In Revelation 5: 5 we read that Christ 'has conquered'. This refers to the accomplished redemption on the cross of Golgotha. In 6: 2 the rider on the white horse is introduced as 'conquering and to conquer'. That conquest is being carried on at present. In 19: 13 the rider upon the white horse is described as clothed with a garment 'sprinkled with blood', that is, the blood of His enemies. Thus, He is going to conquer in the great day of judgment. Thus also we are told that He now wears a crown (6: 2). By and by He will have on His head 'many diadems' (19: 12), for He will have conquered many. Frankly, we do not see how anyone is justified in saying that the rider on the white horse in 6: 2 means one thing, and in 19: 11 ff. something else. Why not permit the Apocalypse to explain its own symbolism?

Fourthly, the idea that the Conqueror upon the white horse is the Christ is in harmony with the very genius and purpose of the book of Revelation. We have indicated that the very theme of this book is the victory of Christ and of His Church. Thus, again and again our Lord Jesus Christ is represented as the One who has conquered, is conquering, shall conquer. (Read carefully the following passages: Rev. 1: 13 ff.; 2: 26,27; 3: 21; 5: 5; 6: 16; 11: 15; 12: 11; 14: 1 ff.; 14: 14 ff.; 17: 14; 19: 11.) The idea of the conquering Christ is as a thread running through this book from beginning to end. If anyone should hesitate to believe this, let him read and study the references which we have just given.

Out of all these references we select just one for quotation in full, namely, 17: 14: 'These shall war against the Lamb, and the Lamb shall *conquer* them, for he is Lord of lords and King of kings; and they also shall conquer that are with him, called and chosen and faithful.'[1]

Therefore, when we say that in 6: 2 the rider upon the white horse is the Christ, we are simply expressing an idea which is in harmony with the entire book.

Fifthly, the view that the rider on the white horse in 6: 2 is the Christ is in harmony with what is found in Matthew 10: 34. Just as in that passage it is Christ who brings the sword, so that Christ and sword follow one another, so here in Revelation

[1] Wherever the original has *nikao* we have translated it by some form of the verb 'to conquer'. Thus the reader is able to see, *e.g.*, that the same word is used in the original in Rev. 5: 5 as in 6: 2.

6: 2,3 the rider on the white horse is followed by the rider on the red horse who receives a sword.[1]

Sixthly, this interpretation is strongly supported by its parallel in Psalm 45: 3–5:

'Gird thy sword upon thy thigh, O mighty one!
Thy glory and thy majesty!
And in thy majesty ride on prosperously
In behalf of truth and meekness and righteousness!
And let thy right hand teach thee terrible things!
Thine arrows sharpened! Nations under thy feet!'

The LXX has 'And in thy majesty ride, and bend the bow, and prosper and reign . . .'

Notice the striking similarities. Revelation 6: 2 pictures the rider going forth conquering and to conquer; so does Psalm 45 ('in thy majesty ride on prosperously'). Revelation 6: 2 tells us that the rider was equipped with a bow; so does Psalm 45 (in the LXX translation). But does Psalm 45 refer to Christ? On this point there can be no doubt. Scripture itself quotes part of the description of the rider of Psalm 45 and tells us that this refers to 'the Son' (Heb. 1: 8).

We see, therefore, that the Old Testament—and remember that the Apocalypse is immersed in the symbolism of the Old Testament[2]—pictures the Messiah, equipped with bow (*cf.* Rev. 6: 2) and sword (*cf.* Rev. 19: 15), riding forth prosperously. Then, why not grant that here, in Revelation 6: 2, the rider on the white horse refers to the same exalted Person?[3]

Seventhly, another parallel passage which may be cited in support of our view is Zechariah 1: 8 ff. The identification of the rider upon the first horse in Zechariah's vision with the Christ is not improbable. (*Cf.* also Hab. 3: 8,9; Is. 41: 2.)

Our Lord Jesus Christ is conquering now; that is, throughout this present dispensation His cause is going forward, for He is exercising both His spiritual and His universal Kingship. By means of the Word (gospel: Mt. 24: 14) and the Spirit, the testimonies and the tears of His disciples, His own intercession and their prayers, the angels of heaven and armies on earth, the trumpets of judgment and the bowls of wrath, our Lord is riding forth victoriously, conquering and to conquer. That, in all probability, is the meaning of the rider on the white horse.[4]

[1] *Cf.* K. Schilder, *Christ on Trial*, p. 381.

[2] See chapter VI, pp. 45–49. [3] See p. 94, note 3.

[4] An objection often advanced is that Christ cannot at the same time be the One who opens the seals and the contents of the first seal. But why

Now the other horses and other riders are introduced. Let us be careful in our interpretation of the meaning of these symbols. A very popular method of interpreting the symbolism of the four horses of the Apocalypse consists in placing in parallel columns Revelation 6 and Matthew 24.[1] Matthew 24 is then viewed as a complete commentary on Revelation 6! It is all so very simple, but perhaps it is too simple. Certainly there are striking similarities between Matthew 24 and Revelation 6, but there are also dissimilarities.[2] Let us remember that the symbolism of the Apocalypse is rooted in the *Old* Testament.[3] For the symbolism of the horses and their riders such passages as Ezekiel 5:17; 14:21; Zechariah 1:8 ff., come into consideration.

Now what do we learn from these Old Testament passages that could be useful in explaining the meaning of Revelation 6?

In Ezekiel the one who afflicts Judah is Babylon. But Babylon,

should this be considered impossible? By the same process of reasoning should we not reach the conclusion that Christ cannot lay His right hand on John (1: 17), for in that right hand He is holding seven stars (1: 16); that a Lamb—with seven horns and seven eyes—cannot take a scroll out of the hand of God (5: 6,7); a star cannot accept a key (9: 1), *etc.*? The symbolism of the Apocalypse again and again surprises us: John is told to look up and see a Lion, and he sees . . . a *Lamb* standing as having been slaughtered (5: 6). Again, he expects to see the bride, and he sees a city, the holy city Jerusalem (21: 9,10). Yet, when we begin to study these seeming irregularities, we find a very good reason for every one of them: what may be impossible as far as the *symbol* is concerned, is entirely reasonable and true with respect to the reality to which the symbol refers. Is not Christ constantly holding the seven stars in His right hand; that is, does He not constantly exercise His authority and His protecting care over the ministers? Yet, can He not at the same time lay His right hand on John? Again, a literal lamb may not be able to take a scroll, but the One to whom the lamb refers, namely Christ, certainly can do, and did do so when He sat down at the right hand of the Father. A bride cannot also be a city, but the Church of God—to which both bride and city refer—can be, and is, both at the same time. And for the same reason Jesus Christ, indeed, opens the seals; He carries out the plan of God in the history of the world. Yet, at the same time, all of history reveals the Christ as the One who is riding forth in triumph conquering and to conquer. He opens the seals *and* He is Himself the content of the first seal.

[1] *Cf.* R. H. Charles, *op. cit.*, p. 158, and several popular treatises and pamphlets.

[2] Matthew mentions several 'signs' not mentioned in Rev. 6, *e.g.*, false prophets, false Christs, the abomination of desolation, heedlessness (as in the days of Noah); while Rev. 6 (see our summary) mentions several signs which do not occur in Mt. 24. Rev. 6 describes what will *follow* Christ's first coming; Mt. 24 what will *precede* His second coming; the point of departure and, in fact, the entire setting, is different.

[3] See chapter VI, pp. 45–49.

in turn, is an instrument in the hand of Jehovah who sends trials in order to purify Jerusalem and to sanctify His people. (See especially Ezk. 11: 19; 33: 11.) Similarly, in Zechariah the second, third and fourth riders are associated with the first: they are in his service.

Possibly the same thing holds with respect to the riders described in Revelation 6. On the basis of the Old Testament passages it would not surprise us if here, too, the second, third and fourth riders are subservient to the first: Christ's instruments for the refining and strengthening of His people. True, it is the wicked world that is persecuting the Church.[1] But that world, in turn, is but an instrument in the hand of the One who has taken the scroll. So Satan is foiled by his own weapons; that which was intended as a means of extermination becomes a means of strengthening the Church, an instrument for the furtherance of the kingdom of God and the salvation of His people.[2]

We turn next to Christ's eschatological discourse, recorded in Matthew 24, Mark 13 and Luke 21. Although these chapters do not furnish a complete and simple explanation of Revelation 6, they should be taken into account. Anyone who reads this discourse of our Lord Jesus Christ immediately observes that among the signs that herald the second coming there are some that have reference to mankind in general, others that more directly concern believers. (See Mt. 24: 6–10; Mk. 13:7–9.) Let us quote Luke 21: 10–13.

(i) Signs that have reference to mankind in general: 'Then he continued to say to them: there shall rise nation against nation and kingdom against kingdom; both earthquakes great and in divers places famines and pestilences there shall be', *etc.*

(ii) Signs that more directly concern believers: 'But before all these things they shall lay their hands on you and shall persecute, delivering you to the synagogues and prisons, being led before kings and governors for my name's sake.'

Although even the woes which belong to the first group and which believers experience along with the rest of humanity are here predicted from the aspect of their significance for believers, the distinction between the two groups is still clear.

If the symbolism of Revelation 6 should reveal a similar distinction so that, let us say, the second and third riders describe particularly what happens to believers because they

[1] See the explanation of the second and third horsemen, pp. 99–103.
[2] A. Plummer, *op. cit.*, p. 184.

remain loyal to their Lord, while the fourth rider discloses what God's children experience along with the rest of the world, this would not surprise us. If Revelation 6 has anything to do with Matthew 24, Mark 13, and Luke 21, we more or less expect this distinction.

b. The red horse. Having now studied the passages which constitute a background for Revelation 6, let us direct our attention to the second horse and its rider. The second 'living one' tells the second rider to be going. 'So another horse went out, red (or fiery) in appearance. And to the one who was sitting thereon it was given to take peace from the earth, and that they should slaughter one another: and there was given to him a great short-sword (*machaira*).'

We believe that this horse and its rider refers to religious persecution of God's children rather than to war between nations; to slaughter and sacrifice rather than to warfare. Believers are slaughtered 'for his name's sake'. It belongs to the category of signs that more directly concern believers: their persecution by the world. We submit the following arguments in favour of this view.

First of all, this explanation is in striking accord with the immediate context. The second horse follows the first; that is, wherever Christ by His gospel, Spirit, *etc.*, makes His entrance, there the sword of persecution follows. This passage is also in accord with Revelation 10: 9.

Secondly, this view is confirmed by the parallel passage, Matthew 10: 34: 'I came not to send peace, but a sword (*machaira*). For I come to set a man at variance against his father, and the daughter against her mother . . . And he that does not take his cross and follow after me is not worthy of me. He that finds his life shall lose it; and he that loses his life for my sake shall find it.'[1]

Thirdly, it must not escape our attention that we read in our passage: 'that they should *slaughter* one another'. This is not the ordinary term which John uses to indicate the act of killing or warfare. Everywhere else in the writings of the apostle John, with only one exception (Rev. 13: 3), this term refers to the death of Christ or the execution of believers. Here are all the passages in which John uses the word, which in its verbal form is peculiar to John. 'Cain . . . slaughtered his brother' (1 Jn. 3: 12): here it is a child of God (Abel) who is said to have been

[1] See chapter III, p. 27 and note 1.

slaughtered or butchered. '. . . A Lamb standing, as having been slaughtered' (Rev. 5: 6): here it is Christ as a sacrifice for sin. '. . . For thou was slaughtered . . .' (Rev. 5: 9): this, again, refers to Christ. 'Worthy is the Lamb that has been slaughtered' (Rev. 5: 12): the reference is clearly to Christ. 'The souls of those who have been slaughtered for the Word of God' (Rev. 6: 9): here the word refers to believers. 'The Lamb that has been slaughtered' (Rev. 13: 8): the reference is to Christ. 'And in her was found the blood of prophets and saints, and all who have been slaughtered upon the earth' (Rev. 18: 24): the reference, clearly, is to believers.

However, in Revelation 13: 3 the 'slaughtered head' belongs to the beast, which arrogates to itself the honour and power belonging to Christ.

Thus it is not improbable that in the only remaining passage also, the one which we are discussing (Rev. 6: 4), the primary reference is to believers. Religious persecution seems to be the point, not warfare in general.

Fourthly, we read that when the fifth seal is opened John sees 'the souls of those who have been slaughtered for the Word of God'. As already indicated, exactly the same word 'slaughtered' is used in the original. But here we are definitely told that those who were slaughtered are believers. They were slaughtered for the Word of God. Does it not seem reasonable to suppose that those who under the second seal are seen as *being* slaughtered are the same as those who under the fifth seal are described as *having been* slaughtered?

Fifthly, we read: 'there was given to him a great short-sword (*machaira*).' The term *machaira* is used in a very wide sense, as any study of Scripture with the aid of a concordance will reveal. Yet it signifies strictly the sacrificial knife,[1] the natural instrument of the slaughter mentioned. It is the word used in the LXX of Genesis 22: 6,10, in the story of Isaac's sacrifice, where also we find the word 'to slaughter, to sacrifice'.[2]

Finally, let us constantly bear in mind that the Lord Jesus Christ in this book is speaking to believers who, when this vision was first revealed, were being persecuted to death. The slaughter of believers was their immediate problem; that, more than warfare in general.

Wherever the rider on the white horse—the Christ—makes His appearance, the rider on the red horse follows. (See Mt. 5:

[1] A. Plummer, *op. cit.*, p. 185.

[2] See also p. 104, first paragraph.

10,11; Lk. 21: 12; Acts 4: 1; 5: 17, *etc.*) Think of Stephen and Paul, Publius and Polycarp, Perpetua and Felicitas, the Inquisition and St. Bartholomew's night, Armenia and Russia, John and Betty Stam.[1] The rider on the red horse does not refer to one definite person. He does not belong to one particular age. No century is without its rider upon the red horse: the world is always persecuting the Church. Christ always brings the sword. Peace is taken from the earth (Mt. 10: 34).

Yet, praise God! the sacrificial knife or short-sword is 'given' to this rider. All things are in the hands of God. The Lamb reigns.

c. The black horse. The third 'living one' addresses the third rider, saying, 'Be going', and he goes out upon his black horse. This rider has in his hand a balance, that is, a pair of scales (*cf.* Ezk. 4: 10). To eat bread by weight refers to a condition of economic hardship. A voice comes from somewhere among the four living ones saying, 'A quart of wheat for a denarius, and three quarts of barley for a denarius . . .' In other words, a whole day's wages for a quantity of wheat that will last one person just one day (*cf.* Mt. 20: 2). At this rate a man could support himself, but what about his family? True, he could buy barley, the coarser food, at one-third the price and thus provide for his family. But is food all a family needs? What about all the other necessities? When such prices prevail it becomes very difficult for a person to make both ends meet. It is not famine, as such, that is indicated here; for these prices, though high, are by no means famine prices.[2] Besides, one can get all the wheat he wants, provided he has the money to pay for it! But that is exactly the point. How can a man who is earning very little provide for his family when prices are so high? A certain class of people is going to be hard-pressed. By and by we shall learn just what group of people is indicated.

The voice continues: 'And the oil and the wine do not damage.' Oil and wine, representing all the comforts of life, are in plentiful supply! But they are utterly beyond the reach of the man who is making hardly enough to provide coarse food for his family. Now we have the entire picture: we see the rich enjoying their food in abundance and all the comforts of life besides. But the poor have hardly enough to keep body and soul together.

[1] N. L. Saloff-Ostakhoff, *Christianity and Communism: Real Russia 1905 to 1932*. Mrs. H. Taylor, *The Triumph of John and Betty Stam.*

[2] See R. C. H. Lenski, *op. cit.*, p. 227.

The question arises, when the seer refers to these poor people who are hard-pressed, of whom is he thinking? The answer is obvious. That believers were poor, lacking the comforts which others enjoyed, is very clear from the book of Revelation. The first readers would immediately understand this symbol. From the Apocalypse itself we receive the following information with respect to the economic conditions prevailing in the Church at that time.

We learn, first of all, that one could hardly remain a member of his trade-guild without sacrificing his religious principles and convictions.[1] And if a person did withdraw from such an organization? It requires very little imagination to realize that the result of such withdrawal would be material loss and physical suffering.

Then, too, we learn that anyone who did not have 'the mark of the beast' was unable to buy or to sell (see Rev. 13: 17).

Has not this been true throughout the ages? Is it not a principle of human conduct to oppress believers and to cause them to suffer physical want? How often have the children of God been crowded out of their job, business, or profession, because they insisted on being true to their convictions? A man, for example, refuses to work on the Lord's Day and is dismissed. As a result he is forced to take another job with lower wages. He has a family to support. It would be vain to look for any comforts or luxuries in his home. Another, for reasons of conscience, refuses to join a labour organization that adheres to a policy of violence, with the result that he, too, loses his job. The rich oppressor, meanwhile, has abundance. No-one damages his wine and oil.

The second and third riders belong together. Both describe the persecution of the people of God. Some believers are slaughtered. Their blood is poured out. These are the martyrs in the more restricted sense of that term. The second (red) horse and its rider describes them. But not all believers suffer actual martyrdom in that sense. Yet, in a broader sense, the others too, are martyrs. They suffer poverty and hardship (*cf.* 1 Cor. 1 : 26). The black horse and its rider may be seen in their mission of woe spreading oppression, injustice, and economic hardship throughout the centuries of the Church's existence.

But this form of persecution is also an instrument in the hand of Christ for the furtherance of His kingdom. The hard-pressed individual feels his dependence on God.

[1] See our explanation of the letter to Thyatira, chapter VIII.

Thus, the second and the third riders describe those woes which in a very special manner affect believers. They symbolize that throughout the entire dispensation the world will persecute the Church in every conceivable way. Let us remember that the two forms of persecution here mentioned, namely slaughter and injustice or economic hardship, represent all forms.

d. The pale horse. But are these the only trials through which the Church must pass on its way to eternal glory? Not so. Just as in Matthew 24, Mark 13, and Luke 21 there is mention of a second group of tribulations, so here. There are woes which the believer suffers along with the world, for the simple reason that he is in the world. To that class of trials the fourth horse and its rider call our attention.

The fourth seal is opened. The fourth living creature says, 'Be going'. Now a livid or greenish horse is seen.[1] It is a horse with a very sickly gruesome colour, symbolical of disease and death. Above[2] this horse sits a rider whose name is the Death. Death in general is meant; yes, death in its most universal form, for the instruments of death here mentioned affect both believers and unbelievers. Trotting behind Death, as always, is Hades.[3] Death cuts down, and Hades—symbolizing the state of disembodied existence—gathers the slain.[4] Yet Death and Hades cannot do as they please. They can do nothing beyond what is allowed by the divine permission. This is emphasized for the consolation of believers. We read that authority is *given* to Death and Hades. Their sphere of activity, moreover, is very definitely restricted. Although the territory is very large, the fourth part of the earth, yet its bounds have been definitely determined in the divine decree which is carried out by the Lamb. It is the fourth part, no more!

Unto them is given authority to kill 'with the sword, famine (or hunger), pestilence (or death), and by the wild beasts of the earth'. These are four woes which have not been described under the second and third seals. This passage is very definitely rooted in Ezekiel 14:21. Notice the very close resemblance: 'But thus says the Lord Jehovah, Even though I should send against Jerusalem my four deadly judgments: the sword and hunger and the wild beasts and pestilence, to cut off from it man and beast, nevertheless, there shall be left a remnant in it . . .'

[1] *Cf.* for the colour, 8: 7; 9: 4.
[2] The preposition here is different from that used in the other cases.
[3] See A. Pieters, *op. cit.*, p. 122.
[4] See chapter VII, p. 57.

Here (Rev. 6: 8) the same four woes are mentioned in almost the same order.

First, to kill with the sword is mentioned. Here we do not read 'to slaughter' as in the second seal, but 'to kill'. Also the term translated 'sword' is different. It is not the *machaira* but the *rhomphaia*. It is not the sacrificial knife or short-sword but the long and heavy great-sword, like the one with which David cut off Goliath's head. In the LXX translation of Ezekiel 14: 21 we find the same word (*rhomphaia*) as is used here in Revelation 6: 8. Here is *war*! Those commentators who hold that the second horse and its rider refer to war get into difficulties when they come to explain the fourth horse. And if, in addition, they have interpreted the third seal as indicating famine, then they are entirely at a loss what to do with the fourth seal which also indicates famine. They seek a way out of their difficulty by teaching either that the woes of the second and third seals are repeated under the fourth—a rather unlikely and unintelligible repetition—or that much of what is described under the fourth seal is an interpolation.[1] This, of course, is a very convenient way of dispatching a problem. Blame it on the scribe!

Careful study reveals, however, that these four seals indicate types of woes that are easily distinguishable. The fourth seal, moreover, describes four[2] universal woes. They are viewed here from the aspect of their significance for the Church. War, not just one particular war but war between nations wherever and whenever it occurs throughout the entire dispensation is mentioned first. That the sword (*rhomphaia*) refers to warfare is clear on the basis of Revelation 2: 16; 19: 21.

Next, hunger or famine is mentioned. This, too, is a very general woe, often mentioned in the Bible. When a city is besieged in time of war, famine often follows.

Famine, in turn, is often followed by or associated with pestilence. Pestilence, both here and in the LXX translation of Ezekiel 14: 21, is called 'death'. Just as even today we call it the Black Death. As it is here mentioned in connection with famine, it is probable that pestilence proper, the bubonic Plague, is meant.[3] Anyone who is interested in a fascinating description of what we consider to be the bubonic Plague should read 1 Samuel 5–7.[4] For the very close connection between famine

[1] See R. H. Charles, *op. cit.*, p. 169.

[2] This is the number of the universe: North, South, East, West.

[3] *Cf.* R. C. H. Lenski, *op. cit.*, p. 231.

[4] The disease suffered by the Philistines after they had taken the ark was,

and pestilence see Jeremiah 21: 6–9; Luke 21: 11.

Finally, just as in Ezekiel, so here the wild beasts are mentioned. (See 2 Ki. 17: 25.) These wild beasts, also, do not distinguish between believers and unbelievers. They tear to pieces and devour whatever they can seize, whether in or outside the Roman amphitheatres.

Thus all four—warfare, famine, pestilence, wild beasts—are general in character. These four, moreover, are symbolical of *all* universal woes which believers suffer along with the rest of humanity throughout the entire dispensation. Yet, with respect to the Church, these woes have a very specific meaning. Our Lord Jesus Christ uses these woes as instruments, for the sanctification of His Church and the extension of His kingdom.[1]

We have reached the following conclusion with respect to the meaning of the four horsemen of the Apocalypse:

The rider on the white horse is our Lord Jesus Christ.

The rider on the red horse represents slaughter.

The rider on the black horse represents economic hardship and poverty due to injustice.

The second and the third seals symbolize the direct persecution of the Church by the world.

The rider on the livid horse represents Death, the sword (warfare), famine, pestilence, wild beasts. These are the common woes of humanity described here from the aspect of their effect upon the kingdom of God.

6. *The cry of the martyrs* (6: 9–11)

'And when he had opened the fifth seal, I saw underneath the altar the souls of those that had been slaughtered for the Word of God and for the testimony which they held. And they cried with a great voice, saying, How long, O Master, the Holy and

in all probability, the bubonic Plague, for the following reasons:

a. In both cases we have as one of the symptoms 'rounded swellings' or suppurating lymph-glands. The 'emerods' are plague-boils.

b. In both cases one of the regions in which these swellings occur is that which includes the groin.

c. In both cases the disease is closely associated with mice or rats. Evidently we have here the rat-flea-man transmission of the plague (see H. Zinsser, *Rats, Lice and History*).

d. Rapid, epidemic spread characterizes both.

e. A very high mortality rate characterizes both. The disease 'destroyed' the men of Ashdod; it 'smote' the inhabitants of Gath.

[1] Both mass conversions *and* moral and religious disintegration result from calamities such as these. (See H. Zinsser, *op. cit.*, pp. 86, 139.)

Genuine One, dost thou not judge and avenge our blood on those dwelling on the earth?'

Do not forget that what John sees is not heaven or the universe itself but a symbolic vision. In this vision the apostle beholds the altar, which here appears as the altar of burnt-offering at the base of which the blood of slaughtered animals had to be poured out (Lv. 4: 7). Underneath this altar John sees the blood of the slaughtered saints. He saw their souls, for 'the soul is in the blood' (Lv. 17: 11). They had offered their lives as a sacrifice, having clung tenaciously to the testimony which they had received concerning the Christ and salvation in Him. These are the souls which under the second seal were being slaughtered.[1] These souls are crying for vengeance on those who have slaughtered them.

The question arises, how can we harmonize this cry for judgment and vengeance with Christ's prayer for His enemies (Lk. 23: 34) and with Stephen's prayer of 'Lord, lay not this sin to their charge'? We answer, these martyrs do not invoke retribution for their own sake but for God's sake. These saints have been slaughtered because they placed their trust and confidence in God. In slaughtering them, the world has scorned Him! Does not God Himself affirm that the blood of His saints cries for wrath? (Gn. 4: 10; *cf.* Heb. 11: 4.) Insignificant individuals, mere earth-dwellers, have defied the holy, true, and sovereign Lord of the universe. They have challenged His attributes. Unless full retribution be rendered, God's righteousness and sovereignty will not shine forth in its full and perfect lustre. No, the saint in glory does not desire personal vengeance any more than did Stephen, but he yearns for the coming of that great day when the majesty and holiness, the sovereignty and righteousness of God in Christ shall be publicly revealed.

To each of these slaughtered ones a white, flowing robe is given, symbolizing righteousness, holiness, and festivity. To them is given the assurance that their prayers will be answered but the time for the judgment day has not yet arrived. Thus these souls of the martyrs must enjoy their heavenly repose 'for a little time' until every elect one has been brought into the fold and the number of the martyrs is full. God knows the exact number. It has been fixed from eternity in His decree. Until that number has been realized on earth the day of final judgment cannot come.

[1] See pp. 99–101.

7. *The final judgment* (6: 12–17)

The sixth seal, accordingly, introduces[1] the judgment day. It describes the one great catastrophe at the end of this age. The dread and terror, the awe and consternation of that day is pictured under the twofold symbolism of a crashing universe and a thoroughly frightened human race.

The terror of that great day refers, of course, only to the wicked. But whereas believers are going to be few in number at the time of the second coming (Lk. 18: 8), we can say that the world in general is seized with alarm. In this connection it is interesting to observe that this final outpouring of the divine wrath upon mankind is described under the sixth seal—six, or rather six hundred and sixty-six, being the number of man (Rev. 13: 18)—and is represented as affecting six objects of creation; and as distributed among six classes of men.[2]

Notice the six objects that are enumerated in this symbolic description of the terror of the judgment day.

First, there is a great earthquake (*cf.* especially Ezk. 38: 19; Joel 2: 10; Am. 8: 8; Mt. 24: 29). Picture it to yourself: the earth rising and falling in rapid waves, as an indication of God's power and anger.

Then, in connection with this earthquake, the sun turns black as sackcloth and the full moon becomes as blood. The darkening of the sky often accompanies earthquakes; yet, more than that is intended by this symbolic description. This is not a mere darkening or even an eclipse, for the very light of the sun is blotted out and the moon assumes the colour of blood. In the picture which John sees this is all very real. We must be careful, however, in arriving at conclusions. Let us take the picture as a whole.[3] We have no right, on the basis of this description, to draw conclusions with respect to the exact changes that will take place in the heavenly bodies at the end of this present age. What we have here is a symbolic picture of the terror of the judgment day. The symbol, taken as a whole, teaches just *one* lesson, namely, that the final and complete effusion of God's wrath upon a world that has persecuted the Church will be terrible indeed.

Three objects have now been mentioned, namely, earthquake, sun, and moon. The fourth is the stars of the heaven falling to the earth, as a fig-tree casts her winter figs when shaken by a violent wind. No doubt John had often seen those winter figs

[1] See chapter IV, p. 35.

[2] *Cf.* R. C. H. Lenski, *op. cit.*, p. 241.

[3] See chapter V, pp. 38ff.

hidden under the leaves until they dry up and come down in showers when a violent wind shakes the trees. In similar showers the stars are seen falling out of their orbits. They fall to the earth. Not comets, or meteors, but stars. You say: how is this possible? The earth is altogether too small for even a single star to fall upon it. Again, we remind you that this is a picture. In pictures things are possible which are not possible in reality. When we say this, we do not deny, of course, that there will be a most thorough-going dislocation of the heavenly bodies and a rejuvenation of the universe, in connection with the end of this present age. Scripture very clearly teaches this (2 Pet. 3: 10, 12, *etc.*). Neither do we at all deny that also our present passage refers to this fact (*cf.* Mt. 24: 39). But the main point of our passage is this: it stresses the terror of the day of wrath for the wicked. The dissolving elements, earthquake, falling stars, *etc.*, add terror to the picture.

In this very vivid and awe-inspiring picture John sees heaven itself curled up like a piece of paper (*cf.* Is. 34: 4). The sixth and last object mentioned is 'every mountain and island'. These mountains and islands completely disappear, being moved out of their place.

Again, try to visualize what John saw, taking the picture as a whole: heaven itself curling up like a piece of paper, rolling up like a scroll; the sun, its light blotted out so that it resembles a black sack used in mourning; the big, full moon, a huge, awe-inspiring bloody ball; the stars, turned out of their orbits and plunging to the earth in great showers; the earth itself quaking violently so that every house crashes to the ground; and every mountain and island suddenly disappearing. What a picture of dread and despair, of confusion and consternation—for the wicked!

Notice now the six classes of mankind upon whom this terror falls.

First, the kings of the earth, the dictators and supreme political rulers of this earth. Second, the princes, those next in authority to the kings. Thirdly, the officers, the military dictators and generals. Fourthly, the rich men, the leaders in commerce and industry. These are the capitalists, the money magnates. Fifthly, the strong men, those who exert a powerful influence in any realm, whether physical or educational. Lastly, every slave and freeman, the entire lower classes, consisting of those who were still serving as slaves or those who had been released from bondage.

Thus, under the symbolism of these six classes, John sees the entire godless world seized with sudden fear. He sees them terror-stricken and fleeing, fleeing from something far more terrible than crumbling mountains and falling rocks. They even seek safety in death itself. If only death would come to them—John hears shrieks of agony uttered by thousands of voices. Kings and slaves, princes and servants, they are all caught in the same self-inflicted agony of despair. The dreadful wail is heard: 'Mountains and rocks, fall on us and hide us from the face of the One sitting on the Throne, and from the wrath of the Lamb. For it came, the day, the great one, of their wrath, and who is able to stand?' The door of grace is closed for ever once that day has arrived!

But although final and complete retribution will not be rendered until the judgment day, even now during this present age judgments are sent upon the earth because the wicked persecute God's children. Throughout history the seals of persecution give rise to the trumpets of judgment. That is a principle in the divine moral government of this world. We should read the events of the day in the light of this principle.

8. *The sealed multitude* (7: 1–17)

These trumpets of judgment which arise out of the seventh seal are described in chapters 8 and 9. But even at the beginning of chapter 7 everything seems to be ready for the execution of these judgments. Then, why do they not fall upon the unbelievers? All is in readiness: the winds of woe are about to set out on their mission of destruction; the four angels—four because they control the agencies of destruction throughout the earth, in every direction, north, south, east, and west—are all prepared for their task of afflicting the earth and the sea (Rev. 7: 2). Then suddenly, dramatically, John sees another angel ascending from the east. He has the seal of the living God. He cries to the four angels who are controlling or holding in check the four winds of judgment. In a loud voice he tells them, 'Do not harm the earth or the sea or the trees till we seal the servants of our God on their foreheads.'

These woes are punishments for the wicked, persecuting world. They are not going to hurt you, if the seal of God is on your forehead. The Lord has laid on Christ the iniquity of all the believers (Is. 53: 6). Rest assured that 'to them that love God all things work together for good, even to them that are called according to his purpose' (Rom. 8: 28).

This sealing is the most precious thing under heaven. Scripture speaks of the seal in a threefold sense. First of all, a seal *protects* against tampering. Thus, the tomb of Jesus was sealed with a guard (Mt. 27: 66; *cf.* Rev. 5: 1). Secondly, a seal *marks* ownership. Thus, we read in the Song of Solomon 8: 6: 'Set me as a seal upon thy heart.' Thirdly, a seal *certifies* genuine character. The decree that all the Jews should be wiped out was sealed with the signet of King Xerxes (Est. 3: 12).

The Christian is sealed in this threefold sense. The Father has sealed him, for the believer enjoys the Father's protection throughout life. The Son has sealed him, for He had bought and redeemed the believer with His own precious blood. He owns us. The Spirit had sealed him (Eph. 1: 13), for He certifies that we are sons of God (Rom. 8: 15).

In the passage which we are discussing the emphasis is on ownership and consequent protection. Notice that the sons of God are sealed 'on their foreheads'. In chapter 14 we again meet this same sealed multitude, the 144,000. There we read that they have on their foreheads the name of the Lamb and the name of the Father. That name, in all probability, is the seal.[1] (*Cf.* also Rev. 22: 4.)

John hears the number of the sealed. He does not see their exact number for these sealed ones are still on earth. Only God knows how many truly sealed people there are on earth. The number is 144,000. This, of course, is symbolical. First, the number three, indicating the Trinity, is multiplied by four, indicating the entire creation, for the sealed ones shall come from the east and the west, the north and the south. Three times four makes twelve. This number therefore indicates: the Trinity (3) operating in the universe (4).[2] When the Father through the Son in the Spirit performs His saving work on earth—the divine (3) operating in the universe (4)— we see in the old dispensation the twelve (3×4) patriarchs and in the new the twelve apostles. In order to arrive at the conception of the Church of the old and of the new dispensation we shall have to multiply this twelve by twelve. This gives us 144.

Entirely in harmony with this representation we read in Revelation 21 that the holy city Jerusalem has twelve gates and twelve foundations. On these twelve gates were written the names of the twelve tribes of the children of Israel. On the twelve foundations were the names of the twelve apostles of the

[1] *Cf.* our explanation of Rev. 2: 17.
[2] *Cf.* C. F. Wishart, *op. cit.*, pp. 22 ff.

Lamb (21: 9–14). We also read that the wall is 144 cubits in height (21: 17).

It is very clear, therefore, that the sealed multitude of Revelation 7 symbolizes the entire Church militant of the old and new dispensations. In order to emphasize the fact that not a small portion of the Church is meant but the entire Church militant, this number 144 is multiplied by one thousand. One thousand is 10×10×10, which indicates a perfect cube, reduplicated completeness.[1] (See Rev. 21: 16.) The 144,000 sealed individuals out of the twelve tribes of literal Israel symbolize spiritual Israel, the Church of God on earth.

To say that the symbol ultimately indicates Israel according to the flesh is wrong. The apostle certainly knew that ten of the twelve tribes had disappeared in Assyria, at least to a great extent; while Judah and Benjamin had lost their national existence when Jerusalem fell, in AD 70. Besides, if Israel according to the flesh were meant, why should Ephraim and Dan be omitted? Surely not all the people in the tribe of Dan were lost. Again, notice the order in which the tribes are arranged. Not Reuben but Judah is mentioned first. Remember that our Lord Jesus Christ was of the tribe of Judah (Gn. 49: 10). Even the fact that exactly twelve thousand are sealed out of every tribe—harmony in the midst of variety—should be sufficient to indicate that we are dealing with a symbol, as already indicated. As to the meaning of this symbol, we are not left in the dark. In the first place, the very number, being the product of one hundred and forty-four and one thousand, is fully explained in Revelation 21 as we have shown. According to that chapter it must indicate the Church of the old and new dispensations. Besides, in chapter 14 we again see this same multitude, the 144,000. Here we are plainly told that they are those who have been purchased out of the earth. They represent those who follow the Lamb wherever He goes, and the entire Church militant, therefore, as is also clearly taught in Revelation 22: 4.[2] Christ, having purchased them by His own precious blood, owns them, and the Father (through Christ, in the Spirit) protects them. Let the winds blow; they will not harm God's people. Let the judgments come; they will not hurt His elect!

After these things John beholds the most glorious vision of

[1] *Ibid.*, p. 23.

[2] That the entire (not only the Jewish) Church is meant is also the view of W. Milligan, *op. cit.*, pp. 861 ff.: a series of very convincing arguments.

all. It is the Church triumphant as in eternity it shall dwell for ever in the immediate presence of God and His throne. It is a great multitude which no man could number, although the exact number is known to the Lord (2 Tim. 2: 19). They were gathered out of every nation and of all tribes and peoples and tongues.[1] It is clear that God's elect out of the people of the Jews are included: both Gentiles and Jews are represented. They stand before the throne and the Lamb who is now seated upon the throne (Rev. 5: 7). To stand before the throne and the Lamb means to have fellowship with, to render service to, and to share in the honour of the Lamb. The countless multitude is clothed around with white, flowing robes. The flowing robes indicate festivity, blessedness; their whiteness symbolizes righteousness, holiness (*cf.* 7: 14). John sees the blessed with palms in their hands. These palms indicate salvation (Jn. 12:13). Accordingly, this immense multitude is heard crying with a great voice:

'Our salvation is the work of God, the One sitting on the throne, and of the Lamb.' Literally we read '*the*' salvation, not salvation in general but that very definite salvation (from sin and all its consequences) which these redeemed are now enjoying. They ascribe this work of salvation to God and to the Lamb and not to their own wisdom or goodness. Similarly, we sing:

> 'Thou art, O God, our boast, the glory of our power;
> Thy sovereign grace is e'er our fortress and our tower.
> We lift our heads aloft, for God, our shield, is o'er us;
> Through Him, through Him alone, whose presence goes
> before us,
> We'll wear the victor's crown, no more by foes assaulted,
> We'll triumph through our King, by Israel's God exalted.'

The angels surround this redeemed multitude. (See the diagram on p. 83.) They render homage to God, and in a double Amen and a seven-fold ascription of praise (7: 12)[2]

[1] See pp. 91ff.

[2] Notice that the definite article precedes each of the seven items of praise. It indicates that in the fullest, deepest sense these excellences pertain to God, and to Him alone. These seven have the following meaning:

a. he eulogia: probably not merely the invocation of blessing but the actual possession of the blessed fullness of the divine attributes upon which our salvation is founded.

b. he doxa: the glory which results when the splendour of God's attributes (sovereignty, righteousness, love, grace, *etc.*) is recognized.

c. he sophia: the wisdom of God revealed in the plan of salvation and in the execution of that plan. God ever employs the best means to reach the highest goal. This wisdom, moreover, implies the reconciliation of

they testify their agreement with the adoration of the Church triumphant (*cf.* 5: 11). 'And there answered one out of the elders, saying to me: "These, the ones clothed around with the flowing robes, the white ones, who are they, and where do they come from?" And I said to him: "My lord, thou knowest." '

Now it is an elder who speaks (7: 13; *cf.* 5: 5). It is one who knows by experience the meaning of salvation. He asks John a question, not in order that the apostle may inform him, but in order to rivet John's attention upon that countless multitude; especially, upon that amazing miracle, namely, that all these individuals who once were sinners are now righteous and holy, clothed around with white, flowing robes. The apostle, by saying, 'My lord, thou knowest', indicates that he desires to hear the explanation of this great miracle.

The explanation given by the elder, in a most sublime and beautiful manner, closes this section, chapters 4–7. Constantly bear in mind that this section has as its theme, *the Church in tribulation.* We have seen the red horse of slaughter, the black horse of poverty and injustice, the livid horse of Death. We have heard the cries of the souls of those who had been slaughtered for the Word of God and for the testimony which they held. It has become clear that all these trials are controlled by the One who is sitting upon the throne. Now, in addition, it is made clear to us that the Church does not remain in the tribulation. The countless multitude is composed of individuals who come 'out of' the great tribulation. We read 'And he said to me: "These are the ones coming out of the tribulation, the great one, and they have washed their flowing robes and have made them white in the blood of the Lamb. Therefore are they before the throne of God, and they worship him by day and by night in his sanctuary, and the One sitting on the throne will spread his tabernacle over them. They shall hunger no more, neither thirst any more; neither shall the sun fall upon them nor any heat, for the Lamb that is in the midst of the throne shall be their shepherd and shall lead them to life's springs of waters and God shall wipe away every tear out of their eyes." '

seeming incompatibilities. (*Cf.* Eph. 3: 10 in the light of the entire preceding context.)

d. and *e. he eucharistia* and *he time:* the thanksgiving and the honour result whenever this wisdom of God in our salvation is recognized.

f. and *g. he dynamis* and *he ischys:* the power and the strength of God (power includes strength) are as clearly revealed in the work of salvation as is His wisdom.

The elder tells John that these people who are clothed around with the white flowing robes come out of 'the tribulation, the great one'. This one tribulation is great because it is all-inclusive: all the persecutions and trials of God's people, symbolized by the seals, are included in it. That gives unity to this entire section, chapters 4–7. The point is that the saints come out of their trials. The Dutch have a term for 'dying' which literally means 'to get over (or beyond) suffering'. It expresses the truth whenever a believer dies.

These saints whom John, in the vision, beholds, have washed their flowing robes and have made them white in the blood of the Lamb (*cf.* 1 Jn. 1: 7; Heb. 9: 14). In other words, they have placed all their trust in the saving blood of Jesus Christ. This blood, representing the complete atonement which our Lord has rendered, has cleansed them of the guilt and the pollution of sin. By means of the red blood of Christ they have been made white.

Therefore are they before the throne of God. Only those who have placed their confidence in Christ and His atonement appear before the throne. They worship Him; that is, they render to Him the spontaneous, glad, and thorough devotion of the heart. It is an unceasing worship. These redeemed saints in glory, moreover, experience the sweetest, fullest, and most intimate fellowship with God through Christ; they worship Him *in His sanctuary*, that is, in His immediate presence. The One who sits on the throne treats them as His own dear children, for such by grace they are; He spreads His presence like a tent over them. Negatively, their salvation consists in this, that they are delivered from every care and hardship, from every form of trial and persecution: no more hunger, thirst, or heat. Positively, their salvation means this, that they enjoy the most perfect bliss; the Lamb is now their shepherd (*cf.* Ps. 23; Jn. 10: 11,14). Think of it, a *Lamb* being a *shepherd*! This Lamb leads His flock to life's springs of water. Water symbolizes eternal life and salvation (Is. 55: 1; Jn. 7: 38,39). The springs of water indicate the source of life, for through the Lamb the redeemed have eternal and uninterrupted fellowship with the Father.

Finally, the sweetest touch of all: 'And God shall wipe away every tear *out of* their eyes.' Not merely are the tears wiped or even wiped away; they are wiped out of the eyes so that nothing but perfect joy, bliss, glory, sweetest fellowship and most abundant life, remains! And God Himself is the Author of this perfect salvation.

CHAPTER TEN

REVELATION 8–11: THE SEVEN TRUMPETS

THE panorama of the history of the Church has twice been unrolled before our wondering gaze. We saw the lampstands and the Son of man moving about among them. We heard His voice of tender admonition, earnest reproof, and generous promise. In seven beautiful letters He seemed to be drawing nearer and nearer to us until we saw Him standing at the very door and knocking. Then, just as we yearned for the full realization of His promise to come in and sup with us, the vision ceased. Yet its imprint upon our soul is indelible. Through the bitterest tears we see our Saviour, very near us, full of tender love and sustaining power. We see Him as the light of the world. That light is shining through us: the churches are the lampstands (chapters 1–3).

Again the ages turned backward in their flight . . . to the very moment of our Lord's ascension. With wide-eyed wonder we beheld a door standing open in heaven. Peering through this door, we saw a throne out of which proceeded flashes of lightning, rumblings and peals of thunder. The surrounding heavenly beings were acknowledging in grateful anthems the sovereignty of the One whose countenance remained concealed behind the flashing lustre of the diamond and the fiery red of the sardius. Suddenly we witnessed that central event, namely, the coronation of Jesus, who took the scroll out of the right hand of the Lord on the throne. We heard an elder saying, 'Weep not; behold the lion . . . of Judah has conquered.'

Consequently, we were not at all surprised when, with the opening of the first seal, we saw that same Jesus going forth conquering and to conquer. But this Rider upon the white horse is always followed by the rider upon the red horse; wherever our Lord Jesus Christ begins to wield His spiritual sceptre, Satan begins to brandish his sword. The seals describe the persecution of the Church by the world and not only persecution, but every form of trial and tribulation. In the vision of the souls underneath the altar we received the assurance that the slaughter of the saints will not remain unavenged. Although the final and complete retribution is reserved for the great day of

Jehovah, even now the seals of persecution are again and again followed by the trumpets of judgment. But before these trumpets are introduced the Church militant is sealed against all harm. Finally, we saw the Church triumphant that has come out of the great tribulation and for ever rejoices in the immediate and glorious presence of the Lamb (chapters 4–7). Now all is ready for the trumpets of judgment.

These trumpets of judgment (chapters 8–11) indicate *series* of happenings, that is, calamities that will occur again and again throughout this dispensation.[1] They do not symbolize single and separate events, but they refer to woes that may be seen any day of the year in any part of the globe. Therefore, the trumpets are synchronous with the seals.

Again, these trumpets of judgment are clearly retributive in character. Terrible calamities befall the wicked in order to punish them for their opposition to the cause of Christ and for their persecution of the saints. Yet even by means of these judgments God is constantly calling the ungodly to repentance. These woes do not symbolize God's final and complete displeasure. On the contrary, they indicate His *initial* judgments. They are charged with serious warning, not with final doom. Remember that trumpets warn and that bowls are poured out. It is for this reason that the trumpets affect a third part—not the whole—of the earth, sea, waters, sun, moon and stars. The very function of the trumpets is to warn (Ezk. 33: 3).

Observe also that these trumpets of judgment affect the various parts of the universe: the land, the sea, *etc.* Nowhere is there safety for the wicked. Yet a certain order is evident. The first four trumpets harm the wicked in their *physical* being; the last three bring *spiritual anguish*: hell itself is let loose!

These judgments are expressed in language which reminds the reader of the ten plagues in Egypt. Notice the 'hail and fire' (8: 7); the 'darkness' (8: 12) and the 'locusts' (9: 3). Yet the description which we find here in Revelation is far more terrible: the hail and fire are mingled with *blood*; the locusts do not hurt grass or trees but *men*! These judgments fall upon the wicked, persecuting world, (Egypt), where also our Lord was crucified (11: 8). They do not harm believers.

1. *The seventh seal* (8: 1–6)

'And when he opened the seventh seal, there occurred a silence in heaven for about half an hour.'

[1] See chapter v, pp. 41ff

Why this silence? Was it in order that the prayers of God's persecuted children on earth might be heard in heaven?[1] We rather incline to the view that here as always we must look for the interpretation in Old Testament symbolism. Now, in the prophets the going forth of the Almighty in judgment is again and again introduced by a reference to silence, *e.g.*, Habakkuk 2: 20: 'But Jehovah is in his holy temple: let all the earth keep silence before him.' (*Cf.* Zp. 1: 7; Zc. 2: 13.) Here in Revelation, in similar vein, the silence is introduced to prepare us for the terrible character of the judgments that are about to be related. This silence makes the manifestations of the wrath of God all the more impressive. So fearful and awful is even this initial retribution which is about to be inflicted upon the wicked that the inhabitants of heaven stand spell-bound, lost for a long time—half an hour—in breathless, in silent amazement. Besides, God does not afflict 'from the heart'. That, too, is indicated by the silence in heaven (Lk. 19: 41; La. 3: 33; Ezk. 33: 11). And now John sees the seven angels that stand before God—a very high order of angels—to each of whom is given[2] a trumpet. Another angel appears on the scene. He stands over the altar, which is here the golden altar of incense.[3] He has a golden censer. Much incense is given to him. Observe that it is *given* to him: the angel does not bring his own offering. Are we stretching the meaning of the symbol when we draw the conclusion that this incense which is given to the angel represents our Saviour's intercession in heaven for His persecuted Church on earth?[4] Is it not that intercession, based upon the atonement, which sanctifies and purifies our prayers? We translate the next clause as follows: 'in order that he should give it for the prayers of all the saints upon the altar, the golden one, the one before the throne'.

These saints in persecution and tribulation are praying. But their prayer life[5] is imperfect. It needs to be incensed with the intercession of Christ. Once these prayers have been incensed, the seer notices that the smoke *ascends* to the very presence of God; that is, the prayers of the saints, which accompany the smoke of the incense, are heard in heaven. The Lord on the throne sees the sighs and sufferings, He hears the requests and

[1] *Cf.* R. H. Charles, *op. cit.*, p. 223.

[2] Throughout the book of Revelation God ever remains the Sovereign of the universe. Notice how often the word 'given' occurs.

[3] In Rev. 6: 9 it appears as the altar of burnt-offering.

[4] *Cf.* R. C. H. Lenski, *op. cit.*, p. 269.

[5] See R. C. Trench, *Synonyms of the New Testament*, p. 176.

the thanksgivings of His children who are in the midst of tribulation. The angel understands this; he realizes that the prayers are heard. So he takes the censer, now emptied of its incense, and fills it with fire of the altar, and empties it upon the earth; that is, *God has heard the prayers of the saints, and the judgments upon earth are His answer to them.* Moreover, to indicate that this is indeed God's view of the matter and not merely the angel's, we read: 'and there occurred peals of thunder, loud blasts, flashes of lightning and quaking'. Because of this, the seven angels prepare themselves to blow the trumpets.

2. *The first four trumpets* (8: 7–13)

The first angel trumpets with the result that there is a storm of hail and fire. Both the hail and fire are seen as having been mixed with blood. This emphasizes their destructive character, and we read that the third part of the earth, the third part of the trees and all the green grass—which includes the herbs—was burnt up. In all probability this first trumpet indicates that throughout the period extending from the first to the second coming, our Lord, who now reigns in heaven, will afflict the persecutors of the Church with various disasters that will take place on earth, that is, on the land. That these calamities, of whatever nature they be, are controlled in heaven, and in a certain organic sense are sent by our governing Lord is clearly indicated by the clause 'they were cast upon the earth'.

The second angel trumpets. John sees what looks like a huge mountain all ablaze hurled into the sea. Notice that he does not see a real mountain but *what looked like* a mountain. What he saw symbolized the terror of God's judgment upon the sea. Not only does our ascended Lord use calamities on *land* as an instrument to punish and warn the wicked; He also employs the *sea* as a tool against them. We are to interpret *all* the disasters that take place on the sea in that light. The figure of a mountain being cast into the sea is the most vivid symbol of awe-inspiring maritime calamities, especially when the mountain is all ablaze! It symbolizes great trouble and commotion (*cf.* Ps. 46: 2; Is. 34: 3; 54: 10; Ezk. 38: 20; Mi. 1: 4; Na. 1: 5; Job 9: 5; *etc.*). This judgment is more severe than the first: one third of the sea becomes blood; one third of all the live creatures in the sea perish; one third of the ships are destroyed and with them, of course, the passengers and crews.

The third angel trumpets. As after the first trumpet God's Son used vegetation, and after the second trumpet the sea, so now the

Lord Jesus Christ uses the inland waters as instruments against the wicked. The message to be passed on is this: 'Persecuted children of God, remember that your Saviour sees your tears and is not unmindful of your afflictions. Nowhere will the wicked persecutors find real rest or lasting enjoyment. Not only the land and the sea but even the fountains and the rivers, throughout this entire age, will be turned against evildoers.' John then sees a huge star blazing like a torch which is dropped out of the sky. What could produce greater fear than this? What better symbol could strike terror into the hearts of men? Remember, moreover, that this huge star blazing like a torch is dropped out of the sky; in other words, these judgments upon the inland waters are the acts of God. That is usually forgotten. The newspapers tell you all about floods and about epidemics originating in the marshes, *etc.*, but they fail to point out that these judgments are God's warning-voices! Do you remember the terrible Ohio River flood? Did anyone view this disaster—as well as all other floods throughout the age—as God's trumpet calling men to repentance? The name of the star is Wormwood, symbolical of bitter sorrow (La. 3: 19). The meaning is, bitter sorrow will fill the hearts of the wicked as a result of the plague indicated. Many men, moreover, die of the waters because they are made bitter.[1]

The fourth angel trumpets. One third of the sun is blasted; also one third of the moon and one third of the stars, with the result that for one third of the day and of the night there is no light. Thus, even the stars in their courses fight against the enemies of God's Church (*cf.* Jdg. 5: 20). The effect of the sun, moon, and stars upon life can hardly be over-estimated. All evils that are due to the abnormal functioning of the heavenly bodies throughout this entire age are here indicated. Thus the entire universe, including even the sun, moon and stars, is used by our Lord as a warning for those who do not serve Him and who persecute His children.

Four angels have blown their trumpets. Now there is an intermission.[2] John sees and hears an eagle (see verse 13, RV).

[1] It is, perhaps, possible to expand the meaning of this plague so that, under the symbolism of making the land-waters bitter, it indicates all calamities which obstruct whatever means man employs in order to satisfy his needs. Water, then, symbolizes that which supplies man's needs, *e.g.* industry, commerce. Hence, the poisoning of fountains and waters would indicate, among other things, the derangement of industry, commerce, *etc.*

[2] Notice, again, the arrangement of the seven into two groups: one of four and another of three. See chapter II, pp. 22f.

It is soaring aloft to the zenith so that it may be seen everywhere. The very fact that this bird is an eagle bodes evil, for the eagle is a bird of prey (Mt. 24: 28). Accordingly, this eagle says in a loud voice, 'Woe, woe, woe, for those dwelling on the earth because of the remaining trumpet-blasts of the three angels that are about to trumpet.'

The voice is loud and clear so that it can be heard everywhere. The meaning is plain; the three remaining woes will be worse than the first four.

3. *The fifth and sixth trumpets* (9: 1–21)

The fifth angel trumpets. John sees a star that has fallen out of heaven to the earth. *Cf.* Luke 10: 18: 'I beheld Satan fallen as lightning from heaven.' That is the devil's present condition; having rebelled against God he has lost his holiness, his position in heaven, his splendour. In the vision the apostle now observes that the prince of darkness receives the key of the shaft of the abyss. In other words, he receives power to open the abyss and to let the demons out. The abyss indicates hell before the final judgment (Lk. 8: 31; Rev. 20: 1,3). After the judgment, hell is called 'the lake of fire' (20: 14,15). When we read that Satan opens the shaft of the abyss, the meaning is that he incites to evil; he fills the world with demons and with their wicked influences and operations. John sees that the shaft, as soon as it is unlocked, begins to belch forth columns of diιty blue-black smoke just like the smoke of a great furnace. It is the smoke of deception and delusion, of sin and sorrow, of moral darkness and degradation that is constantly belching up out of hell. So thick and murky is that smoke that it blots out the light of the sun and darkens the air.[1] The power to bring this about is 'given' to the devil; that is, by God's permissive decree he is not prevented from carrying out his wicked designs in the hearts of the children of men, a wickedness for which he—not God—is responsible. Let us bear in mind that this, too, is one of the *trumpets*. God uses even the work of the devil as a punishment and as a warning for the wicked, a warning in order that they may repent (9: 21).

[1] We do not think it at all necessary to allegorize sun and air. It is possible to look upon sun and air as indicating the literal sun and the literal air as these appear in the vision. In the vision, so thick and black is the smoke that even sun and air were darkened by it. Hence, the picture, taken as a whole, symbolizes a very grievous moral and spiritual darkening by the forces of evil.

Now, out of the smoke, locusts descend on the earth. A more terrible plague than that of locusts is hardly conceivable. We have a very graphic description of this kind of plague in Exodus 10: 4–15, and especially in the prophecies of Joel which one should study very closely.[1] Observe the effect of this plague upon vegetation and upon men (Joel 1: 7–12).

'He has laid waste my vine,
And blighted my fig-tree;
He has stripped off its bark and thrown it away;
Its branches have become white . . .
The vine is withered . . .
Even all the trees of the field are withered
So that joy has withered away from the sons of men.'

The destruction, the utter ruin, the desolation and despondency caused by a locust storm can be understood only by the person who has seen and experienced it. These locusts, unbelievably terrible in their destructive power, are a fit symbol of the far more terrible and destructive *hellish* locusts which the apostle is about to picture. Under the symbolism of a locust plague John describes the powers and influences of hell operating in the hearts and lives of wicked men. No ordinary locusts are these; they do not destroy vegetation; they do not even harm it. They harm the men who have not been sealed (*cf.* Rev. 7: 1–8). Yet —glory be to God—the duration of their destructive work has been definitely determined by God's permissive decree: five months, no longer.[2]

There follows a very graphic description of these hellish locusts (9: 7–11). We should take the picture as a whole.[3] The locusts like horses prepared for battle; those crowns of pseudo-gold foreboding victory; those faces like human beings who are bent only on destruction; that hair as of furies; those teeth as of lions; those breastplates of iron portending invincibility; that sound of wings like the noise of countless prancing horses and jolting chariots on the field of battle; and last but not least, that exceedingly painful and burning, yet not fatal, scorpion-sting, striking terror into the hearts of men and filling their souls with the worst conceivable dread and utter hope-

[1] The entire prophecy of Joel centres around these three themes: Plague 1: 1–2: 11; Penitence 2: 12–17; Promise 2: 18–3: 21. Note the very vivid description of the locusts in 2: 2b–11.

[2] So many explanations of these 'five months' have been given that we think it best to say no more than this.

[3] See chapter v, pp. 38ff.

lessness, so that they seek death but cannot find it—can you conceive of a more frightful and horrible *and true* picture of the operation of the powers of darkness in the souls of the wicked during this present age? Here are the demons, robbing men of all light, that is, of all true righteousness and holiness, joy and peace, wisdom and understanding. And their king is 'the angel of the abyss', whose name, in two languages—Hebrew and Greek—is Destroyer. The entire symbolic picture emphasizes this one idea: terror and destruction, for that is Satan's work!

Hear God's warning voice, 'The first woe is past: behold there come yet two woes hereafter.'

The sixth angel trumpets. And now the same powers of darkness that carry on the work of destruction in the hearts of men change men into devils, as it were. For in times of war wicked men seem to become incarnate demons. The sixth trumpet describes war; not one particular war is indicated but *all* wars, past, present and future. Yet we are convinced that the symbol refers especially to those most frightful wars that shall be waged toward the close of this dispensation. You remember, of course, that war was also symbolized by the fourth seal. *There* it is mentioned as a trial or tribulation which believers, along with the rest of the world, must endure. *Here*, in the vision of the trumpets, war is described as a punishment and a warning voice for *unbelievers*. Throughout this dispensation God again and again hears the prayers of His persecuted children, the prayers that have been incensed with the merits of Christ's atonement and of His intercession. From the altar of incense we saw those prayers and that incense ascending heavenward (8: 3,4). The answer to these prayers is here, in 9: 13, also represented as coming 'from the horns of the golden altar'.

Says the voice coming from the horns of the golden altar to the sixth angel, 'Release the four angels, those that have been bound at the river, the great one, Euphrates' (9: 14). This river represents Assyria, Babylon, that is, the wicked world. These four angels are not the same as those mentioned in 7: 1.[1] They are *evil* angels here. They relish the idea of plunging mankind into war. Yet they can do nothing unless God permits. And—let us never forget it!—in finally permitting them to be released God uses war as a voice of warning for the wicked (9: 20). Thus, war also is included in God's decree, its very hour and day and month and year having been determined.

[1] The four angels of 7: 1 stand 'at the four corners of the earth'. The four angels of 9: 14 are bound at the great river Euphrates.

John now sees the armies on the field of battle. There are so many horsemen that he is unable to count them. He *hears* their number: two hundred million! This is a symbolical number, of course, indicating a tremendous host. Moreover, horsemen and 'horses' have one purpose, namely, to destroy. In order to indicate the perfect harmony between horsemen and 'horses', the former are described as having breastplates whose colour resembles fire, smoke, and brimstone, while the mouths of the latter are said to belch forth fire, smoke and brimstone. It should be clear by this time that these are not ordinary horses. They clearly symbolize war engines and war tools of every description. All this terrible death-dealing war machinery, causing destruction on every side (verse 19) is included in the symbolism of these 'horses'. They kill one third of mankind.

The general meaning of these trumpets is clear. Throughout this entire period, extending from the first to the second coming, our exalted Lord Jesus Christ, who rules all things in accordance with the scroll of God's decree, will again and again punish the persecutors of the Church by inflicting upon them disasters in every sphere of life, both physical and spiritual. The blood of the martyrs is precious in the sight of the Lord. The prayers of all the saints are heard. God sees their tears and their suffering. Yet, in spite of all these warning voices, mankind in general does not repent. Foolish and stubborn men continue to transgress both the first (verse 20), and the second table of the law (verse 21). The persecuting world becomes the impenitent world. It is impenitence that brings about not only the outpouring of the bowls of final wrath (chapters 15, 16) but also the culmination of this wrath in the final judgment. Delay is now no longer possible.

4. *The angel with the little book* (10: 1–11)

In order to announce that third and final woe—the final judgment—another angel appears. John sees him in the act of coming down out of heaven. This angel is a giant. His feet are as pillars of fire, columns so immense in size that while the left foot is firmly planted on earth the right foot rests far out on the ocean, so that, let us say, he is able to step across with one tremendous stride. His face is like the sun and a cloud is thrown around him. His sun-like face shining into the cloud produces a rainbow which encircles his head. The symbolism clearly indicates that this angel is very closely associated with the Christ (*cf.* 1: 7, 17; 4: 3). Look up these references and see the close resemblance between Christ and the angel. Yet the two figures do not indicate the same person.[1] God's holiness is symbolized by the angel's face, and His judgment is indicated by the cloud (Zp. 1: 15; Ps. 97: 2), but His mercy and His covenant faithfulness are expressed by the rainbow.

Why does this angel stand upon the sea and upon the land and why does he utter a great shout like the roar of a lion? Because his message concerns the entire universe and must be heard by all. In answer to his shout the seven thunders—(*cf.* Ps. 29)[2]—raise their voices in seven distinct messages. John is about to write them down but he hears a voice from heaven saying, 'Seal the things which they have spoken, the seven thunders, and do not write them.' The meaning is clearly this: never shall we be able to know and to describe *all* the factors and agencies that determine the future. We know the meaning of the lampstands, the seals, the trumpets, the bowls, *etc.*, but there are other forces at work; there are other principles that are operating in this universe, namely, the seven thunders. What they are we do not know. So let us be very careful in making predictions regarding the future: we may be leaving out a very important factor.

The angel, whose glory again is emphasized, now raises his right hand to heaven (*cf.* Gn. 14: 22; Dn. 12: 7) and swears by the eternal and omnipotent God who created the entire universe that there shall be delay no longer. No more delay! The final judgment is about to come. The mystery of God—*mystery* not because it is something entirely unknown, but because it would have remained unknown if God had not revealed it—this mystery of God's decree with respect to the history of the world is about to reach its culmination in the final judgment. Then God's people will receive their final glorious inheritance, their full salvation as promised to His servants, the prophets.

So now the final judgment can come. We expect that the next sentence will read: 'And the seventh angel sounded'. We expect the judgment day. Yet it is not definitely introduced until 11: 15 ff. Just as after the sixth seal the seventh does not immediately follow but is preceded by a very beautiful and comforting paragraph (chapter 7) in which the safety and final victory of the Church is set forth, so here the description of the sixth trumpet is not immediately followed by that of the

[1] Christ is not called 'an angel' in the Apocalypse. Besides we do not read that John worships this angel as he worships the Christ (1: 17).

[2] Notice that the expression 'the voice of Jehovah' occurs seven times in this psalm in which God's greatness in the storm is set forth.

seventh. First, the suffering, power, task, and final victory of the Church must be set forth so that believers may receive consolation when judgments are inflicted on the wicked. Again, the inevitable character of the final judgment will become even clearer when it is pointed out that the wicked world not only fails to heed God's warning voice revealed in the six plagues, but in addition rejects the very clear and definite testimony of the 'two witnesses' (chapter 11).

But is not this a delay after all? The angel has sworn very solemnly that there would be no delay, yet here we seem to have a delay. But the delay is apparent only. What we have in 10: 8–11: 13 does not intervene chronologically between the sixth and the seventh trumpets. It is simply a description of the present dispensation from a different aspect, namely, from the aspect of the suffering, power, task, and final victory of the Church, as already indicated.

When John saw the angel, he noticed that this glorious being had a little scroll open in his hand (verse 2). The apostle now receives the command to take this scroll. So he asks the angel to give it to him. The angel, complying with this request, says to John, 'Take it and eat it. And it shall make bitter thy belly, but in thy mouth it shall be sweet as honey.' (*Cf.* Ezk. 2: 9 ff.; 3: 1.) Psalm 119: 103 makes clear what is meant: the scroll is the Word of God, His gospel in which the mystery of salvation is set forth. That gospel is in itself glorious and sweet. But its proclamation is always followed by bitter persecution. In the same way the first rider (6: 2), namely the Christ, is always followed by the second, namely slaughter. So, in the vision, John takes the little scroll out of the angel's hand and eats it. In his mouth it is, indeed, sweet as honey; but when he had eaten it, it made his belly bitter. The meaning is very clear: the apostle must not merely understand and digest the message of the gospel; he must experience both its sweetness and the suffering, the cross-bearing, which is always the portion of those who truthfully proclaim it. Was not John an exile on the isle of Patmos? Was he not writing to Christians in tribulation for the Word of God and the testimony of Jesus? (*Cf.* 1: 9.) But this very suffering for Christ's sake enables believers to persevere in the proclamation of the Word. For this reason heavenly messengers assure the apostle that he must prophesy again concerning many peoples and nations and tongues and kings (*cf.* Rev. 17). In that chapter John is actually prophesying concerning nations and kings.

5. *The measuring of the Temple* (11: 1,2)

In very close connection with 10: 8–11, chapter 11 now gives us a description of the 'bitter' experiences which the true Church must endure when it preaches the 'sweet' gospel of salvation. In a vision[1] someone gives John a reed which is thick and heavy like a measuring-rod. He is told to measure the sanctuary of God and the altar and those who worship in connection with it. He must not measure the court which is outside the sanctuary. That court he must reject. 'And the court, the one outside of the sanctuary, cast out, and do not measure that, because it was given up to the heathen; and the city, the holy one, they shall trample upon it for forty-two months.'

Why this measuring? What does it mean? On the basis of the immediate context, the parallel expression (21: 15), and the Old Testament background (Ezk. 40: 5; 42: 20; Zc. 2: 1), we arrive at the conclusion that measuring the sanctuary means to set it apart from that which is profane; in order that, thus separated, it may be perfectly safe and protected from all harm. The sanctuary is 'accepted' while the court is 'rejected'.

It is of the utmost importance that we bear in mind that here, as elsewhere, the apostle receives a vision. Therefore, the assumption that the Herodian Temple must still have been standing in Jerusalem, and that the Apocalypse must have been written before the destruction of the Jewish nation by the Romans, is baseless. In a vision one can see things which no longer exist in literal reality.

Again, judging by the context it appears probable that what the apostle sees in the vision is indeed the Herodian Temple at Jerusalem. At any rate, he sees the Temple of the Jews as it had existed on earth. He is told to measure the sanctuary, that is, that part of the Temple which comprised the Holy place and the Holy of holies. The outside court, namely, the court of the Gentiles, is to be rejected. It must not be measured. There were, of course, several additional courts but these are not mentioned; perhaps because they have no symbolical significance. Then, outside the court of the Gentiles lies Jerusalem, which is still called 'the holy city', as in Matthew 27: 53. The apostle is not thinking of the heavenly Jerusalem but very definitely of the earthly city which had rejected the Christ. It is called the 'holy city' here and in Matthew 27: 53 for the simple reason that

[1] See the emphasis that this is all vision and symbolism, in R. C. H. Lenski, *op. cit.*, p. 325.

it used to be holy. Even today earthly Jerusalem is often styled the 'holy city'. The fact that in the vision John sees earthly Jerusalem—and therefore the earthly Temple—is also clear from what follows: 'and the city, the holy one, they shall trample upon it for forty-two months'. This is the Jerusalem which will be 'trampled upon' by the heathen. Luke 21: 24, a very close parallel, clearly indicates that earthly Jerusalem is meant.

That is the picture, the symbol and the vision. Let us see it clearly. The apostle views earthly Jerusalem with its earthly Temple. He measures the inner sanctuary but rejects the outside court. The 'holy city' Jerusalem and even the outside court of the Temple are trampled upon by the heathen for forty-two months.

Now the question arises, what does this picture mean? That is the question with respect to every picture or symbol. What is its ultimate, spiritual significance? The picture is one thing. The ultimate symbolical significance is another matter. Although these two are always very closely related, they should never be confused. A highly spiritual meaning is often expressed in earthly symbolism. Let us illustrate what we mean. According to 1: 12 John saw seven golden lampstands. In the vision they were golden lampstands in the literal sense of that term. But these lampstands, in turn, have a meaning. They have symbolical significance. They 'represent' something else. They indicate or symbolize 'the seven churches' (1: 20). So also here. In the vision the apostle sees, indeed, earthly Jerusalem, the earthly Temple, the earthly sanctuary, the earthly outside court, *etc.* The next question is, what does all this symbolize?

The answer is that this 'sanctuary of God' symbolizes the true Church, that is, all those in whose hearts Christ dwells in the Spirit. All true children of God, who worship Him in spirit and truth, are measured, that is, protected. They are safeguarded, while the judgments are being inflicted upon the wicked, persecuting world. To be sure, these saints are going to suffer severely but they will never perish; they are protected against eternal doom. But this divine protection does not extend to 'the court', that is, to those who although outwardly belonging to the Church are not true believers. Just as in the vision the heathen trample upon Jerusalem and even upon the outside court of the Temple, so the world tramples upon the outside court of merely nominal Christendom. The world invades this false church and takes possession of it. Worldly church members welcome the ideas of the world; they feel themselves perfectly at home with the world; they have a good time in worldly company; in voting for political offices they are prompted by worldly considerations; in brief, they love the world. This condition lasts throughout the forty-two months, that is, throughout the gospel age. More about these forty-two months will be said later.

Our interpretation is supported by the following arguments: first of all, observe that the term 'sanctuary of God' is a very common name for the true Church (*cf.* 1 Cor. 3: 16,17; 2 Cor. 6: 16; Eph. 2: 21). God dwells in His Church through the Spirit. Hence, the Church is His temple, or rather His sanctuary.

Secondly, the concept 'sanctuary of God' is defined in our passage as meaning 'the altar (of incense) and those who worship in connection with it'. While incense was being offered on the altar of incense, the worshippers were reverently bowing their heads in prayer. It is clear, then, that the term 'sanctuary of God' symbolizes people, those people who offer to God the incense of prayer, all who are true Christians.

Thirdly, we read: 'And the court, the one outside of the sanctuary, cast out.' The reference is clearly to people, namely, unfaithful church members who must be cast out or excommunicated (*cf.* Jn. 9: 34). The term 'sanctuary of God' must refer to the faithful, those who are not cast out but protected.

Fourthly, just as in Revelation 7 all true believers on earth (*cf.* 22: 4) are numbered and receive the seal of God on their forehead; so here, in chapter 11, all those who worship in connection with the altar, that is, all true worshippers (*cf.* 8: 3) are said to be measured. Both numbering and measuring refer to their protection. Furthermore, just as in Revelation 7 the Church militant was described under the symbolism of Israel's earthly tribes, so here the true Church on earth is symbolized by Israel's earthly sanctuary. The physical sanctuary symbolizes the spiritual sanctuary, namely, the people of God.

Fifthly, this interpretation is in harmony with the symbolism of the Old Testament. Ezekiel's Temple symbolizes the Church (*cf.* Ezk. 43: 4 ff.; 47: 1 ff.).[1]

Finally, the best interpreter of Revelation 11 is Revelation 11 itself! According to verse 8 the earthly Jerusalem is clearly the symbol of whatever opposes the true Church of God. It is the centre and symbol of antichristianity, that is, of immorality (Sodom) and of the persecution of God's children (Egypt).

[1] We do not mean that Ezekiel had arrived at the New Testament representation of the Church as the body of Christ.

From this it would seem to follow that the term 'sanctuary of God' must also be taken symbolically as indicating God's true people, His faithful ones.

6. *The two witnesses* (11: 3–14)

This point having been established, it is not difficult to grasp the meaning of the rest of the chapter. The true Church is now represented under the symbolism of two witnesses. These witnesses symbolize the Church militant bearing testimony through its ministers and missionaries throughout the present dispensation. The fact that there are two witnesses emphasizes the missionary task of the Church (*cf.* Lk. 10: 1). The Lord sends His missionaries two by two; what the one lacks the other supplies. Now the Church as an organization, functioning through its ministers and missionaries, will carry on this work for twelve hundred and sixty days. This is the period that extends from the moment of Christ's ascension almost until the judgment day (*cf.* Rev. 12: 5,6,14). It is, of course, exactly the equal of forty-two months, for forty-two times thirty is twelve hundred and sixty—and of 'a time, and times, and half a time', which is three years and a half (Rev. 12: 14). It is the period of affliction; the present gospel age. The question may arise, why is that period expressed now in terms of months (verse 2) then in terms of days (verse 3)? Here our answer is a mere guess: in verse 2 we have the picture of a city that is being besieged and finally taken and trampled upon. Now, the duration of the siege of a city is very often expressed in terms of months. In verse 3, however, the two witnesses are described as prophesying; this is a day-by-day activity. Every day they bear witness, throughout the entire dispensation. They preach repentance and for this reason they are clothed in sackcloth.

In order that we may receive a very clear picture of the Church as a powerful missionary organization throughout the present gospel age, it is here described under a fourfold symbolism.

First of all, just as 'the two olive-trees and the two candlesticks', Joshua and Zerubbabel(?) (*cf.* Zc. 4), represented the offices through which God blessed Israel, so throughout the gospel era He blesses His Church through the offices, that is, through the preaching of the Word and the administration of the sacraments.

Secondly, just as the missionaries were sent out two by two (Lk. 10: 1), so throughout this gospel age the Church, as an organization, fulfils its mission in the world.

Thirdly, just as the fire of judgment and condemnation proceeded out of Jeremiah's mouth devouring God's enemies (Je. 5: 14), even so when the Church of today, through its offices, condemns the wicked, on the basis of God's Word, this condemnation will actually result in their destruction (Mt. 18: 18).

Fourthly, just as Elijah received power to shut the heavens (1 Ki. 17: 1), so that it did not rain, and just as Moses received authority to turn waters into blood (Ex. 7: 20), even so the mighty missionary Church of this present gospel age, if its message is rejected, has authority to judge and condemn the world.

This power is not imaginary but very real. Not only does the Lord constantly rain woes upon the wicked world in answer to the prayers of the persecuted saints (8: 3–5), but He also assures His Church that, whenever it is engaged in the official ministry of the Word and is true to the Word, its judgments are His judgments (Mt. 16: 19; 18: 18,19; Jn. 20: 21–23).

Indeed, in a most real sense, the Church still smites the earth with every plague! The wicked world should be careful, for if anyone is fully determined to harm the Church, fire proceeds out of the mouth of God's witnesses. But even if anyone would like to[1] harm the true ministers and missionaries, he will be destroyed similarly (verse 5).

This gospel age is, however, going to come to an end (*cf.* Mt. 24: 14). The Church, as a mighty missionary organization, shall finish its testimony. The beast that comes up out of the abyss, that is, the antichristian world, urged on by hell, shall battle against the Church and shall destroy it. This is the Battle of Harmagedon[2]. The beast will not kill every believer. There are going to be believers on earth when Christ comes again, although they will be few in number (Lk. 18: 8). But the Church itself, as a mighty organization for the dissemination of the gospel and regular ministry of the Word, will be destroyed. By way of illustration, think of conditions in Communist China at the present time; to be sure, there are sincere believers in Communist China, but where is the powerful, official, unhindered and public proclamation and dissemination of the gospel? And is not this condition spreading to other countries? Thus, just before the second coming, the corpse of the Church, whose public and official testimony has been silenced and smothered by the world, lies on the great city's High Street. This is the High Street of immoral and antichristian Jerusalem.

[1] Notice the difference in the two forms of the verb in the original.

[2] See pp. 143, 162–165, 182f., 195.

Jerusalem crucified the Lord. Because of its immorality and persecution of the saints it has become, spiritually, like Sodom and Egypt (*cf.* Is. 1: 10; 3: 9; Je. 23: 14; Ezk. 16: 46). It has become the symbol of Babylon and of the immoral and antichristian world. So when we read that the corpse of the Church is lying on the broad avenues of the great city,[1] this simply means that in the midst of the world the Church is dead: it no longer exists as an influential and powerful missionary institution! Its leaders have been slaughtered; its voice has been silenced. This condition lasts three days and a half, which is a very brief time. (Mt. 24: 22; *cf.* Rev. 20: 7–9.) The world does not even allow the dead bodies of the witnesses to be buried. In the High Street lie these corpses, exposed to insects, birds, and dogs. The world has a grand picnic: it celebrates. People send each other presents and gloat over these witnesses (*cf.* Est. 9: 22).

Their word will not torment them any more. Foolish world! Its joy is premature.

The corpse suddenly begins to stir; the breath of life from God has entered into it; the witnesses stand upon their feet. In connection with Christ's second coming the Church is restored to life, to honour, to power, to influence. For the world the hour of opportunity is gone, and gone for ever. On the day of judgment when the world shall see the Church restored to honour and glory, the world will become frozen with fear. The Church—still under the symbolism of the two witnesses—now hears a voice, 'Come up hither'. Thereupon the Church ascends to heaven in a cloud of glory. 'And their enemies beheld them.' This is no secret rapture!

We now again direct our attention to the wicked world. While the summary of the history of the Church has carried us to the day of judgment and beyond it, let us now return to the events that take place just before this final day. As all of these events group themselves around the second coming, it is evident that the expression 'in that hour' does not forbid us to do this. In the vision the apostle sees that the earth is quaking. We have here the same picture as in 6: 12. There also the earthquake immediately precedes the final judgment. Already the tenth part of the city falls; in other words, the work of destruction begins. So terrible is the earthquake that it kills seven thousand people. This is probably simply a symbolic representation of the alarming happenings on the very eve of the final judgment. The

[1] The term 'great city' always refers to Babylon and never to the New and Holy Jerusalem.

number seven thousand must not be taken literally; the complete number of those destined for destruction by the earthquake is indicated. Not all the wicked were thus destroyed. Those who remain alive are terrified and 'they gave glory to the God of heaven'. This, of course, does not mean that they were converted. Far from it! They were simply struck with terror. King Nebuchadnezzar, in his day, again and again glorified the God of heaven (Dn. 2: 47; 3: 28; 4: 1 ff.; 4: 34; 4: 37). But this does not imply that he was a converted man.

Now all is ready for the final judgment; for, in spite of all these trumpets of warning, the world has remained impenitent and in addition has rejected the testimony of the two witnesses—the Church as an organization—and has killed them (verse 7). Therefore, now the final reckoning must come. So we read: 'The second woe is past. Behold, the third woe comes quickly.'

7. *The seventh trumpet* (11: 15–19)

The seventh angel trumpets. Again, the final judgment is not described but introduced.[1] Moreover, the significance of the judgment day with respect to God, His Christ, believers and unbelievers is pointed out. Notice the double chorus.

First, the angels sing. In the spirit the apostle hears their glorious, soulful, swelling anthem of praise and adoration. 'The dominion over the world[2] became the dominion of our Lord and of his Christ; and he shall reign for ever and ever.'

To be sure, God always reigns. Yet that power and authority which He exercises with respect to the universe is not always apparent. At times it seems as if Satan is the supreme ruler. But once the judgment day has arrived, the full royal splendour of God's sovereignty will be revealed, for all opposition will then be abolished. Then it will be clear to all that the world has become the province of our Lord and of His Christ. And He shall reign for ever and ever. If you wish to know what these words mean, go and hear Handel's *Messiah* and its Hallelujah chorus the next time you have an opportunity to do so. For, while I am writing, the words of that most wonderful musical composition are ringing in my heart. And that is but a foretaste of heaven! When the judgment day arrives, then the full meaning of Psalm 2: 7 ff., and of Daniel 7: 14 (*cf.* Lk. 1: 33) is going to be revealed.

[1] See chapter IV, p. 35.

[2] The term rendered 'kingdom' in our English translation often means kingship, rule, dominion, sovereignty. See the author's *Sermon on the Mount*, p. 31.

The entire redeemed multitude, represented by the twenty-four elders, responds to this song of the angels by rendering homage to God in the most humble manner—the elders fall on their faces—and by saying 'We render thanks unto thee, O Lord God, the Almighty, the One who is and the One who was, because thou hast taken thy power, the great one, and didst begin to reign. And the heathen were wroth, and it came: thy wrath and the season for the dead to be judged, and to give the reward to thy servants, the prophets, and to the saints and to those fearing thy name, to the small and to the great, and to destroy those destroying the earth' (11: 17,18).

Observe that in this anthem the Lord is no longer called 'the One who is and who was and who is to come', as in 1: 8, for He has come. The Church rejoices in the fact that the Lord has reached the zenith of His power and authority, now publicly displayed. The heathen were furious; they had made war with the witnesses, conquered them, killed them, and gloated over their misery (11: 7 ff.). But at last God's wrath became fully revealed, namely, on the day of final judgment which has now arrived. On that same day all those who fear the Lord receive their reward, while the destroyers are destroyed (*cf.* Mt. 25: 31 ff.).

In order to understand the final paragraph of this chapter be sure to remember that this is still a vision. The apostle sees not heaven itself but a symbolic picture. In this picture the sanctuary of God in heaven is now wide open. Nothing remains veiled. Nothing remains hidden or concealed. The ark of the covenant, so long hidden from view, is now seen. That ark of the covenant is the symbol of the superlatively real, intimate, and perfect fellowship between God and His people—a fellowship based on the atonement. Think of the mercy-seat. We read in Exodus 25: 22, 'And there I will meet with thee, and I will commune with thee from above the mercy-seat . . .'

Hence, when this ark is now seen, that is, fully revealed, the covenant of grace (Gn. 17: 7)[1] in all its sweetness is realized in the hearts and lives of God's children.

But for the wicked that same ark, which is God's throne, is a symbol of wrath. Also this wrath will now be fully revealed. Because of this there follow flashes of lightning, and rumbling and peals of thunder, and quaking, and a great hail-storm (*cf.* 4: 5).

[1] See also the author's *Covenant of Grace*.

CHAPTER ELEVEN

REVELATION 12–14: THE CHRIST VERSUS THE DRAGON AND HIS ALLIES

AS in each of the preceding sections, so here we return to the beginning of our present dispensation in order once more to traverse the same ground. In each vision we make a journey that takes us through the entire course of this era, from the first to the second coming of Christ. In unmistakable symbolism the seer carries us back to the moment of Christ's birth and ascension (12: 1–5). The vision does not end until we see 'One sitting like the Son of man, having on his head a golden crown and in his hand a sharp sickle' (14: 14 ff.). The judgment day has again arrived.

Yet, as we have already indicated,[1] chapter 12 is the beginning not only of another minor section, namely, the fourth, but also of the second major division of the book. This major division covers chapters 12–22. It forms a unit. The main characters that arise in opposition to Christ and His Church are introduced in chapters 12–14. They are the dragon, the beast out of the sea, the beast out of the earth, Babylon, and the men that have the mark of the beast. The visions that follow show us what happened to each of these antichristian forces, to those having the mark of the beast (chapters 15,16), to the harlot Babylon and to the two beasts (chapters 17–19), and, finally, to the dragon (chapters 20–22).

It is clear, therefore, that the central theme of the first main division (chapters 1–11) is continued in the second. That theme is, as has been indicated,[2] the victory of the Christ and of His Church over the dragon and his helpers. But whereas the first main division pictures the outward struggle between the Church and the world, the second part of the book reveals the deeper background. We now see more clearly than in the preceding division that the conflict between the Church and the world is but the outward manifestation of the war between the Christ and Satan (the dragon).

[1] See chapter II, pp. 22f.

[2] See chapter I, pp. 8f.

It is noteworthy that in chapter 12 the dragon is first pictured as purposing to destroy the Christ (verses 1–12). Failing in this, he persecutes the woman because she brought forth the Christ (verses 13–17a). Unsuccessful in this also, he makes war with the rest of her seed (verse 17b).

1. *The woman, the child and the dragon* (12: 1–6)

These six verses contain the first symbolic picture. The scene is heaven. Here John sees a woman gloriously arrayed: the sun is her garment, the moon her footstool and a wreath of twelve stars her crown. This woman is about to give birth to a child. She cries because she is in labour. Suddenly John sees standing in front of the woman a fiery red dragon. Think of a winged serpent with crested head and destructive claws, cruel, savage, malignant, vicious; but remember that this is a picture, a symbol. Now this beast has seven crowned heads and ten horns. So immense in size is this dragon that its mammoth tail furiously lashing across the sky sweeps away one-third of the stars of heaven and flings them to earth! Why does this terrible monster stand in front of the woman who is about to give birth to a child? In order to devour her child as soon as it is born! Does the dragon succeed? He does not. The woman gives birth to a son, a male, a mighty one, who is to shepherd the heathen with an iron rod. Then suddenly . . . but let us hear what happened in the apostle's own words: 'And snatched away was her child unto God and unto his throne.' Having failed in his attempt to devour the child, the dragon now directs all his fury against the radiant, all-glorious woman. But the woman flees into the wilderness where God has prepared food and shelter for her for 1,260 days. We shall read more later about the dragon's attempt to destroy the woman (see verse 13).

That, briefly, is the picture. But what does this picture mean?

There are three characters. First, there is the radiant woman. That woman symbolizes the Church (*cf.* Is. 50: 1; 54: 1; Ho. 2: 1; Eph. 5: 32). Scripture emphasizes the fact that the Church in both dispensations is one. It is one chosen people in Christ. It is one tent; one vineyard; one family—Abraham is the father of all believers whether they are circumcised or not—one olive tree; one elect race, royal priesthood, holy nation, people for God's own possession; one beautiful bride; and in its consummation one new Jerusalem whose gates bear the names of the twelve tribes and whose foundations are inscribed with the names of the twelve apostles. (*Cf.* Is. 54; Am. 9: 11; Mt. 21:

33 ff.; Rom. 11: 15–24; Gal. 3: 9–16,29; Eph. 2: 11; 1 Pet. 2: 9 (*cf.* Ex. 19: 5,6); Rev. 4: 4; 21: 12–14.)

On earth this Church may appear very insignificant and open to scorn and ridicule; but from the aspect of heaven this same Church is all-glorious: all that heaven can contribute of glory and of splendour is lavished upon her.[1] She is clothed with the sun, for she is glorious and exalted. She has the moon under her feet, for she exercises dominion. She has on her head a wreath of twelve stars, for she is victorious. She was pregnant, for it was her task to bring forth the Christ 'as concerning the flesh' (Rom. 9: 5).

Secondly, theie is the child, the seed of the woman. This mighty child is the Christ.[2] He is the One 'who is to rule all the nations with a rod of iron'. This expression is clearly borrowed[3] from Psalm 2: 9, a messianic psalm, while Christ applies it to Himself in Revelation 2: 27. The appellation 'the son (or seed) of a woman' is used elsewhere to indicate the Christ (Gn. 3: 15; Gal. 4: 4). If anyone should still hesitate to believe that the child of the woman indicates the Christ, let him compare verse 5 with verse 10; when the child is caught up to God and His throne and the dragon cast down, heaven sings, 'Now is come the salvation . . . of our God and the authority of his Christ.'

Thirdly, there is the dragon. It symbolizes Satan (Rev. 20: 2). The seven crowned heads indicate the devil's world-dominion (*cf.* Eph. 2: 2; 6: 12). See also our explanation of Revelation 13: 1 and 17: 9. These crowns, however, are not wreaths of victory but merely crowns of arrogated authority. The ten horns indicate Satan's destructive power; he stands in front of the woman in order to devour her child! When Satan fell, he dragged along with him in his ruin 'one-third of the stars of heaven', that is, a vast number of evil spirits (*cf.* Job 38: 7; 2 Pet. 2: 4; Jude 6).

Let us now study the main thought. It is this—the dragon stands in front of the woman who is about to be delivered so that when she is delivered he may devour her child; that is, Satan is constantly aiming at the destruction of the Christ. Thus viewed, the entire Old Testament becomes one story, the story of the conflict between the seed of the woman and the

[1] See A. Pieters, *op. cit.*, p. 161.

[2] Nearly all commentators of all schools agree that the child is Christ.

[3] Not borrowed in the ordinary sense, however; for Christ wrote Psalm 2 and revealed the Apocalypse.

dragon, between Christ and Satan. In this conflict Christ is, of course, victorious.

Let us view the history of the Old Testament from that aspect.

a. The initial promise (Gn. 3: 15). Revelation 12 is very clearly based on this verse. The same characters appear in both; the same truth is proclaimed in both. The words of the promise are, 'And I will put enmity between thee and the woman, and between thy seed and her seed; he shall bruise thy head, and thou shalt bruise his heel.' The 'serpent' of Genesis 3 is the 'dragon' of Revelation 12. The woman's 'seed' of Genesis 3 is the 'son, a man child' of Revelation 12. Also in Genesis 3: 15 the expression 'her seed' indicates the Christ. Here in Genesis 3 the conflict is announced.

b. From Seth to the Flood. By and by children are born to Adam and Eve—Cain and Abel. But Cain slays Abel. Then Seth is born. Does Satan realize that the family of Seth has been predestined to bring forth the promised seed, the Messiah? One is inclined to think so, for the devil now begins to do all in his power to destroy Seth. He whispers into the ears of Seth's sons that they must marry the daughters of Cain. He tries to destroy Seth's generations in order thus to annihilate the promise concerning the Messiah. Does the dragon succeed? It looks as if he does. Read Genesis 6: 12. Satan has triumphed . . . no, not entirely. Among the families that descended from Seth there is one which fears the Lord, that of Noah. God saves this one family, while the Flood destroys the rest. In this one family the promise is continued.

c. From the Flood to Jacob. Again the dragon stands in front of the woman in order to destroy the child. The promise concerning the Messiah is now given to Abraham, and Sarah his wife. Humanly speaking, however, that promise will never be fulfilled, for Abraham is old and Sarah is barren. The dragon has almost triumphed when the miracle happens and Isaac is born. The promise is now given to Isaac. But the Lord orders Abraham to offer Isaac as a burnt-offering. 'And Abraham stretched forth his hand, and took the knife to slay his son . . .' What now will become of God's promise? Surely the dragon now triumphs. But does he? We know the answer. The Angel of the Lord appears, that is, Christ Himself appears, in order to safeguard His own birth according to the flesh. Even during the old dispensation it is constantly Christ Himself who prepares all things for His own birth. The Angel of the Lord, that is, Christ Himself says to Abraham 'Lay not thy hand upon the lad, neither do thou anything unto him; for now I know that thou fearest God, seeing thou has not withheld thy son, thine only son, from me . . . and in thy seed (the Angel of the Lord might have said: *in myself*) shall all the nations of the earth be blessed.'

The seed that was going to destroy the serpent's head would be born from the generations of Isaac and Rebekah. But Rebekah was barren (Gn. 25: 21). Again Jehovah, the God of the promise, performs a miracle, and Rebekah conceives so that the promise is continued in the line of Jacob.

But see what happens. Jacob deceives his father and receives the blessing which Isaac had intended for Esau. Jacob has to flee. Even years afterwards when he returns to his own land he is greatly afraid. Yet Esau did not kill Jacob. The promise concerning the son of the woman is saved again.

d. From Jacob to the Jews in the desert. Again the dragon stands in front of the woman. He attacks Jacob's descendants, the Jews. This time it surely seems as if he will be successful, for though the Lord in tender mercy has led His people out of Egypt, they reject Him and are dancing around a golden calf.

'And Jehovah said to Moses . . . Let me alone that my wrath may wax hot against them, and that I may consume them.'

Is the dragon actually going to triumph? He is . . . unless there be an intercessor. And there was! Moses intercedes and the promise is saved again. And remember that it was the greater Mediator, Christ, who created in the heart of the lesser mediator, Moses, the spirit of intercession.

e. From the Jews in the desert to David, the king. Again history moves on. Out of the tribe of Judah God chooses one family, that of David. The promised Messiah will be born as the seed of David (2 Sa. 7: 12 ff.; Ps. 89: 29,35,36; Je. 23: 5; Acts 2: 30). So the devil now aims his arrow at David. David must be destroyed. We read, 'And Saul had his spear in his hand; and Saul cast the spear; for he said, I will smite David even to the wall.' Saul did this because an evil spirit came mightily upon him. Did the dragon succeed? No, for David escaped from Saul's presence twice. Even during the old dispensation the Christ is at work on earth, safeguarding the promise concerning Himself.

f. From David to Queen Athaliah. Athaliah, the wicked daughter of wicked parents—Ahab and Jezebel—is reigning. In order that she may have absolute power she conceives in her heart to destroy all the seed of David. Thus again the coming of the Mediator in human form is threatened. The dragon stands in front of the woman; his wrath is directed against the child. And now, finally, Satan is successful. At least, so it seems. For we read 'Now when Athaliah the mother of Ahaziah saw that her son was dead, she arose and destroyed all the seed royal.' Of course, if all the seed royal is destroyed, then the Christ cannot be born as the legal son and heir of David. Then God's plan is frustrated and the promise has failed. Athaliah destroyed all the seed royal. But read on (2 Ki. 11: 1,2 ff.): 'Jehosheba . . . took Joash, the son of Ahaziah, and stole him away from among the king's sons that were slain, even him and his nurse, and put them in a bedchamber; and they hid him . . . from Athaliah, so that he was not slain.'

How wonderful are God's ways. How marvellous His providence!

By and by we see Joash again, and on his head there is a crown. We hear people shouting, 'Long live the king!' Again, the promise is saved. Christ will be born of David's line. Unless the dragon should still prevent it.

g. From Athaliah to King Ahaz. And now the combined forces of Israel and Syria are gathered against Judah. Their purpose is to blot out the house of David with which were connected the hopes and promises concerning the Messiah, and to set up a foreign king 'in the midst of Judah, even the son of Tabeel' (Is. 7: 6). It is a critical moment in history. Will the Christ ever be born of the seed of David? Jehovah orders the prophet Isaiah to meet King Ahaz of Judah to encourage him. Ahaz, however, disdainfully refuses to ask for a sign as a pledge of Jehovah's aid. Surely, the dragon—the serpent of Genesis 3: 15—will be successful now, for against the house of David is assembled the host of Syria and of Israel and the wickedness of King Ahaz himself! Satan laughs. Again, however, he laughs too soon, for we read, 'Therefore the Lord himself will give you a sign: behold, a virgin shall conceive, and bear a son, and shall call his name Immanuel.' God's purpose must stand. Immanuel must be born, from the family of David.

h. From King Ahaz to Esther. It is the fifth century BC and King Ahasuerus is reigning. At the request of Haman, the king issues a decree that throughout his vast domain all the Jews should be put to death (Est. 3: 15). This decree is sealed with the king's ring. But Jehovah's promise concerning the Mediator, to be born of the seed of David, was sealed with the oath of the King of kings. Need I relate what happened? Read the book of Esther for yourself. The Jews, again, were saved.

i. From Esther to Bethlehem. Now occurs the final act in this mighty drama. The scene is Bethlehem. There in a manger lies the Christ-child. But although He is now actually born, the dragon still tries to destroy Him. In fact, Revelation 12, though covering with a few words the entire previous history of Satan's warfare against the Christ, refers directly and specifically to the events that took place in connection with Christ's birth. 'And the dragon stands in front of the woman who is about to be delivered, that when she is delivered he may devour her child.'

The wise men from the East are in the audience room of Herod. 'Be sure', says Herod, 'to report to me as soon as you shall have found the child, that I also may come and worship him.' His intention was to kill the child. But the wise men, warned of God, returned to their country another way after they had found and worshipped the Christ. Still the dragon refuses to admit defeat. The infants of Bethlehem and district, two years old and under, are slain. But Herod failed. So did the dragon. The Christ-child was safe in Egypt (Mt. 2: 13). God's purpose can never be frustrated. Christ's birth in Bethlehem is God's victory over the dragon. The Saviour's death on the cross for His people is His further victory. 'And snatched away was her child to God and to His throne.' This refers to Christ's ascension and enthronement (Rev. 5: 7; *cf.* Phil. 2: 9). Those who oppose Him will be treated to 'the iron rod'. This is true throughout this entire dispensation. Christ triumphs and the angels sing 'Glory to God in the highest!'

2. *The expulsion of the dragon* (12: 7–12)

The second symbolic picture shows us the effect of Christ's birth, atonement, and ascension to the throne in heaven. As always, let us first see the picture as a whole. There is a battle in heaven. Michael, as leader of the good angels and defender of God's people (Dn. 10: 13,21; 12: 1; Jude 9) makes an attack upon the dragon, the leader of the evil angels and the opponent of God's people. Two generals and two armies oppose each other. Notice, however, that it is Michael and his army that do the attacking. The result is that the dragon is defeated and cast out of heaven.

'And he was hurled down, the dragon, the great, the serpent, the old, the one called the devil and Satan, the one deceiving the whole world; hurled down was he to the earth, and his angels with him were hurled down.'[1]

The picture which John sees is fully explained by the words which he hears. The battle in heaven and the hurling down of the dragon are not to be understood literally. Satan is 'hurled down from heaven' in this sense, namely that he has lost his place as an accuser of the brethren. Whereas Christ was born and rendered satisfaction for sin, Satan has lost every semblance of justice for his accusations against believers. True, he continues to accuse. That is his work even today. But no longer is he able to point to the unaccomplished work of the Saviour. Christ's atonement has been fully accomplished; complete satisfaction for sin had been rendered when He ascended to heaven (*cf.* Rom. 8: 33: 'Who shall bring any accusation against God's elect?'; *cf.* also Rom. 8: 1 and Lk. 10: 18). Notice the threefold effect of this defeat of Satan and his host.

First, because of this defeat the salvation wrought by God in Christ becomes manifest; God's power is vindicated; His royal rule in the hearts of His people established; His authority revealed (verse 10). As a result, there is a mighty acclaim in heaven.

Secondly, because of this defeat God's people, who bear witness concerning their faith—in the blood of the Lamb—and prove its genuine character by perseverance even to death, triumph (verse 11). Accordingly, let the heavens and those who live there rejoice.

Thirdly, because of this defeat, Satan is filled with wrath. He knows that his time is short: this, his second defeat, forebodes that other, final discomfiture at the close of history (verse 12). Consequently, let heaven ring with jubilation.

3. *The final assaults of the dragon* (12: 13–17)

In this third symbolic picture, the dragon, having been hurled down to the earth, persecutes the woman because she was the one who gave birth to the male. This explains his attempt to destroy the woman and is in reality another phase of his wrath against her child. Let us be sure to notice this point. The woman

[1] For Satan's names see our explanation of Rev. 20: 2, p. 186.

received the two wings of the eagle (Ex. 19: 4; Dt. 32: 11; Is. 40: 31) so that she flew to the wilderness. In that wilderness God had prepared a place for her (verse 6). Here she is nourished for a time and times and half a time, that is, for a thousand two hundred and sixty days (verse 6). Here she resides 'away from the face of the serpent'. The dragon, not yet willing to give up, tries to engulf the woman with a stream of water which he pours from his mouth; but the earth swallows up this stream. So the dragon is furious, filled with wrath against the woman. Yet, having failed, not only in his attempt to destroy the child but also in his assault upon the woman, he slinks away to do battle against the rest of her seed, those keeping the commandments of God and adhering to the testimony of Jesus.

We interpret the picture as follows. Satan, having failed to defeat the Christ, continues his attack upon the Church. He directs his fury against the Church because the Church has brought forth the Christ. But the Lord protects His people: He bears them on eagles' wings. In the desert of affliction, this earthly sojourn, He has prepared a place for them and nourishes them with the manna of the Word. Here the Church resides 'away from the face of the serpent', that is, away from Satan's most direct and deadly attack. The devil cannot destroy her. This is the millennium of Revelation 20. True, the evil one tries to engulf the Church in a stream of lies, delusions, religious '-isms', philosophical falsehoods, political utopias, quasi-scientific dogmas, but the true Church is not fooled. Worldly people, on the other hand, are ready to swallow the entire river! This failure to deceive the Church makes the devil very angry. He is determined to direct his attack against 'the rest of the woman's seed', that is, against individual believers.

This period of time during which the Church experiences both bad and good, the persecution of Satan and the special care of God which makes it impossible for the evil one to launch a direct attack on the Church and destroy it; this twilight period during which God's people are nourished with the manna of the Word and enjoy a certain degree of tolerance and security on earth, the Lord having prepared a place for them in the desert, is described as 'a time, and times, and half a time'.

This is the period during which the witnesses (chapter 11) prophesy; the gospel is being proclaimed far and wide. It is followed by 'three days and a half' during which the witnesses are killed and their dead bodies lie in the High street of the great city (Rev. 11: 7 ff.). This is the Battle of Harmagedon. These three days and a half are, in turn, followed by the judgment day. It is clear, therefore, that the period described as 'a time, and times, and half a time' begins at the moment of Christ's first coming—His birth, ministry, cross, coronation—and extends to a point of time very near to His second coming in judgment. A careful study of Revelation 20 confirms our view. There, too, the long period during which the Church is nourished 'away from the serpent' so that Satan's influence is curbed is followed by a very brief span of time during which the devil marshals the armies of Gog and Magog against 'the camp of the saints'. There, too, this brief span is followed by the second coming of Christ to judge the world (20: 11 ff.).[1] In all these chapters we have the following order.

(i) A long period (the gospel era) '42 months', 'a thousand years', 'a time, times, half a time', and 1,260 days (Rev. 11: 2,3; 12: 6,14; 13: 5; 20: 2–5).

(ii) A very short period of 3½ days (Rev. 11: 7,9; 13: 7; 20: 7–10).

(iii) The judgment day (Rev. 11: 11,12,16 ff.; 14: 14 ff.; 20: 11 ff.).

We immediately see that the three ways of designating this period which we find in chapters 11, 12 and 13 differ but slightly. In fact, forty-two months is equal to 1,260 days; both are equal to 'a time, times, and half a time', if the term 'time' be interpreted as meaning one year, and 'times' as indicating two years. In all three cases we are dealing with a period which is designated as three years and a half.

It is in order to ask why the term 'three years and a half' is used to characterize this long period. To answer this question we must remember that during the old dispensation there was a period of three years and a half which God's people could never forget. It was a period of affliction, yet also a period during which the power of God's Word was exhibited (1 Ki. 17; Jas. 5: 17). When you compare James 5: 17 with Revelation 11: 6, you immediately see that the apostle was thinking of the days of Ahab and Elijah. During that period of three and a half years God's Church was persecuted (1 Ki. 18: 10,13) yet not destroyed (1 Ki. 18: 4,39; 19: 18). God's Word showed its great power (1 Ki. 17: 1). Elijah and others were nourished by Jehovah in a miraculous manner (1 Ki. 17: 4,9 ff.). Similarly, throughout the present long period of gospel activity, beginning

[1] Compare chapters 11, 12 and 20 of Revelation: a very striking parallel.

with Christ's first coming and extending nearly to the second coming, the Church is persecuted but not destroyed, God's Word exerts a powerful influence, and God's people receive spiritual nourishment.

The expression 'a time, and times, and half a time' occurs first in the book of Daniel 7: 25; 12: 7. It is the period of the antichrist. John emphasizes the fact that the spirit of the antichrist is in the world already (1 Jn. 4: 3). In the Apocalypse this period of three years and a half refers to the entire gospel age. It is followed by the 'three days and a half' during which 'the beast that comes up out of the abyss'—the antichristian world in its final phase—will kill the witnesses and will silence the voice of the gospel (*cf.* Rev. 11: 7 ff.).

4. *The helpers of the dragon* (13: 1–18)

Chapter 13 shows us the agents, instruments, or tools which the dragon uses in his attack upon the Church. Two beasts are described. The first is a monster of indescribable horror. The second has a harmless appearance and for that very reason is even more dangerous than the first. The first beast comes up out of the sea. The second arises from the land. The first is Satan's *hand*. The second is the devil's *mind*. The first represents the persecuting power of Satan operating in and through the nations of this world and their governments. The second symbolizes the false religions and philosophies of this world. Both these beasts oppose the Church throughout this dispensation; yet the apostle describes them in terms that indicate the form which they assumed during the closing decade of the first century AD.[1]

In 14: 8 a third agent is mentioned, namely, Babylon, the harlot. So, in all, three agents are employed by Satan in his attack upon the earth. They are antichristian persecution, antichristian religion, and antichristian seduction.

John notices that the dragon goes to the sea-shore in order to summon help. The dragon, accordingly, must be viewed as standing at a place where sea and land meet; on one side is the sea, on the other the land. The first ally comes up out of the sea. The second arises from the land. The apostle beholds a monster of indescribable horror coming up out of the sea. Very gradually the beast emerges out of the water. First, John sees nothing but the horns. There are ten of them covered with diadems.

[1] See chapter VI, pp. 44f.

Next the heads appear. This beast has seven heads and on these heads are names of blasphemy. The body now comes to view. It is that of a leopard, large and fierce, swift to spring upon its prey (*cf.* Dn. 7: 6; Ho. 13: 7; Hab. 1: 8). Now the beast is stepping out of the water. John sees its feet. They are the feet of a bear. Think of the familiar figure of the bear robbed of her whelps (2 Sa. 17: 8; Pr. 17: 12; Ho. 13: 8); it is ready to rend and tear, anxious with its great and terrible feet to crush its enemy. As the mouth is the main point of the figure, it is mentioned last. This horrible beast has the mouth of a lion: growling and roaring, it is eager for its prey, anxious to destroy (Ps. 17: 12; Ho. 5: 14; 1 Pet. 5: 8). To this monster the dragon gives his power and authority. John now notices, looking closely, that one of the seven heads seemed to have received a mortal wound, but the wound has been healed. The whole world follows the beast in wonder and amazement, in the spirit of adoration and worship, saying: 'Who is like unto the beast? and who is able to fight it?' In worshipping the beast, men are also rendering homage to the dragon who gave his authority to it. The beast now begins to speak; it utters great boasts and blasphemies. This continues for forty-two months. The blasphemies are directed against God and all those who dwell in the heavenly tabernacle. And as far as the inhabitants of the earth are concerned, 'it was given unto him to do battle against the saints and to conquer them: and there was given to him authority over every tribe and people and tongue and nation. And they shall worship him, all those dwelling on the earth, whose-ever name has not been written from the foundation of the world in the book of life of the Lamb, the one having been slaughtered' (13: 7,8).

We interpret the picture as follows. The sea represents nations and their governments (*cf.* Is. 17: 12, where the roaring of peoples is compared to the roaring of the sea; and the surging of nations to the surging of mighty waters).[1] Revelation 17: 15 proves the point. The beast that comes up out of the sea is very closely associated with the beast that comes up out of the abyss (11: 7). The latter is the final guise which the former assumes. The sea-born beast symbolizes the persecuting power of Satan embodied in all the nations and governments of the world throughout all history. World-dominion directed against God's people wherever and whenever it appears in history, that is the beast. This beast assumes different forms; it has seven heads.

[1] See also K. Schilder, *op. cit.*, p. 141.

Now it is Old Babylonia; then Assyria; next, New Babylonia; Medo-Persia; Macedonia; Rome, *etc.* But though the forms differ, the essence remains the same: worldly government directed against the Church. In this beast the persecuting power of Satan becomes visible. This accounts for the great resemblance between the dragon and the beast; both are cruel monsters having ten horns and seven heads. Observe, however, that in the case of the beast the horns—and not the heads—are crowned, while the dragon wears his diadems of arrogated authority on his head. In other words, it is the dragon, Satan, who rules: his plans are executed by the governments of the world. It is true that earthly rulers, too, wear crowns; think of the crowned horns symbolical of crowned cruelty. But these earthly rulers are subject to and receive their inspiration from Satan! This is true with respect to every worldly ruler who persecutes the Church. These rulers and governments blaspheme God and demand for themselves divine titles. Thus, in the days of John, Roman emperors demanded that their subjects address them as 'Lord', and 'Saviour'. The fact that this beast represents every form of wordly government which persecutes the Church, whenever and wherever it appears in history, becomes very clear when we observe that, according to verse 2, the four beasts which Daniel saw in his vision (Dn. 7) have been combined into one beast here. In Daniel these four beasts represent four successive world empires.[1] But here this composite beast cannot symbolize merely one empire or government. It must indicate all antichristian governments.

One of these seven heads had received a mortal wound, but the wound had been healed. In order to give a correct interpretation of this statement we must bear in mind that the seven heads symbolize seven antichristian empires that succeed one another in history (*cf.* 17: 10). Therefore, the statement that one of the heads received a death stroke and that this death stroke was healed must mean that one of these seven empires ceased, for a while, to be a fiercely persecuting power but afterward resumed its former rôle. Accordingly, the explanation which we regard as the most probable is as follows. The head of which John speaks represents Rome, the Rome of his day. When Nero was emperor (AD 54–68) that cruel tyrant, in order to divert from himself the suspicion that the conflagration of Rome was his act, instigated the persecution of Christians. Some believers were crucified. Others were covered with pitch or oil, nailed to

[1] See chapter VI, p. 46.

posts, and burned as torches for the amusement of the mob.[1] But in the year AD 68 Nero committed suicide. As persecutor, Rome received its death-stroke. But under Domitian the persecution of believers was resumed. The death-stroke was healed. Rome appears again as the Satan-inspired persecutor of the Church.[2] In the days of the apostle the world, in general, worshipped Rome and paid homage to the emperor.

Throughout this entire gospel age—the forty-two months, which we have already discussed[3]—the governments of this world place themselves on the throne; arrogate to themselves the authority that belongs to God (think of the totalitarian governments of the present day) and blaspheme God and heaven. This condition will finally result in the complete destruction of the Church as a mighty and influential organization for the spread of the gospel. For finally every tribe and people and tongue and nation will worship antichristian government (Rev. 13: 7 and 11: 7 should be compared).[4] But even in these most dreadful days that shall precede Christ's second coming there will be believers on earth, those whose names have been written from eternity in the Lamb's book of life (*cf.* 17: 8).[5] Because of the fact that God has elected them from eternity to salvation in sanctification of the Spirit and belief of the truth (2 Thes. 2: 13), these individuals cannot perish. The government of antichrist may destroy their bodies, but it cannot destroy their souls. Let believers wait patiently for this time of severest tribulation, knowing that all things are included in God's decree; and knowing, in addition, that when the world makes use of the sword in its warfare against the Church, God Himself will avenge this wrong. The individual who understands this will exercise endurance and will persevere in his faith. If anyone has an ear, let him hear these admonitions and take them to heart (verses 9,10). It is not Satan but God who rules supreme.

Afterwards John sees another beast. It rises from the earth. According to James 3: 15 antichristian 'wisdom' comes from the earth (*cf.* Phil. 3: 19). But let us see the picture first of all. This beast does not have ten horns but merely two: two little

[1] See P. Schaff, *History of the Christian Church*, I, p. 381.
[2] See A. Pieters, *op. cit.*, p. 236.
[3] pp. 142ff.
[4] See our explanation of 11: 7 ff., p. 130ff.
[5] The words 'from the foundation of the world' modify 'written', as in ASV.

horns just like a lamb. But it speaks like a dragon! This second beast is the servant of the first; that is, it fully co-operates with the first. It performs many tricks and pseudo-miracles to deceive the masses. It brings down fire from heaven; that is, it makes it appear as if fire descends from heaven. It also orders the people to make an image or statue in honour of the first beast. And then it makes the image speak. At last, the people, sunk in superstition and ignorance, are deluded so that they actually believe that speech issues from the image. Furthermore, this second beast orders all who refuse to worship the image of the first beast to be killed. Finally, it orders the mark of the beast to be impressed on the right hand or forehead of everyone as an evidence of loyalty. Those who refuse to receive this mark are boycotted. They are not permitted to buy or sell, or carry on any business. This mark of the beast is at the same time its name or the number of its name. Whoever has a mind, that is, whoever has received wisdom, can explain this number; for it is the number of man, namely 666.

This is, perhaps, the most difficult paragraph in the entire book of Revelation. The main ideas are clear; the details are obscure. Of the many interpretations we regard the following as the most reasonable. We emphasize, however, that in the explanation of the details certainty is wholly lacking.

The second beast is the false prophet (19: 20). It symbolizes false religion and false philosophy in whichever form these appear throughout the entire dispensation. Although this beast outwardly resembles the Lamb it inwardly conceals the dragon.[1] In other words, whatever strikes the eye is very appealing and attractive. The beast looks very innocent: a nice little lamb, a pet for the children. But speech reveals the inner thought, life, essence and character. And this lamb speaks like the devil himself! This second beast, accordingly, is the lie of Satan dressed up like the truth. It is Satan masquerading as a shining angel (2 Cor. 11: 14). It symbolizes all false prophets in every era of this dispensation. They come disguised as sheep, but inwardly they are ravenous wolves (Mt. 7: 15).

The two beasts—antichristian government and antichristian religion—work in perfect co-operation. That is invariably the case. It was already true in the days of the apostle: the heathen

[1] Although the definite article is omitted in order to emphasize the character of this beast, yet we immediately feel that this monster is the devil's imitation of the true Lamb of God. In reality, this second beast is inspired by 'the' dragon, Satan.

priest was the friend of the proconsul. The priestly influence supported and upheld the secular power of the state in its persecution of believers. Heathen religion and heathen politics co-operated with one another in their battle against the Church. The priests of the pagan temples did their utmost in order to impress on the minds of the people the lie of Satan: Caesar is Lord! They even resorted to tricks and pseudo-miracles in order to deceive the people. They ordered the inhabitants of the various districts to make statues in honour of the emperor. Think of Pergamum.[1] Whoever refused to perform an act of worship in front of such a statue or whoever refused to say, 'The emperor is Lord' was put to death.[2] Does the apostle actually intend to tell us that in his day pagan priests, in order to entrench the state religion or emperor-worship more firmly in the minds of the people, would resort to the tricks of causing fire to burst forth without apparent cause and, by the art of ventriloquism, cause speech to issue from the emperor's statue?[3] Or do these details belong merely to the picture and must we assign a symbolical interpretation to them? Either way, the ultimate meaning seems to be that throughout this entire dispensation—and in an increasing manner as the coming of the Lord draws near—false prophets, by showing great signs and wonders (Mt. 24: 24), shall try to deceive the masses and to strengthen the hand of the government when it bears down upon the Church. Notice, however, verse 15: 'And it was given unto him.' Beyond the sphere of God's permission Satan can do exactly nothing!

Now, to all—small and great, rich and poor, free and bond—the false prophet gives a mark. It is the mark of the first beast. Here the false prophet, in outward appearance, resembles the Lamb. Have not the followers of the Lamb been sealed on their foreheads?[4] Hence the followers of the beast must be marked or branded on their foreheads or right hands. But what is meant by this 'mark of the beast'? Various amusing answers have been given.[5] These theories err in this respect, namely, that they interpret this mark as a single, individual, outward, visible

[1] See chapter VIII, p. 66.

[2] See W. M. Ramsay, *op. cit.*, p. 98.

[3] *Ibid.*, pp. 100 ff.

[4] See pp. 68ff., 109ff.

[5] The mark of the beast has been interpreted as meaning, *e.g.*, the symbol of freemasonry; the fasces on an American dime; the mono-mark; the observance of the Sabbath on the first day of the week; antichrist's initials appearing on the forehead of the wicked, and so on.

sign that will appear on the forehead or hand of the wicked at one particular moment in history; then, and then only. But the beast *always* persecutes the Church and indicates every form of secular power that tries to destroy believers. Wherever and whenever the beast appears, you will also find the mark of the beast. The two go together and cannot be separated.

In order to understand the expression 'mark of the beast' we must remember that not only cattle but slaves also were branded or marked. The mark meant that the slave belonged to his master. Very soon the expression 'to receive the mark of someone' began to mean to belong to someone, to serve or worship someone. Let us prove this point. In Revelation 14: 9 we read: 'If any man worships the beast . . . and receive the mark on his forehead'. Here 'receiving the mark of the beast' seems to mean 'worshipping the beast'. Similarly, in Revelation 14: 11: 'They that worship the beast . . . and receive the mark of his name' (*cf.* also Rev. 20: 4). So 'receiving the mark of the beast' seems to mean 'belonging to the beast and worshipping the beast'. The 'mark of the beast' is the God-opposing, Christ-rejecting, Church-persecuting spirit of antichrist, wherever and whenever it shows itself. This mark is impressed on the forehead or right hand (*cf.* Dt. 6: 8). The forehead symbolizes the mind, the thought-life, the philosophy of a person. The right hand indicates his deed, action, trade, industry, *etc.* Therefore receiving the mark of the beast on the forehead or right hand indicates that the person so characterized belongs to the company of those who persecute the Church; and that—either preeminently in what he thinks, says, writes or more emphatically in what he does—this antichristian spirit becomes evident.

This interpretation harmonizes entirely with our explanation regarding the seal which the believer receives on his forehead. This seal indicates that he belongs to Christ, worships Him, breathes His spirit and thinks His thoughts after Him. Similarly, the mark of the beast symbolizes that the unbeliever, who persists in his wickedness, belongs to the beast and therefore to Satan, whom he worships. Observe, however, that there is a difference. The believer receives a seal, the unbeliever a mere mark.[1] Throughout the dispensation it has been true (think of Thyatira)[2] that those people who have not received the mark of the beast and have not worshipped his image have been thwarted in their business pursuits. They are the ones who are

[1] See R. C. H. Lenski, *op. cit.*, p. 409.

[2] See chapter VIII, pp. 71f.

crowded out and oppressed. They are not allowed to buy or to sell as long as they remain loyal to their principles. As we approach the end this opposition will increase. Nevertheless, let not the believer despair. Let him remember that the number of the beast is the number of man. Now, man was created on the sixth day. Six, moreover, is not seven and never reaches seven. It always fails to attain to perfection; that is, it never becomes seven. Six means missing the mark, or failure. Seven means perfection or victory. Rejoice, O Church of God! The victory is on your side. The number of the beast is 666, that is, failure upon failure upon failure![1] It is the number of man, for the beast glories in man; and must fail!

5. *The triumph of God's Church* (14: 1–16)

This chapter is divided into three parts. The clause, 'And I saw', in verses 1, 6 and 14, indicates the beginning of the three paragraphs.

a. The blessedness of the redeemed (verses 1–5). The first of these paragraphs shows us the Lamb standing on mount Zion. This is that Zion 'which cannot be moved but abides for ever' (Ps. 125: 1). It is heaven (Heb. 12: 22) because we read, 'And I heard a voice from heaven.' With the Lamb the apostle sees 144,000 having His name and the name of His father written on their foreheads. This is the sealed multitude of chapter 7. There these saints were still living on earth, surrounded by enemies. Here they are enjoying the blessedness of heaven after the final judgment. Although the dragon has tried his utmost to make them unfaithful to their Lord, and although he has employed the two beasts to assist him, not a single one of the 144,000 is missing 'when the roll is called up yonder'.

The apostle hears a sound coming out of heaven: the 144,000 are singing the new song. It was like the sound of many waters and as the voice of a great thunder, constant, majestic, sublime. Think of mighty Niagara, with the sound of an ever-increasing crescendo, which reaches a thunderous roar when the waters strike the depths. That is what the new song is like! Whatever is trivial and petty will be absent from it. Yet although it will be majestic, sublime, constant, it will at the same time be the most lovely, sweet, and tender song you have ever heard, like

[1] See C. F. Wishart, *op. cit.*, p. 25. The attempts to arrive at an interpretation by adding the numerical values in the name Nero, Plato and so on, lead to nothing just because they lead to everything. The Apocalypse is a book of symbols; it is not a book of riddles!

'harpers harping on their harps'. The majestic and the tender, the sublime and the lovely, are beautifully combined in this new song. It will be a *new* song, for it records a *new* experience: the 144,000 have been purchased out of the earth. Each of the redeemed sings this song before the throne—for upon it are seated God and the Lamb—and before the cherubim, and before the entire Church in glory. As this song records the experience of having been purchased out of the earth by the precious blood of the Lamb, it follows that only those who had this experience could learn this song. These 144,000 are virgins, that is, they are not defiled. They did not become unfaithful to Christ. They follow Him wherever He goes (*cf.* 2 Cor. 11: 2). 'They were purchased away from men, first-fruits for God and for the Lamb.' Christ died for them. One of the results of His death for them was the cleansing work of the Holy Spirit in their hearts whereby they were separated from the sinful life and conversation of men (*cf.* 1 Cor. 6: 20).

Observe especially that these 144,000 are first-fruits for God and for the Lamb in the sense that they were purchased away from men. In other words, there was a separation; the first-fruits were for the Lord. As such they were set apart from men in general (*cf.* Jas. 1: 18). The world of humanity, which is ripening for the final judgment, is often likened to a harvest (Mt. 9: 37; 13: 30; Lk. 10: 2; Jn. 4: 35). We have this symbolism in this chapter (Rev. 14: 14 ff.). Here, too, the first-fruits are for the Lord (verses 14–16); the rest is for Satan (verses 17–20). The symbolism rests upon the Old Testament law with respect to the first-fruits. All the first-fruits were offered to the Lord, after which the Israelite was at liberty to use the rest (Ex. 23: 19; Nu. 18: 12). Similarly, here we have a contrast between first-fruits on the one hand, and men in general on the other. All the redeemed, the full number of the elect, are included in these first-fruits. Whatever does not belong to these first-fruits is not for the Lord and is not elect. These 144,000 are not first-fruits versus other believers. They do not constitute a kind of select group in heaven, a group of super-saints. They are the first-fruits 'purchased away from men'. This is also evident from the fact that these 144,000 'had his name and the name of his Father written on their foreheads'. As such they are the opposite of 'the small and the great, the rich and the poor, and the free and the bond' who receive the mark of the beast on their right hand or on their forehead (13: 16). All believers without exception are sealed with the name of God and of the Lamb.

Similarly, all the reprobate, all those who harden themselves in sin and unbelief, are marked or branded. Again all the redeemed—not merely a select number of super-saints—sing the new song in glory. None of the others can learn it. Chapter 7: 1–8 describes the Church militant here on earth. Chapter 7: 9–17 pictures the Church triumphant in heaven. Here, in chapter 14, the same Church triumphant is described from the aspect of its heavenly blessedness and holiness.[1] These 144,000 have not accepted Satan's lie. Consequently, in Christ, they are without blemish (*cf.* Ex. 12: 5; Lv. 1: 3; 9: 2; Mt. 5: 48).

b. Warnings to mankind (verses 6–13). Just as in Revelation 11: 12 believers are described as 'ascending into heaven in the cloud', while the next verse takes us back to conditions on earth before the judgment day, so here in chapter 14 after the blessedness of the redeemed has been pictured, we return to the events that will occur just before the second coming. The three angels of verses 6, 8 and 9 belong together. They have one purpose, namely to warn mankind with respect to the coming judgment in order that men may turn to God in true faith.

The first angel is sent to those who 'sit on the earth'. That characterizes men in general on the eve of the judgment: they sit on earth. They are easy-going, indifferent, unconcerned, listless and careless. Think of the artist who found a convenient spot on top of an ocean rock from which to paint the beauty of the village and its surroundings. He is altogether unaware of the fact that the returning tide is surging about the base of the rock. So absorbed is he in his painting that he pays no attention to the lashing of the waves against the rock. He fails to heed the warning voices. He just sits and sits absorbed in his painting. By and by the waves will bury him. Similarly, just before the final judgment people in general will be fascinated with earthly charms to such an extent that they will not realize that the judgment is creeping upon them, coming closer and closer. They are unconscious of their peril . . . until it is too late (*cf.* Lk. 17: 26 f.). To these indifferent people an angel appears, flying in mid-heaven so as to be heard by all, saying, 'Fear God, and give him glory, for the hour of his judgment is come.' No-one who continues in unbelief is going to escape, for God is the Almighty One who made 'heaven and the earth and sea and fountains of waters'. Yet for God's people this announcement of the approaching judgment day is 'eternal good tidings'

[1] See R. C. H. Lenski, *op. cit.*, p. 425.

for it means their deliverance (Hab. 3: 13 ff.; Mal. 4: 1 ff.). Besides, all the promises of God will then attain a blessed realization that will last for ever.

The second angel follows, saying: 'Fallen, fallen is Babylon the great, who from the wine of the passion of her whoring has been giving all the nations to drink.'

Babylon is the world as centre of seduction. Its future fall is spoken of here as if it had already occurred, so certain is the event. So, let the wicked be converted from their whoring, their apostasy and their worship of the beast. Notice that the dragon has helpers; the beast out of the sea, the beast out of the earth and Babylon.

A third angel follows. He announces in very solemn language (verses 9 and 10) that all those who are attached to this world are going to perish with the world. If you choose to serve Satan, you must expect to suffer the consequences. You cannot sin and get away with it. The wrath of God will be visited on those who worship the beast. Here on earth this wrath is still mixed with grace. The Lord makes His sun to rise on the evil and the good, and sends rain on the just and the unjust (Mt. 5: 45). By and by, in hell, the wrath will be unmixed. It will be torment with fire and brimstone. Yet, so thoroughly just will be this punishment that the angels and the Lamb will acquiesce in it. And this judgment never ends, according to the very vivid language of verse 11. The fact that this never-ending punishment awaits those who persecute the Church and hate the Lord should encourage believers to hold out under affliction and trial (verse 12). Even if these believers should be put to death because they keep the commandments of God and the faith of Jesus, their blessedness is assured.

c. The harvest of the end (verses 14–16). 'And I heard a voice out of heaven saying, Write: Blessed are the dead, the ones dying in the Lord from now on. Yea, declares the Spirit, that they may rest from their labours; for their works follow with them.' The blessedness of the redeemed has been described. (See chapters 2; 3; 7; 14: 1–5.) Those who die in the Lord from now on see face to face the One who has died for them and ever lives to make intercession for them. They now see Him as the Lamb that has been slaughtered. They see Him in the glory of His human nature which He has taken with Him to heaven. They see Him as the One who has conquered sin, death and Satan. They rest from their toil. Their works, however, follow with them. This is true, not only in the sense that their works are the result of their character, which when thoroughly sanctified, goes with them to heaven but also in the sense that these works are about to be rewarded with the reward of grace and glory.

Thus the final judgment has again arrived. It is described[1] under the symbolism of a twofold harvest. The apostle sees a white cloud, white indicating holiness and the cloud symbolizing judgment (see 1: 7). On the cloud sits 'One like unto the Son of man', Jesus (*cf.* Dn. 7: 13; and see our explanation of Rev. 1: 13). On His head is not the crown of thorns, but the crown or wreath of victory, the golden stephanos.[2] In His right hand He has a sharp sickle. He is prepared for the harvest. This harvest is His own, for the men symbolized by it are the first-fruits. Whereas the time for the final judgment has now arrived, an angel comes out of the sanctuary, the place of God's holiness. He conveys God's message to the Mediator, Christ. Says this angel, crying in a loud voice, 'Send forth thy sickle and reap; for it has come the hour to reap; for dried out is the harvest of the earth'. Matthew 3: 12 is a sufficient commentary: 'And he will gather his wheat into his garner.' Thus the sickle was thrown to the earth, and the earth was reaped and the elect were gathered to Him.

6. *The judgment of the wicked* (14: 17–20)

This judgment is carried out by two angels. An angel is coming from the sanctuary, that is, after he has received orders from the holy God. In his hand he holds a sharp vine-knife. Another angel now comes from the altar (see 6: 9,10; 8: 3–5). This is the altar in connection with which the incense prayers of all the saints have ascended to the throne. The judgment of the wicked is God's final answer to these prayers. This second angel cries to the first, 'Send forth thy vine-knife, the sharp one, and gather the clusters of the vine of the earth, for her grapes are fully ripe.' (*Cf.* Is. 63: 1–6.) The vine of the earth symbolizes the entire multitude of evil men; its grapes are the individual unbelievers. Just as grapes are trodden, pressed, crushed, so the wicked are going to be destroyed and punished everlastingly.

[1] 'Described' is the right wor now. See chapter IV, pp. 35f.

[2] See R. C. Trench, *Synonyms of the New Testament*, p. 74, on the distinction between *stephanos* and *diadema*. Yet, although the *stephanos* is the victor's wreath, that victor is sometimes viewed as a king, so that the distinction between the two terms is not always sharp.

The grapes are cast into the great winepress of the wrath of God and crushed. In the picture which John sees, a lake of blood results. It is so deep that horses can swim in it. It spreads out in all directions to the extent of sixteen hundred stadia. Remember that four is the number of the universe and the earth. This is the judgment of the wicked. Ten is the number of completeness.[1] So, sixteen hundred, which is the product of four times four, times ten times ten, would seem to indicate that this is the thoroughly complete judgment of the wicked. And the winepress of God's wrath was trodden down outside the Holy City!

[1] See C. F. Wishart, *op. cit.*, p. 23.

CHAPTER TWELVE

REVELATION 15, 16: THE SEVEN BOWLS

IN the history of the world a definite and ever-recurring order of events is clearly evident.

Through the preaching of the Word applied to the heart by the Holy Spirit churches are established. Again and again this happens. They are lightbearers—lampstands—in the midst of a world that lies in darkness. They are blessed with the constant spiritual presence of Christ (chapters 1–3).

Again and again God's people are persecuted by the world. They are subjected to many trials and afflictions (chapters 4–7).

Again and again the judgments of God are visited upon the persecuting world. These judgments again and again fail to move men to repentance (chapters 8–11).

Again and again this conflict between the Church and the world points to a deeper, more fundamental warfare between Christ and Satan, between the 'seed of the woman' and 'the dragon' (chapters 12–14).

The question which now arises is what happens whenever in history the trumpets of judgment, the initial plagues, fail to result in penitence and conversion? Does God permit such impenitence, such hardness of heart, to go unpunished until the final judgment of the last day? Must we conceive of God's wrath as being completely pent up until the second coming, until the vintage described in chapter 14? This question is answered in our present vision. The answer, in brief, is this: whenever in history the wicked fail to repent in answer to the initial and partial manifestation of God's anger in judgments, the final effusion of wrath follows. It is final, though not complete until the judgment day. These plagues are the last. They leave no more opportunity for repentance. When the wicked, often warned by the trumpets of judgment, continue to harden their hearts, death finally plunges them into the hands of an angry God. But even before they die they may have crossed the deadline, the line between God's patience and His wrath (Ex. 10: 27; Mt. 12: 32; Rom. 1: 24; 1 Jn. 5: 16).

Throughout the history of the world God's final wrath again and again reveals itself: now it strikes this one, then another.

It is poured out upon the impenitent (Rev. 9: 21; 16: 9). Thus, a very definite connecting link is established between the vision of the trumpets (chapters 8–11) and that of the bowls (chapters 15, 16). Trumpets warn; bowls are poured out. Yet the connection between chapters 12–14 and chapters 15, 16 is just as close. These impenitents are the men who receive the mark of the beast (13: 16). They worship the dragon and are the friends of the two beasts and of the harlot, Babylon.

Thus conceived, we notice that the vision of the bowls of wrath runs parallel with all the others and like them covers the entire dispensation. Let us prove this point.

First of all, the very close resemblance between the vision of the trumpets and that of the bowls—which has already been indicated—would seem to imply that the two refer to the same period of time.[1] If the vision of the trumpets refers to this present dispensation, so does that of the bowls.

Secondly, this vision of the bowls ends just like the preceding ones, namely, with a judgment scene (Rev. 16: 15–21). It would seem to follow, therefore, that the first six bowls refer to series of happenings that precede the final judgment.

Thirdly, observe the very interesting fact that this fifth vision of the bowls has an introduction which is almost identical with the one which opens the fourth vision. (*Cf.* Rev. 15: 1 with Rev. 12: 1.) Revelation 12 very clearly carries us back to the moment of Christ's birth and ascension. Is it not reasonable to assume that Revelation 15, 16 does the same thing, and that it likewise describes the entire period between the first and second coming?

Fourthly, notice that the bowls are poured out upon the men who have the mark of the beast. That characterization is, as we have seen, very general and applies to all those who worship the dragon throughout the history of the world, particularly throughout this entire dispensation.

Finally, our attention is called to the fact that we have in this fifth vision a description of exactly the same forces of evil as in the fourth. The dragon, the beast coming up out of the sea, and the beast coming up out of the earth, in the vision of the trumpets, correspond exactly to the dragon, the beast, and the false prophet in the vision of the bowls (16: 13). Thus the two visions evidently span the same period, the entire era between Christ's first and second coming.

[1] See Principal Fairburn's splendid paragraph quoted in S. L. Morris, *op. cit.*, p. 96.

Yet this spirit of independence reveals itself more and more clearly as we approach the final day. For the vision of the bowls, though covering this entire dispensation, is especially applicable to the judgment day and to conditions that will immediately precede it.

John sees another sign in heaven, a great and marvellous sign. He had seen the sign of the radiant woman and her child (12: 1,2); also, the sign of the great red dragon that opposed them (12: 3). Now he sees another sign which completes the trio—the seven last plagues by means of which God smites those who worship the dragon. Seven angels pour out these seven plagues in which God's burning wrath is brought to its goal. The goal is the final judgment. These seven plagues—seven symbolizes divine perfection and completeness—lead to this goal. Once God withdraws His Spirit from the wicked, so that they become hardened, there is really nothing that can stop their doom in the day of the final judgment. So by means of these seven plagues that cover this entire dispensation God's anger is brought to its *telos* or goal.

1. *The sea of glass mingled with fire* (15: 1–4)

The apostle is going to tell us about these seven angels with their bowls of wrath. But before he does so he shows us the Church triumphant after the last day. After all these bowls of wrath will have been emptied, what is this company of victors going to say? John beholds a sea. On the seashore stands a victorious multitude. They are playing their harps and singing the song of Moses and the song of the Lamb. Clearly, this vision is based on the story of the drowning of Pharaoh's host in the Red Sea. Then also a victorious people stood by the sea and sang the song of deliverance and victory:

'I will sing to Jehovah, for he has triumphed gloriously:
The horse and the rider has he thrown into the sea.'

This victory over the Egyptians was a foreshadowing of the victory of all God's redeemed over the beast, his image, his number. Therefore, the song which the Church triumphant is singing is called the song of Moses and of the Lamb. In both cases it was the Lamb who gave the victory. Moses was simply doing God's will, and is therefore called God's servant.

Observe, however, that the sea which John beholds is of glass mingled with fire: it symbolizes God's transparent righteousness revealed in judgments upon the wicked (*cf.* 15: 4b: 'for thy righteous acts have been made manifest').

Now, just as Israel ascribed its victory to God, so this victorious company which John sees loudly proclaims that God is the One who has granted triumph to His people. Even their harps belong to God; He has given them to these victors. Consequently, they praise God's works of judgment, His ways—the principles underlying the works—and His name or revelation. They declare, moreover, that in the end the entire universe will have to acknowledge the righteous character of all God's sentences. Have not the wicked been warned by means of the trumpets of judgment? Therefore, when, instead of repenting, they harden themselves, is not the fault wholly theirs? Thus the justice of God's final sentences, of His bowls of wrath, is displayed. After the final judgment the Church triumphant will see this clearly and will glorify God.

2. *The opening of the sanctuary* (15: 5–8)

Whereas God's final plagues are righteous in every respect, indeed, so transparently righteous that the Church triumphant will praise God because of the just punishments which He has inflicted on the impenitent, the apostle now leaves the triumphant multitude of the future and returns to the present dispensation. What does he see? The sanctuary of the tabernacle of the testimony is opened. This is the sanctuary which contains the ark of the covenant, and that ark contains 'the testimony' (Ex. 25: 16,21). This sanctuary is now opened, so that we may understand that the wrath which is about to be revealed is God's wrath. Out of the opened sanctuary the seven angels proceed. These angels are robed in pure, dazzling linen, their breasts encircled with golden belts. One of the four cherubim places in the hands of each of these seven angels a bowl. These bowls are of gold, for they are used in the service of God. They are full, to indicate the fierceness and unmitigated character of God's wrath. It is everlasting wrath for it proceeds from the ever-living God. The sanctuary is filled with smoke: a symbol of the full and thorough operation of God's holy anger (Is. 6: 4; Ps. 18: 8). No-one could enter the sanctuary until the seven plagues of the seven angels should be finished, that is, intercession was no longer possible. God had in anger shut up His tender mercies (Ps. 77: 9).

3. *The seven bowls of wrath* (16: 1–21)

John now hears the voice of the Almighty. It was a loud voice for the Lord is filled with anger because of the impenitence of

Satan's followers. The voice said, 'Go and empty the seven bowls of the wrath of God into the earth.' In studying these bowls notice their striking resemblance to some of the plagues of Egypt. These plagues recorded in Exodus 7–11 foreshadow all the manifestations of God's wrath upon the wicked (*cf.* Dt. 28: 20). Throughout history, especially during this entire new dispensation, God is using every department of the universe to punish the wicked and impenitent persecutors of His people. Whoever refuses to be warned by the trumpets of judgment (Rev. 8: 11) is 'destroyed' by the bowls of wrath. For one individual a certain calamity may be a trumpet of judgment, while for someone else that same event may be a bowl of wrath. Thus, the disease which hurled King Herod Agrippa I into hell served as a warning to others. Those who remain impenitent are cursed in the city and cursed in the field (Dt. 28: 16).

At times our Lord uses vicious and incurable ulcers or any other incurable disease to hurl the wicked into hell. These come from *the first bowl* (16: 2; *cf.* Ex. 9: 10; Dt. 28: 27; Acts 12: 23). Think of Herod, and remember that throughout this entire dispensation our Lord is constantly doing this very thing. For believers in Christ the afflictions of the flesh are never bowls of wrath (*cf.* Rom. 8: 28). For this reason we read that this plague affected only those who had the mark of the beast (*cf.* Rev. 13: 15–17).

Sometimes the sea is used as the instrument of destruction. This is the purpose of *the second bowl* (16: 3; *cf.* Ex. 7: 17-21; 15: 1; Pss. 48: 7; 78: 53). The sea, as John beholds it in the vision, is turned into blood like a dead man's, and as coagulated blood it emits a foul odour. Here again we must remember that although the symbol is rooted in Old Testament history, the sea is constantly being used for that same purpose. Just as all maritime calamities constitute warnings for the wicked, so also by means of some of these disasters the impenitent are hurled into hell. This happens again and again throughout history.

The third bowl (16: 4–7) brings curses upon rivers and fountains, turning them into blood (*cf.* Ex. 7: 24; 1 Ki. 17: 1; 18: 5,40). The angel of the waters proclaims the justice of God who punishes the impenitent in this way. It is righteous retribution. Underneath the altar the souls of the martyrs had cried for vengeance (*cf.* Rev. 6: 9; 8: 3–5). So when this vengeance is rendered, it is the altar that replies: 'Yea, Lord God, the Almighty, genuine and righteous are thy judgments.'

Frequently, the Lord causes the sun to scorch the wicked,

the calamity produced by *the fourth bowl* (16: 8,9; *cf.* Dt. 28: 22: 'Jehovah will smite thee with . . . fiery heat'). But these men are not sanctified through suffering. On the contrary, they become even more wicked and blaspheme the God of heaven who has the power over these plagues. They do not repent. We readily see that this description is true with respect to all impenitent persecutors of Christ and of His Church throughout this entire dispensation.

Also upon the throne of the beast God's wrath is at times poured out. This is accomplished by *the fifth bowl* (16: 10,11). This throne of the beast is the centre of antichristian government (*cf.* Na. 3: 1; Hab. 3: 12–14). When Assyria falls, or Babylon, or Rome, the whole universe of the impenitent seems to collapse (*cf.* Rev. 17: 9 ff.). The wicked lose all courage. They despair. They keep on gnawing their tongues for pain, not only because of this plague but also because of their ulcers received when the first bowl was emptied.

Notice that in the bowls the aspect of finality is emphasized. Whereas only one-third of the living creatures in the sea died during the second trumpet, the destruction wrought by the second bowl is complete; 'every living soul' died. Again, while in the third trumpet the third part of the waters was turned into wormwood, here the whole supply is turned into blood, *etc.* This is God's final wrath.

The sixth bowl (16: 12–16) produces Har-Magedon. Of late it has been raining sermons and lectures on Har-Magedon or Armageddon,[1] but in order to arrive at the correct interpretation

[1] The following are amongst the views we reject:

a. Those according to which the battle of Har-Magedon is between two groups of nations existing today; for example, Russia and the Muslim nations against the Anglo-Saxon world; or Russia, Italy, Japan against Britain, France, U.S.; or Germany, Italy, Japan against France, Britain, U.S.

b. The theory by which the battle of Har-Magedon is the struggle between paganism and the gospel of Christ. The sword proceeding out of Christ's mouth is interpreted to mean the gospel. But according to Rev. 2: 16 this sword is evidently used for destruction, not for conversion. (See also Rev. 19: 15: 'that with it he should smite the nations'.) The entire setting is one of wrath and destruction. Notice the expression: 'the winepress of the fierceness of the wrath of God'. Hence, we cannot agree with the view of Dr. A. Pieters, *op. cit.*, pp. 275 ff.

c. The theory commonly advocated by premillennialists, that this battle must be viewed literally; that it takes place just after the seven years of tribulation here below and of the wedding of the Lamb above; that wicked nations besiege Jerusalem, and that Christ and His saints

of this battle, let us begin by briefly reviewing the Old Testament story in which this symbol is probably rooted. We find it in Judges 4, 5. Israel is in misery again. This time, King Jabin, the Canaanite, is the oppressor. The spoilers go out to ravage the fields and plunder the crops of the Israelites. So numerous are these spoilers that the Israelites go in hiding and are afraid to appear on the highways (Jdg. 5: 6). But can they not wage war and drive out these Canaanites? No, King Jabin and General Sisera are strong, for they have nine hundred chariots of iron. Israel has not even a spear or a shield (Jdg. 5: 8). Must the people perish?

In the highlands of Ephraim lives Deborah who one day tells Barak the judge, 'Up, for this is the day in which Jehovah is to deliver Sisera into your power. Is it not Jehovah who has gone forth in front of you?' A battle is fought at Megiddo and Israel's enemy is routed. It was Jehovah Himself who had defeated them. 'From heaven fought the stars; from their courses they fought against Sisera' (Jdg. 5: 20).

For this cause, Har-Magedon is the symbol of every battle in which, when the need is greatest and believers are oppressed, the Lord suddenly reveals His power in the interest of His distressed people and defeats the enemy. When Sennacherib's 185,000 are slain by the angel of Jehovah, that is a shadow of the final Har-Magedon. When God grants a little handful of Maccabees a glorious victory over an enemy which far outnumbers it, that is a type of Har-Magedon.

But the real, the great, the final Har-Magedon coincides with the time of Satan's little season (see Rev. 11: 7–11). When the world, under the leadership of Satan, antichristian government and antichristian religion—the dragon, the beast and the false prophet—is gathered against the Church for the final battle, and the need is greatest; when God's children, oppressed on every side, cry for help; then suddenly, dramatically, Christ will appear to deliver His people. That final tribulation and that appearance of Christ on clouds of glory to deliver His people, that is Har-Magedon. It is for this reason that Har-Magedon is the sixth bowl. The seventh is the judgment day. As we have indicated, this sixth bowl, as well as the preceding ones, is evident again and again in history. Yet, like the other bowls, it reaches its final and most complete realization just before and in connection with the last day.

suddenly descend from the sky to rescue the beleaguered Jews. See C. E. Brown, *The Hope of His Coming*, p. 231.

John sees that the sixth bowl is emptied upon the Euphrates river. This river represents Assyria, Babylonia, the wicked world. When the river is said to dry up, the road is prepared so that all the antichristian powers can make the attack upon the Church. The apostle sees proceeding out of the mouth of the dragon (Satan) and out of the mouth of the beast (antichristian government) and out of the mouth of the false prophet (antichristian religion) three unclean spirits. These spirits or demons are compared to frogs in order to indicate their abominable, loathsome and repulsive character. They represent satanic, hellish ideas, plans, projects, methods and enterprises, hell-born and introduced by hell into the sphere of thought and action. Thus, when the kings of the earth gather to battle against believers, this battle or persecution is inspired by hell itself. Here very little is said about this final battle. But we must remember that this same conflict of Har-Magedon is described in Revelation 11: 7 ff. (see our explanation); and especially in Revelation 19: 11 ff.; 20: 7 ff.[1]

Now, at this moment of tribulation and anguish, of oppression and persecution, Christ suddenly appears (verse 15). He comes as a thief, suddenly, unexpectedly (*cf.* Mt. 24: 29 ff.; I Thess. 5: 4; II Thess. 2: 8 ff.; II Peter 3: 10). Therefore the believer must be vigilant. Let him keep his garments of righteousness unspotted, lest men see his sins (*cf.* Rev. 3: 18; 7: 14).

This section dealing with the bowls, like the preceding ones, ends with a very vivid description of the terror of the final judgment, which is symbolized by *the seventh bowl* (16: 17–21). The final fall of Babylon is the crushing blow for those who bear the mark of the beast. All that delights them now collapses. It is utterly ruined. This bowl is emptied upon the air. When a curse falls upon the air, life on earth perishes. John hears a loud voice from the sanctuary—it was the voice of God Himself—saying, 'It has happened.' The final and complete exposure of God's wrath, so long restrained, has come: the judgment day has arrived. In the picture the apostle sees flashes of lightning, and hears the rumblings and peals of thunder and he witnesses an earthquake, the greatest of all time. The great city, Babylon, is broken into three pieces; it falls apart. Thus, the entire antichristian empire, viewed as a centre of seduction, the whole kingdom of the world, falls apart and is destroyed. Its cities and nations are ruined. In this great day of judgment it becomes

[1] See our comments on these paragraphs, pp. 130ff., 181ff., 193ff.

evident that, after all, God has not forgotten the sins of Babylon. His anger so long pent up now fully explodes. The world receives the cup of the wine of the fierceness of His wrath (*cf.* Rev. 14: 10). Every island flees and the mountains are not found (see our explanation of Rev. 6: 14). John, being in the Spirit, now sees great hailstones, every stone almost a hundred pounds in weight, falling down upon these hardened, impenitent men. The meaning is that in the final judgment the entire empire of evil is destroyed. It goes down into utter ruin. Moreover, these stones fell from heaven; they symbolize God's judgment, the final and complete effusion of His wrath. But even in hell these impenitent sinners blaspheme God because of the greatness of the plague and because of the hardness of their hearts!

CHAPTER THIRTEEN

REVELATION 17–19: THE FALL OF THE DRAGON'S ALLIES

FIVE enemies of the Christ have been introduced: the dragon, the sea-born beast, the earth-born beast or false prophet, the harlot Babylon, and the men who bear the mark of the beast. We have seen what happens to the men who receive this mark (chapters 15, 16). In the present vision the apostle shows us by means of symbolic pictures what befalls Babylon, the sea-born beast, and the false prophet. The dragon's defeat will be described in Revelation 20.

Broadly speaking, this section may be subdivided as follows: Chapter 17 describes the nature and tells the history of the great harlot, Babylon. Chapter 18 shows us the inevitable, complete, and irrevocable character of Babylon's fall. Chapter 19 introduces us to the rejoicings in heaven because of the complete overthrow of Babylon and because of the wedding of the Lamb. It also presents the Author of this victory, the Rider upon the white horse, who triumphs over Babylon, the beast, and the false prophet, and executes final judgment on all His enemies.

I. THE JUDGMENT OF BABYLON

1. *The woman and the beast* (17: 1–6)

One of the seven angels that had the seven bowls appears to John. The fact that one of these angels appears indicates that the vision is one of woe for the wicked and of weal for the Church (*cf.* Rev. 21: 9). This angel speaks with John in a friendly manner, saying, 'Hither! I will show thee the judgment of the harlot, the great one, the one sitting upon many waters.' So, in the Spirit (see Rev. 1: 10) John is carried to the wilderness where he sees a scarlet beast.[1] It is the sea-born beast and symbolizes the world as the centre of persecution. This spirit of persecution finds expression in the governments and peoples of this world, particularly in the great world empires that follow one another in history. John sees this beast in the wilderness,

[1] See pp. 144–147.

for the radiant woman of Revelation 12, representing the Church, had fled there.

The beast is not alone. There is sitting upon it a woman. This woman must not be confused with the radiant woman of Revelation 12. The two are enemies. The woman of Revelation 17—the one sitting upon the beast—is the great harlot. She is gorgeously arrayed and excessively adorned. She is 'gilded with gold'. She is clothed with purple and scarlet, for she sits as queen. Precious stones and pearls are her ornaments. Kings of the earth are her paramours. Worldly people are made drunk with the wine of her whoring. In her hand she holds a cup filled with abominations: the unclean things pertaining to her whoredom. On her forehead, possibly on a band attached to her forehead, is a name written: Babylon the great, the mother of the harlots and of the abominations of the earth. Not only are her paramours drunk, she herself is also drunk, namely with the blood of the martyrs of Jesus. John wonders greatly. He does not grasp the meaning of this picture, so the angel explains its meaning.

This harlot, evidently, is Babylon[1] (17: 5,18; 19: 2,3). The question is, what does Babylon represent?[2] In order to arrive at the correct view with respect to the symbolical meaning of this figure, we must bear in mind, first of all, that Babylon is called the great harlot.[3] In other words, the symbol indicates that which allures, tempts, seduces and draws people away from God.

Secondly, we must remember that this harlot is a worldly city, namely, Babylon. It reminds us of pleasure-mad, arrogant,

[1] A. Pieters, *op. cit.*, p. 260.

[2] We reject the following views:

a. That Babylon is the literal city which will be rebuilt on the bank of the river Euphrates.

b. That Babylon is the apostate church (the view held by Dean Alford, W. Milligan, S. L. Morris, and many others). But the Babylon of Rev. 17–19 is the harlot not the adulteress. Besides, Rev. 18—especially verses 11,13—suits the description of the city of the world; it can hardly be said to harmonize with the idea of the false church. Finally, the entire Old Testament basis in the prophets suggests the world as opposed to God's people. We consider the 'false church' conception quite impossible.

c. That Babylon is Rome. This is true but too restricted. See our explanation. We need not discuss the view that Babylon symbolizes the Roman Catholic church.

[3] Babylon is never called *moichalis*, 'adulteress'; always *porne*, 'harlot'. Hence, Babylon was never the Lamb's wife. She is not the false church See under note [2] above.

presumptuous Babylon of old.[1] The description of this symbolical Babylon of Revelation 17–19 also recalls to our mind that heathen centre of wickedness and seduction, Tyre. Observe the striking similarity between Revelation 17–19 and Ezekiel 27, 28. Moreover, when we study the catalogue of goods found in Babylon (18: 11 ff.) it becomes evident that the symbol has reference to a great industrial and commercial metropolis. Babylon, therefore, must indicate the world as a centre of industry, commerce, art, culture, *etc.*, which by means of all these things seeks to entice and seduce the believer, that is, to turn him away from God. It symbolizes the concentration of the luxury, vice, and glamour of this world. It is the world viewed as the embodiment of 'the lust of the flesh, the lust of the eyes, and the vainglory of life' (1 Jn. 2: 16).

Thirdly, Babylon thus viewed is past, present and future. Its form changes; its essence remains. Let us remember that the harlot, Babylon, is very closely associated with the beast, so closely, in fact, that she is said to be sitting on the beast (17: 3). The beast is the entire antichristian persecution movement throughout history, embodied in successive world empires. The beast, very clearly, is past, present, and future. (Read Rev. 17: 8–10.) Therefore we conclude that the harlot also represents the world as the centre of antichristian seduction at any moment of history. That the harlot, Babylon, was present in one form or embodiment in John's day is clear from Revelation 17: 9: 'the seven heads are seven hills on which the woman sits'. Here the reference is clearly to Rome. The imperial city attracted to her pleasures the kings of the nations, the rulers in every domain of life, art, industry, commerce, *etc.* (See Rev. 17: 2.) The apostle sees the Rome of his own day, filled with vanity, luxury and pleasure. It was a pleasure-mad city. Even the saints were torn to pieces in its circuses for the amusement and entertainment of the public. The harlot was drunk with the blood of the saints (17: 6). When, in Revelation 18: 4, the admonition is given: 'Come forth my people, out of her, and have no fellowship with her sins', that command was intended not only for people living close to the end of the world's history, but also for believers in John's own day and age; indeed, for believers in every age.

[1] The Scripture passages which should be studied, as forming the foundation for this New Testament symbolism, are: Gn. 10: 10; 11: 11; Is. 13; 14; 21; 46; 47; 48; Je. 25; 50; 51; Dn. 2; 4: 30; 7; Hab. 3; also Ezk. 27, the fall of Tyre.

Babylon, then, is the world as the centre of seduction at any moment of history, particularly during this entire present dispensation. The harlot, Babylon, always opposes the bride, new Jerusalem (Rev. 21 : 9 ff.). Both symbols are introduced by 'one of the seven angels who had the seven bowls', but they are opposites. For Babylon's fall refers not only to the final destruction of the world, viewed as a centre of antichristian culture and seduction, at the moment of Christ's second coming, but also to the demolition of every preceding concentration of worldly enticement. Babylon's fall takes place throughout history but especially on the great day of final judgment. The fall of the last great Babylon—Babylon in its final form—coincides with the coming of our Lord unto judgment.

According to the figure employed, the harlot holds in her hand a golden cup. A golden cup entices one to drink; for one expects the most precious drink from such a precious vessel. Yet the cup contains nothing but abominations, the unclean things pertaining to the woman's whoredom. Whatever is used by the world in order to turn believers away from their God is in this cup: pornographic literature, sports in which one becomes completely absorbed, luxuries, worldly fame and power, the lusts of the flesh, and so on. Let everyone make his own list. It includes things that are bad in themselves as well as things which become bad because one does not view them as a means but as an end in themselves: art for art's sake, *etc.* The angel tells John the mystery of the woman and of the beast that carries her (verses 7–18). Observe the close association between beast (the empire of the world) and woman (seduction). This is true in a two-fold sense: first, worldly people drink the wine of the woman's whoredom and indulge in her pleasures; secondly, the world as the centre of persecution and the world as the centre of luxury, antichristian culture, and pleasure always work in close co-operation in opposing the Church. The prophet Balaam was aware of this, so he advised Balak to make use of the cunning art of deception in order to ensnare and destroy Israel (Nu. 31: 16; Jude 11; Rev. 2: 14). In the days of John, Rome not only persecuted the Church with the sword but also tried to entice believers by means of the allurements of the great city. The same holds true even today. Antichristian governments do not destroy every church building; they change some of them into places of worldly amusement! Thus, throughout history 'beast' and 'woman' are always associated. Always until . . . the beast turns against the woman (17–19).

2. *The history of the beast* (17: 7–18)

In verse 8 the angel begins to relate the history of the beast. It was, and is not, and is about to come up out of the abyss. First, the beast *was*, for example, in the form of Old Babylonia, the kingdom of the mighty Nimrod, in the land of Shinar: 'let us make us a name' (Gn. 10: 8–11; 11: 4). Or in the form of Assyria with its proud capital in Nineveh. Or, again, of the spirit of worldly arrogance and oppression which manifested itself in New Babylonia (think of Nebuchadnezzar and the captivity of the Jews); or in the kingdom of the Medes and Persians; and, very definitely, in the Greco-Macedonian Empire out of which came forth the great precursor of the final antichrist, Antiochus Epiphanes of Syria (175–164 BC). 'And is not.' All of these kingdoms in which the beast had been embodied perished. The beast, in the form of Old Babylonia, Assyria, New Babylonia, Medo-Persia or Greco-Macedonia, is no more. Yet—and this excites the wonder and admiration of men whose names from the foundation of the world were not written in the book of life—this beast seems to have the ability to raise its head anew after every defeat! Worldly men wonder when they see the beast 'how that it was, and is no more, and yet shall be present'. They fail to see that, under every form and in every embodiment, the beast goes into perdition. This statement, as a comparison between verses 8 and 11 indicates, is true especially with respect to the final manifestation of the power of antichrist just before the second coming of Christ. That antichristian empire will also go 'into perdition'. Thus, again and again the beast appears in a new embodiment. The forms change, but the essence remains throughout this entire dispensation, even throughout the history of the world until the judgment day.

The angel is now about to interpret the meaning of the beast's seven heads and ten horns. The meaning is not clear on the surface. Wisdom is needed to interpret them (*cf.* 13: 18). The seven heads have a twofold symbolical significance. They indicate both the present embodiment of the beast and all of its embodiments throughout history. First of all, then, these seven heads symbolize seven mountains, the seven hills of Rome, viewed as the capital of the Roman Empire.[1] It is the great city which rules over the kings, the mighty ones, of the earth. It was,

[1] Most commentators, whether preterists or parallelists (and even some futurists) grant this point.

in John's day, the centre of antichristian persecution. But it was also the centre of antichristian seduction, allurement and enticement; the woman, the harlot, sits on these seven hills. Secondly, these seven heads also symbolize seven kings, that is, kingdoms.[1] As we have already indicated, the Book of Daniel clearly proves that these seven heads do not symbolize seven individual kings or emperors but seven antichristian world-empires. Five fell, namely, Ancient Babylonia, Assyria, New Babylonia, Medo-Persia and Greco-Macedonia. One is, namely Rome. The seventh is not yet come, but when it comes it will have to remain some little while. The emphasis is on the word 'remain'. Is this seventh head the collective title for all anti-christian governments between the fall of Rome and the final empire of antichrist that is going to oppress the Church in the days just preceding Christ's second coming?[2] In the language of the Apocalypse this entire gospel age is but a little while (*cf.* Rev. 11: 2,3; 12: 6,14; 13: 5). The beast that 'was and is not' is the eighth and final, most terrible dominion of anti-christ toward the close of history (*cf.* 2 Thes. 2: 3 ff.). Does the clause 'and is of the seven' indicate that, in some sense, one of the former antichristian empires will be re-established and, if so, which one?[3] At any rate, 'he goes into perdition' (see Rev. 19: 20).

The ten kings are really all the mighty ones of this earth in every realm: art, education, commerce, industry, government, in so far as they serve the central authority. Self-aggrandizement in opposition to Christ is their goal. In order to reach this goal they are willing to give their power and authority to the beast. They reign 'in company with' the beast for just 'one hour'. Every worldly ruler has his satellites and they, too, generally last only 'one hour'. All these 'horn-kings' have one design, namely to help the beast in its conflict with Christ and His Church. That this is their unanimous purpose is clearly stated in verse 14. That verse, as already indicated, states the theme of the entire book: 'These shall war against the Lamb, and the Lamb shall overcome ('conquer') them, for he is Lord of lords and

[1] See chapter VI, p. 46.

[2] Some make this seventh head the papacy; others, the nominally Christian Roman Empire beginning with Constantine the Great; still others, the Germanic nations that overwhelmed Rome.

[3] Some say Rome; others hold that, in some form or sense, the ancient Babylonian Empire will be re-established, or that conditions existing in that empire shall return.

King of kings; and they also shall overcome ('conquer') that are with him, called and chosen and faithful.'

Throughout history, especially throughout this entire dispensation, the Lamb constantly defeats and shall defeat every form of antichristian dominion. Every kingdom of antichrist perishes. This will appear especially when the Lamb shall crush the power of the last great antichrist at the close of the world's history (*cf.* Rev. 11: 11; 16: 14 ff.; 19: 11 ff.; 2 Thes. 2: 8). For a while it may seem as if antichristian forces have gained the upper hand (Rev. 11: 7; 13: 7). But when antichrist seems to be completely victorious, his utter ruin is imminent! Thus, Christ ever reveals Himself as King of kings and Lord of lords (Dt. 10: 17) and believers conquer together with Christ. By the irresistible grace of God they were called (1 Pet. 2: 9; Rom. 8: 30). This 'internal' call proves the fact that they have been chosen for salvation and victory from eternity (Eph. 1: 4). Moreover, their own faithfulness or loyalty to Christ furnishes further evidence that they are, indeed, God's children (*cf.* Rev. 1: 5; 2: 10; *etc.*; for 17: 15 see 13: 1). Evidently, John had seen in the desert a kind of lake or pool. In this pool he had seen the beast and upon the beast the woman. The waters of this lake symbolize the surging nations, peoples, *etc.* of this world, that are constantly opposing and persecuting the Church (*cf.* Je. 51: 13).

For a while all seems to go well: the world in general and especially its mighty ones commit whoredom with the great harlot. They drink of her golden cup and they become drunk with the wine of whoredom. They carry the woman: they yield entirely to her allurements and enticements, her antichristian culture. They are fond of the luxuries of the world. The 'lust of the flesh, and the lust of the eyes, and the vainglory of life' please them immensely. But, in the end (verses 15, 16) these very people who constitute 'the antichristian world' turn against the whore. Worldly people, including also the mighty ones of this earth—the ten horns—in the end hate the whore—they cast her off and strip her of her extravagantly gorgeous garments and costly ornaments; they devour her flesh; and burn her utterly with fire.

The meaning is that there will come a time when these same worldly people who together with their antichristian governments constitute 'the beast' and who were infatuated with the 'harlot', that is, with the seduction of this world, its pleasures and allurements, its culture and luxury, come to see what great fools they have been. But then it is for ever too late. Thus, for example, Judas Iscariot, who drank of the golden cup—Mammon was his god—and for a while considered the thirty pieces of silver so enchanting, finally experienced a revulsion of feeling, and flung the money before the priests and elders, and afterwards hanged himself (Mt. 27: 3 ff.; Acts 1: 18). The pleasures of sin disappoint in the end. Foolish girls may admire the veiled prophet; once the veil is removed and they see his hideous features, they are filled with despair. God Himself finally hardens the hearts of those who have hardened themselves against His repeated warnings (verse 17). Revelation 17: 16,17 is a lesson for every day. It reveals the course of worldly individuals: first, they become infatuated with the pleasures and treasures of the world, and harden themselves against God; then they are hardened; finally, when it is too late, they experience a revulsion of feeling. They are punished by the results of their own foolishness.[1]

When the world offers us her treasures we should follow the example of Jesus (Mt. 4: 8 ff.). Be sure to read that passage and to take it to heart.

3. *The fall of Babylon* (18: 1–24)

And now John sees another angel coming down out of heaven. He has great authority and his effulgence lights up the earth. With a strong voice he cries:

'It fell, it fell, Babylon the Great!
(*Cf.* Is. 21: 9; Je. 50: 2; 51: 8)
And it became a habitation of demons,
And a prison of every unclean spirit,
And a prison of every unclean and hated bird.
For of the wine of the passion of her whoring all the nations have drunk.[2]
And the kings of the earth committed whoring with her;
And the merchants of the earth have grown rich from her excessive luxury.'

Here Babylon's fall is announced as if it had already occurred; so certain is its fall. Let this serve as a warning for all! The utter desolation of Babylon is vividly described when it is said that even the unclean spirits and the unclean and hated birds

[1] Hence the world, in a sense, destroys itself.

[2] This seems to be the correct reading, rather than 'have fallen'. *Cf.* R. H. Charles, *op. cit.*, p. 96.

consider it a prison (*cf.* Is. 13: 20 ff.; Je. 50: 39,45; 51: 37,42; Zp. 2: 14). The reason or justification for Babylon's fall is given in Revelation 18: 3: the nations and kings and merchants allowed themselves to become infatuated with Babylon's pleasures and treasures. These merchants represent all those who have set their hearts on the wares of the world.

A voice from heaven is addressed to believers:

> 'Come forth, my people, out of her,
> That you may have no fellowship with her sins,
> And that you may not receive of her plagues;
> For glued together were her sins, even up to heaven,
> And God has recollected her unrighteous deeds.'

The admonition to leave Babylon is addressed to God's people in all ages (*cf.* Is. 48: 20; 52: 11; Je. 50: 8,41–44; Zc. 2: 7). From this fact it also appears that Babylon is not only the city of the end-time. It is the world, as centre of seduction, in any age. To depart from Babylon means not to have fellowship with her sins and not to be ensnared by her allurements and enticements. Those who set their heart on the world shall also receive of her plagues. It may seem as if God has forgotten Babylon's sins. In the day when Babylon falls it will become evident that He has most certainly remembered them.

Then Babylon will receive the 'double' according to her works. This does not mean that she will receive twice as much punishment as she deserves; but that she will receive the exact amount of punishment which she has earned. The punishment is the 'double', the counterpart, of the sin. The torment and mourning (verse 7) are the exact equivalent for her pride and arrogance. The scales balance exactly. In her self-glorification, presumption, and boastfulness she has said in her heart—which is even worse than saying it to others—'I sit as queen, and a widow I am not, and mourning I shall not see' (*cf.* Is. 14: 13,14; 47: 8; Je. 50: 29). Therefore, death, mourning, and famine will ruin her in one day, because the Lord God, whom she has opposed, is strong.

The next section (verses 9–20) presents a threefold lamentation, on the part of kings, merchants, and navigators, followed by the rejoicings of heaven.

First, the kings or mighty men, the men of influence of the earth, utter their lament. They have committed whoredom with this harlot, Babylon or, in other words, they have yielded to her temptations and have enjoyed her luxuries, so when they see the smoke of Babylon's great conflagration, they shall stand afar off for fear of her torture and say,

'Woe, woe! The city, the great one!
Babylon! The city, the strong one!
For in a single hour your judgment has overtaken you.'

Next, the merchants—all those who set their hearts on the goods and luxuries of the world—wail and mourn because their cargoes have suddenly become worthless (*cf.* Lk. 12: 16–21). All that delighted them is suddenly destroyed. They can do nothing to save it. They stand 'from afar'. Babylon, the pleasure-mad world, the seductress, perishes in utter helplessness.

Notice the list of cargoes which had been Babylon's delight. There were cargoes of gold, silver, precious stones and pearls (*cf.* the gorgeous apparel and embellishments of the great harlot, Rev. 17: 4). None of these things has abiding value. They all perish. 'The fashion (*schema*, outward appearance and glamour) of this world passes away' (1 Cor. 7: 31). Then, in close connection with the foregoing, various kinds of costly garments are mentioned: fine linen, purple, silk, and scarlet. (Again *cf.* Rev. 17: 4; also Lk. 16: 19.) Next, various materials that are used in the construction of articles of luxury are listed; thyine wood, used for inlaying and as incense, ivory vessels, and other utensils made of precious wood, brass, iron or marble. Also listed are spices and ointments: cinnamon, amomum (an aromatic herb), perfume, and frankincense. The emphasis is on luxury.

The best in the line of food and drink comes next: wine, oil, fine flour, wheat. Here is the oil and the wine of the wicked rich, and the finest flour besides. But this also is destined to perish. Livestock and marketable animals such as cattle and sheep, are mentioned next. The concluding items are horses and chariots and bodies, even the souls of human beings. These wicked people trade in bodies and souls of slaves as if they constituted mere articles of merchandise. They did anything and everything to enrich themselves. The apostle's picture is based entirely on conditions prevailing round about him at the very time when he saw and wrote these visions. Yet essentially the picture of Babylon which he receives and reproduces is true for every age.

Observe that to this catalogue of cargoes which belong to Babylon and which perish, every department of existence makes its contribution: the mineral kingdom (gold, silver, *etc.*), the plant kingdom (fine linen, silk, *etc.*), the animal kingdom (ivory, cattle, sheep, *etc.*), and even the kingdom of man (bodies and souls of men). The result is that when Babylon perishes, the economic chaos is complete; the world of the unbeliever, on which he has pinned his hopes and built his trust, collapses! This is true with respect to the fall of every Babylon—whether it is literal Babylon, or Nineveh, or Rome. It is true especially with respect to the final kingdom of antichrist at the close of history. Thus, the harlot Babylon sees the heyday of the lust of her life slipping away from her; the dainty and sumptuous things perish away, so that men cannot find in her anything that is attractive. In the end the harlot proves to be a great and bitter disappointment (see Rev. 17: 16). Utterly helpless is Babylon; the merchants stand 'afar off' and wail when they compare the former splendour of the harlot—her fine linen, her purple, her scarlet, her gold, her precious stones and her pearls, with her present condition. In a single hour this vast wealth has been destroyed!

The third lamentation proceeds from the mouths and hearts of seafaring men. Four classes are mentioned: the captains, the passengers intent on business, the sailors, and as many as gain their living by the sea, *e.g.* exporters, importers, fishermen, those who dive for pearls, *etc.* All these see from afar the smoke of Babylon's conflagration. They recall its former greatness and splendour. They can hardly believe their eyes when they see the total ruin and thorough collapse of all their hopes and desires. They heap dust on their heads as a token of grief (Ezk. 27: 30) and they exclaim,

> 'Woe, woe! The city, the great one!
> In whom were made rich all those having the ships in the sea by reason of her luxury!
> For, in a single hour she was made desolate!'

Because the wicked base their entire hope upon the luxuries and pleasures of this life, when the 'fashion' of this world perishes they perish with it. Their 'all' vanishes.

But the saints, apostles and prophets of God are summoned to rejoice from their heavenly home, for Babylon's fall is God's just retribution which is visited upon the world because it persecuted the Church.

The final paragraph of this chapter indicates the thoroughgoing, irrevocable, and irreparable character of Babylon's fall. The symbol used is very striking (*cf.* Je. 51: 63,64). An angel appears. Observe that it is a *strong* angel. What he is about to do requires strength. By himself he picks up a millstone, not an ordinary stone from a handmill but a great millstone, that is, one from a mill turned by an animal. What does the angel do with this great millstone? Does he drop it upon the land? No, he drops it into the sea so that it may disappear completely. Does he merely permit it to fall? No, he lifts it up and then hurls it into the sea so that it may be buried deeply in the ocean bed. So thorough-going and complete will be Babylon's fall. Never will the great millstone be retrieved. Thus, this wicked world, as the centre of seduction, will perish for ever.

Notice the fact that the phrase 'no more at all' (verses 21–23) occurs six times. Observe also the climax in the arrangement of the six: 'No more at all' shall Babylon be found. The city as such is gone. That is a general statement, not nearly as vivid as what follows. Next we read 'No more at all' the sound of harpists and musicians, flute players and trumpeters. All music has disappeared (*cf.* Je. 25: 10). What is the world without music? Yet one can live without it. In fact, some people seem to prefer to do without it. What follows makes matters more serious. 'No more at all' shall be found in thee any craftsman of whatever craft. Try to imagine life in any great city without any craftsman. But in what follows one of life's basic needs seems to be taken away. 'No more at all' shall be heard in thee the sound of a millstone (*cf.* Je. 25: 10). The passage is beginning to reach its terrible climax. 'No more at all' shall the light of a lamp shine in thee (*cf.* Je. 25: 10). Utter darkness reigns supreme, a darkness that can be felt, a darkness which symbolizes the final and complete effusion of God's wrath upon this wicked, pleasure-loving, seductive world! And that condition lasts throughout all eternity.

Now the final touch: whatever imparts unity, whatever inspires love, every love-relationship, has disappeared completely and for ever: 'No more at all' shall the voice of the bridegroom and of the bride be heard in thee (*cf.* Je. 25: 10). The reason for this terrible sentence was because Babylon's merchants were the 'great ones' of the earth (*cf.* Rev. 6: 15). God was completely forgotten. The merchants had one ambition—to be great; to be like God in power and authority. To this is added: 'By thy magic all the nations were deceived' (*cf.* Is. 47: 9 ff.). The gold and glamour of this world deceived the wicked. The beast out of the earth—also called 'the false prophet'—had been successful in his attempt to lead people astray. In addition, the harlot had caused them to wander away farther and farther from God. Finally, the blood of all God's prophets, saints and even of all Christian martyrs, was found in Babylon. Babylon slaughtered them all. Here is one more reason why we conceive of the term 'Babylon' as indicating the world as a past, present, and future reality, and not merely as the city that shall exist in the last days. The main point for us to observe, however, is this, that the pleasure-mad, arrogant world, with all its seductive luxuries and pleasures, with its antichristian philosophy and culture, with its teeming multitudes that have forsaken God and have lived according to the lusts of the flesh and the desires of the mind, shall perish. The wicked suffer eternal despair. This doom will not be complete until the day of the final judgment.

II. REJOICINGS IN HEAVEN

1. *The marriage of the Lamb* (19: 1–10)

We now hear the hallelujahs of heaven when Christ has come in glory to take for Himself His bride, the Church (19: 7). Heaven celebrates God's victory over the harlot, Babylon. John hears first a great sound of a great multitude. The hosts of angels ascribe salvation and glory and power to God. They declare that in judging the great harlot God has perfected the salvation of His people. Thus the glory of His attributes has become manifest, and His power has been revealed. It is God, and He alone, who has wrought salvation (*cf.* Rev. 12: 10). Moreover, in bringing about the fall of Babylon Jehovah's righteousness has been displayed (*cf.* Rev. 15: 3 f.), for this harlot had corrupted the entire earth with her whoring (*cf.* Rev. 14: 8; Je. 51: 7). Self-exaltation and leading people farther and farther away from God had been her chief delight. Besides, she had brought about the slaughter of the saints (Rev. 17: 6; 18: 24). Now God has rendered vengeance (Rev. 8: 5; Je. 50: 13). The angels rejoice exceedingly in the salvation of God's people. They are filled with gladness of heart when they ponder the fact that all opposition has been quenched for ever. Again they give expression to this joy by crying, 'Hallelujah!' Their hearts seem to be filled with ecstasy to the very breaking-point, and in their rapture they cry 'Praise Jehovah'. That is the meaning of 'Hallelujah', which is found only here in the New Testament. Babylon's smoke goes up for ever and ever (Rev. 14: 11; 18: 8,9,18,21 ff.; Is. 13: 20 ff.; Mt. 25: 46). Never again will she rise to vex the Church.

Next, the twenty-four elders, symbolizing the entire Church, praise God, and so do the four cherubim, representing all the cherubim (Rev. 4: 2–6; 5: 14; 7: 15). So filled are they with thanksgiving that they can utter but two words: 'Amen—Hallelujah!' They express their adoration to God who is seated upon the throne, and who is highly exalted, glorious and sovereign.

Then John hears a solo-voice—one of the cherubim or one of the other angels?—coming from the region of the throne, exclaiming: 'Give praise to our God, all you servants of His, those fearing Him, the small and the great!' The lowliest angel and the highest saint, all are summoned to glorify God, the Author of salvation; for all serve Him out of reverence.

John now hears the voice of all the hosts of heaven, both angels and men. It resembles the sound of many waters and mighty thunders, for these hallelujahs, spontaneous and majestic, issue from lips innumerable (14: 2).

These voices proclaim in unison that the Lord, God, the Almighty has now revealed Himself in the full majesty of His royal glory and power (verse 6). Each exhorts his neighbour to rejoice and to be glad exceedingly, and, above all else, to give to God all the glory (1: 6; 14: 7). The reason for this burst of jubilation is given in these words:

> 'For it has come, the wedding of the Lamb,
> And his wife has made herself ready!
> And it was given to her that she be clothed in fine linen,
> glistening, pure;
> For the fine linen is the righteous acts of the saints.'

In order to understand the meaning of this sublime passage we must briefly review the marriage customs of the Hebrews.[1] We distinguish the following elements in a Jewish marriage. First comes the betrothal. This is considered more binding than our 'engagement'. The terms of the marriage are accepted in the presence of witnesses and God's blessing is pronounced upon the union. From this day groom and bride are legally husband and wife (2 Cor. 11: 2). Next comes the interval between betrothal and the wedding-feast. During this interval

[1] L. Berkhof, *Biblical Archaeology*, p. 63; G. M. Mackie, *Bible Manners and Customs*, p. 122; J. S. Wright, J. A. Thompson, art. 'Marriage', *New Bible Dictionary*.

the groom pays the dowry to the father of the bride if this has not yet been done (Gn. 34: 12). Sometimes the dowry is in the form of service rendered (Gn. 29: 20).

Then comes the procession at the close of the interval. The bride prepares and adorns herself. The groom, arrayed in his best attire and accompanied by his friends, who sing and bear torches, proceeds to the home of the betrothed. He receives the bride and conveys her, with a returning procession, to his own home or to the home of his parents (Mt. 9: 15; *cf.* also Mt. 25: 1 ff.). When the groom had to come from afar, the feast was at times spread at the home of the bride. Finally there is the wedding-feast, which includes the marriage supper. The usual festivities last seven, or even more, days.

Scripture again and again compares the love-relationship between a bridegroom and his bride to that which exists between Jehovah and His people, or between Christ and His Church (Is. 50: 1 ff.; 54: 1 ff.; Eph. 5: 32; Rev. 21: 9). Indeed, the former is a symbol, a faint reflection of the glory and beauty of the latter.

Now, the Church is 'betrothed' to Christ. Christ, moreover, has paid the dowry for her; He has bought His bride, the Church:

'From heaven He came and sought her
To be His holy Bride,
With His own blood He bought her,
And for her life He died.'

The 'interval' of separation has come. It is this entire dispensation between Christ's ascension to heaven and His coming again. During this period the bride must make herself ready. She arrays herself in fine linen, glistening and pure. The fine linen symbolizes her righteous acts, her sanctified character (7: 13). Her deeds have been washed by the blood of Christ. Remember, however, that this righteousness is 'given to her' by God's sovereign grace.

At the end of this dispensation the Bridegroom, accompanied by the angels of glory (Mt. 25: 31), comes to receive His bride, the Church. The wedding-feast begins. To that most glorious moment our passage refers in the words:

'It has come, the wedding (or wedding-feast) of the Lamb,
And his wife has made herself ready!'

The feast lasts not one or two weeks but throughout all

eternity! This feast is the climax of that entire process by means of which the Bridegroom, Christ, comes to His bride, the Church. It is the goal and purpose of that ever-increasing intimacy, union, fellowship, and communion between the Redeemer and the redeemed. In Christ the bride was *chosen* from eternity. Throughout the entire Old Testament dispensation the wedding was *announced*. Next, the Son of God assumed our flesh and blood: the *betrothal* took place. The price—the *dowry*—was paid on Calvary. And now, after an *interval* which in the eyes of God is but a little while, the Bridegroom returns and 'It has come, the wedding of the Lamb'. The Church on earth yearns for this moment, so does the Church in heaven. Then we shall all be with Him for evermore. It will be a holy, blessed, everlasting fellowship: the fullest realization of all the promises of the gospel.

Even during this present dispensation—this 'interval' of separation—those who are 'effectually called' (not merely 'bidden') to the marriage supper of the Lamb are blessed (verse 9). Before the supper itself even begins the 'called ones' are blessed; and these are true words of God. They are genuine and real. Filled with ecstasy, the apostle falls down before the feet of the speaker in order to worship him. Did he mistake him for the Lord Jesus Christ Himself?[1] At any rate, the speaker, who was probably either one of the cherubim or another angel, prevents the intended worship, adding: 'To God render worship.' For the testimony of Jesus is the spirit of the prophecy. The spirit and inner content of all true prophecy—that is, of the entire Bible—is the testimony of Jesus, the testimony which He revealed to us. That revelation which He gave us forbids us to worship anyone besides God (Mt. 4: 10).

The harlot, Babylon, having been disposed of, we now turn our attention to the beast and the false prophet. What happens to them? From the hallelujahs of heaven at and after the judgment day we return to the moments just preceding the final judgment.

2. *The glorious Victor* (19: 11–21)

John sees heaven itself opened, not merely a door opened in heaven (Rev. 4: 1). On a white horse, as in Revelation 6: 2, Christ is seated. He is called 'Faithful and Genuine'. This is our Lord at His second coming, to judgment: to judge and make war. He is about to judge righteously, for His penetrating

[1] See the argument in R. C. H. Lenski, *op. cit.*, p. 549.

eyes are a flame of fire (1: 14). On His head the apostle sees many royal diadems or fillets, for He is King over all (*cf.* 'diadem' with *stephanos,* victor's wreath) (Rev. 6: 2). His name no-one knows but He Himself.[1] Does it express the inner character of His relation to the Father? Whereas He has arrived for judgment, He wears a garment sprinkled with blood, not the blood of the cross but—symbolically, of course—the blood of His enemies (Is. 63: 1–6; Rev. 14: 20). His name is called 'The *Logos* (or Word) of God' (Jn. 1: 1). Only He Himself knows the full meaning of this name. All we can say is that He is called 'the Word of God' because in Him God fully expresses and reveals Himself (Jn. 1: 18,10–30).

At His second coming the armies of heaven, that is, the holy angels, accompany Him (Mt. 25: 31). Because they are holy angels, they are clothed in fine linen, which is white and pure. Out of His mouth proceeds a sharp sword (Rev. 1: 16; 2: 12,16). This sword is not the comforting story of the gospel. It is symbolical of destruction, as is clearly indicated by the entire context. He comes to 'smite the nations', and to 'shepherd them with a rod of iron' (2: 27; 12: 5). He treads the winepress of the fierceness of the wrath of God, the Almighty. He comes to carry out the sentence of God Almighty (Mt. 25: 31 ff.; Jn. 5: 22; Acts 17: 31). He now fully reveals Himself, by means of the destruction of the beast and his allies, as being indeed King of kings and Lord of lords. So certain is the victory of Christ over the beast and false prophet, and over all those who worship them, that an angel standing in the sun already summons all the birds to come and be gathered together for the supper, the great one, of God, in order to eat the flesh of kings, captains, mighty men, horses and their riders, yes, the flesh of all the wicked, both free and bond, small and great (*cf.* Rev. 6: 15; 17: 12,15). It is an immense slaughter, the slaughter of Har-Magedon. Remember that Har-Magedon consists of two elements: the final attack of the anti-christian power—the beast—upon the Church, and Christ's victory over this vast army at His coming unto judgment.

John sees the beast, the persecuting power embodied in world government and directed against Christ and His Church, and the kings of the earth, and their armies gathered together against the Rider on the white horse and His army.[2] Hence,

[1] See our explanation of Rev. 2: 17.

[2] On the final attack of the antichristian forces against the Church in the days just preceding Christ's second coming, see pp. 162–165, 195.

the apostle sees the whole world of unbelief gathered for the final assault upon the Church. Please observe that the battle itself is not described. This battle of Har-Magedon is not a protracted struggle with now this, and then that, side winning. No, 'with the breath of his mouth' Christ, at His coming, defeats the foe. By the 'manifestation of his presence' He vanquishes His enemies (2 Thes. 2: 8). So also here in Revelation. We are simply told that the antichristian forces are gathered together against Christ and His army, and that they are put to rout. The beast (Rev. 13: 1 ff.) is taken. So is the false prophet—that is, the beast out of the earth, the great deceiver (13: 13,14). These two are cast alive into the lake of fire burning with brimstone (20: 10). As these are the leaders—respectively of antichristian persecution and antichristian religion and philosophy—they are said to be cast alive into perdition; while the men who worship them are first killed, and then also cast into the lake of fire and brimstone. The meaning is that at Christ's second coming Satan's persecution of the Church and his power to deceive on earth shall cease for ever. Every influence of Satan—whether in the direction of persecution or of deception—goes with him to hell, never again to appear anywhere outside hell.[1] Christ, the Rider upon the white horse, completely triumphs. So complete is His victory over His enemies, that according to the symbolism begun in verse 17, all the birds gorge themselves upon the flesh of the wicked (verse 21). Thus, in symbolic language, the judgment day has again been described.

We have seen the end of the men who bear the mark of the beast (Rev. 15, 16). We have also witnessed the fall of Babylon (17: 1 f.). We have read the description of Christ's victory over the beast and the false prophet (19: 11 ff.). All go down in defeat. Their discomfiture is not complete until the day of Christ's coming in judgment. Then all go down together, even though their histories have been presented under different symbols and in separate paragraphs. One foe, the leader of them all, remains. It is the dragon, Satan. His ruin is described in the final section of the Apocalypse.

[1] R. C. H. Lenski (*op. cit.*, pp. 562 ff.) ably argues that Rev. 19: 20 in no way proves that the beast and the false prophet are here viewed as two actual persons living at the parousia.

CHAPTER FOURTEEN

REVELATION 20–22: VICTORY THROUGH CHRIST

I. FROM THE BINDING OF SATAN TO THE FINAL JUDGMENT

REVELATION 19 : 19 ff. carried us to the very end of history, to the day of final judgment. With Revelation 20 we return to the beginning of our present dispensation. Thus, the connection between chapters 19 and 20 is similar to that between chapters 11 and 12. Revelation 11 : 18 announces 'the time of the dead to be judged'. The end has arrived. Yet with Revelation 12 we return to the beginning of the New Testament period, for Revelation 12: 5 describes the birth, ascension, and coronation of our Lord. Similarly, with chapter 20 we begin anew.

Now, there is a very striking parallel between chapters 11–14 on the one hand, and chapter 20 on the other. Both divide history into the same periods, though the approach differs. Observe the parallel.

REVELATION 11–14	REVELATION 20
12: 5–12. In connection with Christ's birth, death, ascension, and coronation, Satan is hurled down from heaven. His accusations lose every semblance of justice.	20: 1–3. Satan is bound and cast into the abyss; his power over the nations is curbed. Instead of the nations conquering the Church, the Church begins to conquer (evangelize) the nations.
11: 2–6; 12: 14 ff. A long period of power and witness-bearing for the Church, which is nourished 'away from the face of the serpent (Satan)'. The devil's influence is curbed.	20: 2. A long period of power for the Church, Satan having been bound. He remains bound for a thousand years, that is, during this entire gospel age. (In heaven the souls of the redeemed are living and reigning with Christ, 20: 4–6.)
11: 7 ff.; 13: 7. A very brief period of most severe persecution. This is Satan's little season: the most terrible and also the final manifestation of the persecuting power of antichrist.	20: 7 ff. A very brief period of most severe persecution: Satan marshals the army of Gog and Magog against the Church. This is the Battle of Har-Magedon.
11: 17,18; 14: 14 ff. The one and only second coming of Christ in judgment.	20: 11 ff. The one and only second coming of Christ in judgment.

Once this 'order of events' or 'programme of history' is seen, Revelation 20 is not difficult to understand. All one needs to do is to remember the sequence: Christ's first coming is followed by a long period during which Satan is bound; this, in turn, is followed by Satan's little season; and that is followed by Christ's second coming, *i.e.* His coming in judgment. It should be clear immediately to anyone who carefully reads Revelation 20 that the 'thousand years' precede the second coming of our Lord in judgment. This second coming in judgment is not described until we reach the eleventh verse. It is clear that the theory of the premillennialists is at variance with the facts here.[1]

Yet, though in Revelation 20 we traverse the same ground as in the preceding visions, namely, this entire dispensation from the first to the second coming of Christ, we view it from a different aspect. You remember that Revelation 12 introduces five enemies of the Church. All go down together! Yet the account of their defeat is spread over several distinct visions. The preceding visions have told us what happens to four of the five foes introduced in chapter 12. Only one is left, namely Satan himself. His defeat is described in our present vision.

In this connection, let us remember the main theme of the entire book.[2] It is the victory of Christ and of His Church over every enemy. When Satan also is hurled into the lake of fire and brimstone (20: 10) not a single enemy is left to vex the Church. We are conquerors; indeed, we are more than conquerors through Him that loved us, for not only do we triumph over every foe but we also live and reign with Christ. And in this supreme joy many of those who formerly opposed us will participate (*cf.* 3: 9). Truly, more than conquerors are we!

1. *The binding of Satan* (20: 1–3)

Let us study, first, this vision in which Satan is bound for a thousand years and hurled into the abyss.

John sees an angel coming down out of heaven. He has a key with which he is going to lock the abyss (*cf.* 9: 1,11). This abyss is a deep hole provided with a shaft (9: 1), and with a lid. This lid can be unlocked (9: 2), locked (20: 3), and even sealed (20: 3). Bear in mind, however, that all this is symbolism.

[1] For the premillennialistic view see A. H. Burton, *The Apocalypse Expounded;* H. A. Ironside, *Lectures on the Revelation*; C. I. Scofield, *The Scofield Reference Bible*; J. Seiss, *Lectures on the Book of Revelation*; W. H. Simcox, *The Revelation of St. John*. See further the bibliography.

[2] See chapter 1, pp. 8f.

Upon the angel's hand lies a chain, the two ends hanging down. Evidently, he is going to bind someone in order to lock him up in the abyss. What happens? John suddenly sees 'the dragon', strong, crafty, ugly. It is 'the old serpent', cunning and deceptive. In order to describe him still more accurately he is also called 'the devil', that is, 'slanderer'; and 'Satan', that is, 'adversary' or 'false accuser'. Being in the Spirit John now notices that the angel overpowers Satan. He renders him helpless and binds him securely and firmly. The devil remains bound for a thousand years. The angel hurls him into the abyss and locks it. He places a seal over it. Thus, Satan remains 'locked up' for a thousand years. After that he must be loosed for a short time.

What is the meaning of this symbol?[1] In order to arrive at the real meaning of 'the binding and hurling into the abyss' of Satan we must first ask the question, just what meaning or value did this passage have for the persecuted Christians of John's day?

Let us, accordingly, forget for a moment the fact that we are living in the twentieth century. Let us 'transplant' ourselves to the world of John the apostle. What a picture of spiritual darkness and desolation! Try to count the many idols that disgrace the streets and sanctuaries of imperial Rome. The abominations, the filth and corruption attendant upon the celebration of pagan festivals, the superstitions, vices, and so on, are truly staggering. Temples and shrines throughout the world are crowded with ignorant, half-despairing worshippers. We see a few scattered churches established through the efforts of Paul and others. For the rest, heathendom is everywhere triumphant.

Now let us move back to that long period which preceded Christ's ascension. All the nations—with the exception of the Jews—are under the thraldom of Satan. Not, of course, in the absolute sense of the term, for God always reigns supreme, but in the sense of Acts 14: 16: 'God . . . in past generations allowed all the nations to walk in their own ways.' If during this present era the devil 'blinds the minds of unbelievers' (2 Cor. 4: 4), that was even more emphatically true during the

[1] We reject the following views on the binding of Satan for a thousand years:

a. That Satan is absolutely bound (see W. Milligan, *op. cit.*, VI, p. 913).
b. That the thousand years is symbolical of eternity.
c. The premillennialistic view (see p.185, note 1).
d. That the thousand years begins with Constantine, Charlemagne, *etc*.

old dispensation. With a sigh of horror we exclaim, 'Is this condition never going to change? Will this Old Testament era continue for ever? Will the devil maintain his rule over the peoples of the earth? Will the light of the glorious gospel never penetrate into the palaces and hovels of Asia and Europe? Will this intense moral and spiritual darkness always continue? Has an angry God forgotten mercy?'

The answer is, 'Rejoice!' For Christ can say, 'I will tell of the decree: Jehovah said to me, "Thou art my son; This day have I begotten thee. Ask of me, and I will give thee the nations for thine inheritance, and the uttermost parts of the earth for thy possession" ' (Ps. 2: 7,8). Again, 'He shall have dominion also from sea to sea, and from the river to the ends of the earth. They that dwell in the wilderness shall bow before him; and his enemies shall lick the dust. The kings of Tarshish and of the isles shall render tribute. The kings of Sheba and Seba shall offer gifts. Yea, all kings shall fall down before him; all nations shall serve him . . . his name shall endure for ever. His name shall be continued as long as the sun; and men shall be blessed in him; all nations shall call him blessed!' (Ps. 72: 8–11,17; *cf.* Gn. 12: 3; Am. 9: 11 f.; Mi. 4: 12).

That was the prophecy. The spiritual darkness that covers the nations shall not continue; Satan shall deceive the nations no more. Late comes the fulfilment. Jesus is born. He begins His ministry. The Pharisees accuse Him of casting out demons by the power of Satan himself. He answers, 'How can one enter into the house of the strong one (namely Satan) and plunder his goods, unless he first binds the strong one? Then he shall plunder his goods.' Please notice that exactly the same word 'binding' is used here in Matthew as in Revelation 20. This work of binding the devil was begun when our Lord triumphed over him in the temptations in the wilderness (Mt. 4: 1–11). As a result, Christ begins to 'cast out' demons. The power and influence of Satan over the deluded masses was beginning to be curtailed.

Again, when the seventy missionaries returned, they said: 'Lord, even the demons are subject to us in thy name'. Observe what follows: 'And he said to them, I beheld Satan falling as lightning from heaven' (Lk. 10: 17,18). Here the devil's 'falling from heaven' is associated with the missionary activity of the seventy. This is a very significant passage which does much to explain Revelation 20.

At another time certain Greeks wished to see Jesus. Jesus

remarks: 'Now is the judgment of this world; now shall the prince of this world be cast out. And I, if I be lifted up from the earth, will draw all men to myself.' Be sure to observe that a word is used which has the same root, in the original, as the term which we translate 'casting' or 'hurling' into the abyss (Rev. 20). Even more important is the fact that here, in John 12: 20–32, the casting out of Satan is associated with the fact that not only the Jews, as was the rule in the past, but 'all men'—Greeks as well as Jews—shall be drawn to Christ. All this shall happen as a result of Christ's suffering on the cross and the sending of the Holy Spirit. Colossians 2: 15 very definitely associates the 'despoiling' of Satan and his armies with Christ's triumph on the cross. Revelation 12: 5 ff. clearly shows that 'the casting out' of Satan was a result of Christ's coronation.

Realize, therefore, that in all these passages the binding and casting out or falling of Satan is in some way associated with the first coming of our Lord Jesus Christ. When we say 'the first coming' we refer to all the events associated with it, from the incarnation to the coronation. We may say, therefore, that the binding of Satan, according to all these passages, begins with that first coming. Again, in some of the texts which we have quoted, this binding, *etc.*, is definitely associated with the work of missions and with the extension of the witnessing Church among the nations. Before the coming of Christ, His victory over the devil in the temptations, His ministry, His death, ascension and coronation, salvation had been largely limited to the Jews. God had suffered Satan to blind the eyes of the nations, so that these nations walked in their own ways. A great change was to take place. The 'truth' of the gospel would gradually replace the 'lie' of the devil. Satan is bound so that he can deceive the nations no more. Christ will draw 'all men' to Himself. The chosen from *every* nation will be saved.

In close harmony with all these scriptural passages—and our exegesis must always be based upon the analogy of Scripture—we conclude that here also in Revelation 20: 1–3 the binding of Satan and the fact that he is hurled into the abyss to remain there for a thousand years indicates that throughout this present gospel age the devil's influence on earth is curtailed. He is unable to prevent the extension of the Church among the nations by means of an active missionary programme. During this entire period he is prevented from causing the nations—the world in general—to destroy the Church as a mighty, missionary institution. By means of the preaching of the Word as applied by the Holy Spirit, the elect, from all parts of the world, are brought from darkness to light. In that sense the Church conquers the nations, and the nations do not conquer the Church. Throughout this entire period churches are established. Not only individuals but institutions and ordinances are affected more or less by the gospel of God's grace. In regions where the devil had been allowed to exercise almost unlimited authority, during Old Testament times, he is now compelled to see the servants of Christ gaining territory little by little. Within a comparatively brief period Christianity spreads throughout southern Europe. Soon it conquers the entire continent. During the centuries which follow it is proclaimed everywhere so that the ends of the earth hear the gospel of the crucified One and many bend the knee before Him.

The Church has become international. This international Church is very powerful: 'Like a mighty army moves the Church of God.' The maps of the *World Missionary Atlas* are full of little red lines underscoring the names of places where there are mission stations. The particularism of the old dispensation has made place for the universalism of the new. The Bible has been translated into more than 1,000 languages. The influence of the gospel upon the thought and life of mankind can scarcely be overestimated. In some countries the blessed truths of Christianity affect human life in all its phases: political, economic, social, and intellectual. Only the individual who lacks the historic sense and is, therefore, unable to see the present in the light of conditions which prevailed throughout the world before Christ's ascension, can fail to appreciate the glories of the millennial age in which we are now living. The prophecy found in Psalm 72 is being fulfilled before our eyes.

Do not misunderstand our interpretation. We are not stating that the world is becoming better and better and that by and by nearly everyone will join the ranks of Christ's army. Many will *hear* the gospel, but will not *heed* it. Moreover, God's trumpets of judgment will not convert a world which is hardening itself in unbelief. The majority will always be on the side of the evil one. We most emphatically reject the dream of a man-made era of peace, prosperity, and universal righteousness on earth preceding the second coming of Christ. Just as definitely do we repudiate the related idea according to which the almighty 'law of evolution' will bring about an ever-upward trend in the course of civilization. We are not closing our eyes to the evils which surround us; nor are we ignorant of the fact that present-day humanism, masquerading under the guise of a new and better interpretation of Christianity, is in reality the rat that is gnawing at the roots of the tree of true religion. Nevertheless, although we are fully aware of all these symptoms of evil and harbingers of woe, the facts which we have set out above remain true, and no amount of argument can cancel them. The Church, indeed, exerts a tremendous influence for good upon almost the entire complex of human life. In that sense—not in every sense—the devil is bound.

We repeat, the devil is not bound in every sense. His influence is not completely destroyed. On the contrary, within the sphere in which Satan is permitted to exert his influence for evil he rages most furiously. A dog securely bound with a long and heavy chain can do great damage within the circle of his imprisonment. Outside that circle, however, the animal can do no damage and can hurt no-one. Thus also Revelation 20: 1–3 teaches us that Satan's power is curbed and his influence curtailed with respect to one definite sphere of activity: 'that he should deceive the nations no more'. The devil can do much, indeed, during this present period of one thousand years. But there is one thing which, during this period, he cannot do. With respect to this one thing he is definitely and securely bound. He cannot destroy the Church as a mighty missionary organization heralding the gospel to all the nations. He cannot do that until the thousand years are finished.

We have seen, therefore, that the 'thousand years' of Revelation 20 have a glorious meaning for God's people on earth. Nevertheless, the glories of heaven during this period far transcend those which relate to the earth. The next few verses (4–6) describe the condition of the victorious saints in heaven, not on earth.

Of course, these two aspects of the millennium, namely, the earthly (verses 1–3) and the heavenly (verses 4–6), the binding of Satan and the reign of the saints, are most intimately related. It is in connection with the personal reign of our divine and human Mediator as a result of His atoning work (see Rev. 5) that Satan is bound so that his influence on earth is partly paralysed. It is in connection with this same personal reign of Jesus in and from heaven that the souls of the departed saints are reigning above (*cf.* Rev. 3: 21). This personal reign of Christ in and from heaven underlies all the visions of the Apocalypse. It is the key to the interpretation of the 'thousand years'.

2. *The reign of the saints* (20: 4–6)

In order to arrive at a proper conception of these verses, we must again go back in our thoughts to the first century AD. Roman persecutions are raging. Martyrs are calmly laying their heads under the executioner's sword. Paul had already done this; also James. Rather than say, 'The emperor is Lord', or drop incense on the altar of a pagan priest as a token of worshipping the emperor, believers confess their Christ even in the midst of the flames and while they are thrown before the wild beasts in the Roman amphitheatres. But Christ is not unmindful of His grievously afflicted disciples. He sustains them in order that they may remain faithful to the end. For that very reason He gives to His sorely-tried Church the vision of 'the souls of them that had been beheaded for the testimony of Jesus' (1: 2,9; 6: 9). He describes these souls—together with those of all departed Christians who had confessed their Lord upon earth—as reigning with Jesus in heaven. He says, in effect, 'Here below: a few years of suffering: there, in that better land above, they live and reign with Christ a thousand years!' What a comfort! Certainly, the sufferings of this present time are not worthy to be compared with the glory which is revealed to the souls of believers reigning with their exalted Lord in heaven!

In connection with this 'thousand year reign' of verses 4–6 we shall answer three questions.

First, where does it take place? According to the passage which we are considering it takes place in three places.

(i) The thousand year reign occurs where the thrones are, for we read: 'And I saw thrones and they sat upon them.' Now, according to the entire book of Revelation, the throne of Christ and of His people is invariably in heaven (Rev. 1: 4; 3: 21; 4: 2 ff.; *etc.*).

(ii) The thousand year reign also occurs where the disembodied souls of the martyrs are, for we read: 'And I saw the souls of them that had been beheaded for the testimony of Jesus.' John sees souls, not bodies. He is thinking of souls without bodies, for we read: 'of them that had been beheaded'. In this entire passage there is not a single word about a resurrection of bodies. The distinction between soul and body is even emphasized: 'the souls of them that had been beheaded'. True, the term 'souls' at times means 'people' (*e.g.* Gn. 46: 27). But in that case you can substitute the term 'people' for 'souls'.

Here in Revelation 20 you cannot do so. The souls reign during this entire present dispensation until Christ's second coming. Afterwards, it is no longer the souls that reign, for then body and soul are together again. Then the saints reign, not for a limited though lengthy period—a thousand years—but 'for ever and ever' (22: 5).

(iii) The thousand year reign also occurs where Jesus lives, for we read 'And they lived and reigned with Christ. . . .' The question is, where, according to the Apocalypse, is the place from which the exalted Mediator rules the universe? Where does Jesus live? Clearly, it is in heaven. It is in heaven that the Lamb is represented as taking the scroll out of the hand of Him that sat on the throne (Rev. 5). Revelation 12 clearly states that Christ was 'caught up to God and to his throne . . . Therefore, rejoice O heavens, and ye that dwell therein'.

We may safely say, therefore, that the thousand year reign takes place in *heaven.*

The next question that has to be answered is, what is its character? The nature of this reign may be summarized in four ways as follows.

(i) It is judging with Christ. The ransomed souls in heaven praise Christ for His righteous judgments. They constantly sing: 'True and righteous are his judgments.' These souls in glory are constantly pictured as taking part in all the activities of the Master: they sit down with Him in His throne (3: 21); they stand with Him on Mount Zion (*cf.* 14: 1); they sing before His throne (*cf.* 14: 3; 15: 3); they shall see His face (*cf.* Rev. 22: 4; *etc.*).

(ii) It is living with Christ: 'they did live and did reign' (see Rev. 7: 9 ff.). In heaven these souls respond in a perfect manner to a perfect environment. And what is life but that?

(iii) It is a sharing of royal glory with Christ. These souls celebrate the Lamb's, and thus their own, victory. With Him they reign. All their prayers are answered; all their wishes are constantly fulfilled.

(iv) It is 'the first resurrection'. The first resurrection is the translation of the soul from this sinful earth to God's holy heaven. It is followed at Christ's second coming by the second resurrection when the body, too, will be glorified.

Our final question is, who participates in this reign? The answer is simple and easy. First of all, all the souls of the martyrs, 'those who had been beheaded for the testimony of Jesus'. Secondly, all other believers who died in their faith, 'such as worshipped not the beast', *etc.* The rest of the dead, that is, all other men who died, the unbelieving dead, lived not until the thousand years are finished. When that period is finished, then there is a change. Then they enter 'the second death'. In other words, they receive everlasting punishment: not only as for the soul but now also for the body. The change is not for better but for the worse. On the other hand, those who have part in the first resurrection are blessed and holy. Over them the second death has no power. Not only shall they reign with Christ, but they shall also worship God in Christ as priests throughout the thousand years (Rev. 1: 6; 5: 10).

3. *The final conflict* (20: 7–10)

When the thousand years are finished, Satan is released from his prison. Then it becomes very clear that the final and most terrible persecution, by means of which antichristian forces are going to oppress the Church, is instigated, in a most direct manner, by Satan himself. The devil musters Gog and Magog for a final attack upon 'the camp of the saints, the beloved city'. The expression 'Gog and Magog' is borrowed from the book of Ezekiel,[1] where the term undoubtedly indicates the power of the Seleucids especially as it was revealed in the days of Antiochus Epiphanes, the bitter enemy of the Jews. The centre of his kingdom was located in Northern Syria. Seleucus established his residence there in the city of Antioch on the Orontes. To the east his territory extended beyond the Tigris. To the north the domain over which the Seleucids ruled included Meshech and Tubal, districts in Asia Minor.[2] Accordingly, Gog was the prince of Magog, that is, Syria. Therefore the oppression of God's people by 'Gog and Magog', refers, in Ezekiel, to the terrible persecution under Antiochus Epiphanes, ruler of Syria.

The book of Revelation uses this period of affliction and woe as a symbol of the final attack of Satan and his hordes upon the Church. Observe the resemblance.

[1] We reject the following interpretations of Gog and Magog:

a. That they symbolize the most distant nations, *e.g.*, China, Japan, India, which will attack the Christian nations in physical warfare.

b. That the same nations will wage a spiritual warfare—the culture and religion of the far away nations invading Christian nations.

[2] For our interpretation of Gog and Magog we are indebted to E. W. Hengstenberg, *The Revelation of St. John*, II, pp. 303 ff.; W. Fairweather, *From the Exile to the Advent*, pp. 133 ff.; *The Background of the Gospels*, pp. 95 ff.; A. H. Sayce, *The Races of the Old Testament*, p. 73.

First, remember that the attack of Gog and Magog (Syria under Antiochus Epiphanes) was the last great oppression which the people of God had to endure in the old dispensation. It is therefore an appropriate symbol for the final attack of anti-christian forces upon the Church during the new dispensation.

Secondly, bear in mind that these armies of Gog and Magog were very numerous. So they could adequately symbolize world-wide opposition to the Church in the days just preceding Christ's second coming.

Thirdly, reflect on the fact that the tribulation under Antiochus Epiphanes, though very severe, was also of very brief duration. Hence, it was well adapted to foreshadow the brief final tribulation which will occur at the close of our present dispensation (*cf.* Mk. 13: 20; Rev. 11: 11).

Finally, remember that the defeat of the armies of Syria—that is, of Gog and Magog—was most unexpected and most complete. It was clearly the work of God. Also for that reason the onslaught of Gog and Magog against Israel could serve as an excellent symbol of the final struggle of the godless world against the Church.

In the passage which we are studying 'Gog and Magog' are identified with 'the nations which are in the four corners of the earth'. This expression, however, does not mean the most distant nations. The term 'the four corners of the earth' simply means 'the whole world'. The entire wicked world is going to persecute the Church. The opposition will be world-wide. There is not the least ground, therefore, for regarding our passage as referring to a final attack by certain 'peripheral' nations—for example, China, Japan, and India—upon the nations of western Europe and America. The New Testament simply does not contain any predictions which apply to certain specific present-day nations or states, to these and to these only. It describes the struggle between the Church and the world. It says nothing that refers exclusively or even specifically to China, Japan, the Netherlands, or Louisiana! The conflict here described is not that between 'civilized' and 'uncivilized' nations. It is simply the last attack of the forces of antichrist against the Church. Our interpretation is also supported by the expression 'They went up over the breadth of the earth' (*cf.* Hab. 1: 6; Is. 8: 8; Gn. 13: 17; Jb. 38: 18).

The meaning, then, is this: the era during which the Church as a mighty missionary organization shall be able to spread the gospel everywhere is not going to last for ever; not even until the moment of Christ's second coming. Observe what is happening in certain countries even today. Are certain regions of this earth already entering Satan's little season?[1]

In other words, we have here in Revelation 20: 7–10 a description of the same battle—not 'war'—which was described in Revelation 16: 12 ff. and in Revelation 19: 19. In all three cases we read in the original, *the* battle. Thus 16: 14: 'to gather them together for *the* battle of the great day of God, the Almighty'. Again, Revelation 19: 19: 'gathered together to make *the* battle against him. . . .' Similarly, here in 20: 8: 'to gather them together to *the* battle'. In other words, these are not three different battles. We have here one and the same battle. It is the battle of Har-Magedon in all three cases. It is the final attack of antichristian forces upon the Church. The 'new' thing which Revelation 20 reveals is what happens to Satan as a result of this battle.

This final onslaught is directed against 'the beloved city', also called 'the camp of the saints'. Thus the Church of God is described here under the double symbolism of a city and a camp.

'And fire came down out of heaven and devoured them.' Notice the sudden character of this judgment upon Gog and Magog. It is as sudden and unexpected as the lightning which strikes from heaven (*cf.* 2 Thes. 2: 8). Thus, suddenly, will Christ appear and discomfit His enemies! This is His one and only coming in judgment. Satan had deceived the wicked world. He had deceived the wicked into thinking that a real and absolute victory over the Church was possible and that God could be defeated! So the devil, that deceiver, is cast into the lake of fire and brimstone—indicating hell as a place of suffering for both body and soul after the judgment day—where the beast and the false prophet are also. The sense is not that the beast and the false prophet were actually cast into hell before Satan was; but that the punishment of the beast and the false prophet has already been described (Rev. 19: 20). They all go down together, Satan, the beast and the false prophet. This must be true, for the beast is Satan's persecuting power, and the false prophet is Satan's antichristian religion. Wherever Satan is, there are also the other two. In this lake of fire and brimstone all three are tormented for ever and ever (Mt. 25:46).

4. *The great white throne* (20: 11–15)

Christ's coming in judgment is vividly described. John sees a

[1] Read pp. 130, 143, 162 ff., 182 f. where this subject is discussed more fully.

great white throne. Upon it is seated the Christ (Mt. 25: 31; Rev. 14: 14). From His face the earth and the heaven flee away. Not the destruction or annihilation but the renovation of the universe is indicated here. It will be a dissolution of the elements with great heat (2 Pet. 3: 10); a regeneration (Mt. 19: 28); a restoration of all things (Acts 3: 21); and a deliverance from the bondage of corruption (Rom. 8: 21). No longer will this universe be subject to 'vanity'.[1] John sees the dead, the great and the small, standing before the throne.[2] All individuals who have ever lived on earth are seen before the throne. The books are opened and the records of the life of every person consulted (Dn. 7: 10). Also the book of life, containing the names of all believers is opened (Rev. 3: 5; 13: 8). The dead are judged in accordance with their works (Mt. 25: 31 ff.; Rom. 14: 10; 2 Cor. 5: 10). The sea gives up its dead; so do Death and Hades.[3] Here is the one, general resurrection of all the dead. The entire Bible teaches but one, general resurrection (read Jn. 5: 28 f.). This one and only and general resurrection takes place at the last day (Jn. 6: 39 f., 44, 54). Nowhere in the entire Bible do we read of a resurrection of the bodies of believers, followed, after a thousand years, by a resurrection of the bodies of the unbelievers. All arise at the same time. Death, the separation of soul and body, and Hades, the state of separation, now cease. Neither in the new heaven nor upon the new earth nor even in hell will there ever be a separation between body and soul after Christ's second coming for judgment. Therefore, symbolically speaking, Death and Hades—now personified—are hurled into the lake of fire. And anyone whose name was not found written in the book of life was also flung into the fiery lake.

II. GOD'S FINAL TRIUMPH

We have reached the final and most beautiful theme. There is a beautiful connection between the first book of the Bible and the last. Scripture resembles a flower. We find the seed in Genesis, the growing plant in the books which follow, the fully developed and beautiful flower in the Apocalypse. Observe the following comparison.

[1] See J. Orr, *The Christian View of God and the World*, p. 195.

[2] See G. A. Gordon, 'The Vision of the Dead' in *Great Sermons by Great Preachers*, ed. J. L. Hurlbut.

[3] See our explanation of Rev. 1: 18; 6: 8.

Genesis tells us that God created heaven and earth. Revelation describes the *new* heaven and earth (21: 1). In Genesis the luminaries are called into being: sun, moon and stars. In Revelation we read: 'And the city has no need of the sun, nor of the moon, to shine in it; for the glory of God lightened it, and its lamp is the Lamb' (21: 23). Genesis describes a paradise which was lost. Revelation pictures a paradise restored (Rev. 2: 7; 22: 2). Genesis describes the cunning and power of the devil. The Apocalypse tells us that the devil was bound and hurled into the lake of fire and brimstone. Genesis pictures that awful scene of man fleeing away from God and hiding himself from the presence of the Almighty. Revelation shows us the most wonderful and intimate communion between God and redeemed man: 'Behold, the tabernacle of God is with men, and he shall tabernacle with them' (21: 3).

Finally, whereas Genesis shows us the tree of life, with an angel to keep the way to the tree of life, 'lest man put forth his hand and take of its fruit', the Apocalypse restores to man his right to have access to it: 'that they may have the right to come to the tree of life' (22:14).

So, again, we ask what is the theme of this book? It is this: Not the devil but Christ is victorious; God's plan, though for a while seemingly defeated, is in the end seen to triumph completely. We are conquerors. No; *more* than conquerors, for not only are we delivered from the greatest curse, indeed from every curse, but we obtain the most glorious blessing besides (Rev. 21: 3).

But what is depicted in Revelation 21: 1–22: 5? The ideal Church as it now is?[1] Or the universe and the Church of the future?[2] Neither of these answers seems complete. We have in this section a description of that which is ideal. Whatever is the result of God's redeeming grace, in the present or in the future, is included here. This redeeming grace and transforming power of God must not be viewed as pertaining only to the future. No, here and now in this present era, it is already working in the hearts of God's children. Consequently, what we find here in Revelation 21: 1–22: 5 is a description of the redeemed universe of the future as foreshadowed by the redeemed Church of the present. Let us prove our point.

Consider Revelation 21: 3: 'Behold the tabernacle of God is with men, and he shall tabernacle with them, and they shall

[1] *Cf.* W. Milligan, *op. cit.*
[2] *Cf.* R. C. H. Lenski, *op. cit.*, pp. 620 ff.

be his people, and God himself shall be with them, and be their God.'

The fact that these words refer to the new heaven and earth, to fully redeemed humanity as it shall exist after the judgment day, is as plain as daylight. The context is very clear. The first heaven and earth have passed away (21: 1). The judgment has taken place (20: 11 ff.). But does this passage refer only to the future? Anyone who is at home with the Bible will be able to answer the question. He will immediately recognize the passage which we have quoted (*cf.* Is. 65: 17; 66: 22). Reflect on the last phrase of Revelation 21: 3, 'and be their God'. Is not that the ancient covenant-promise which is found throughout Scripture? Look up Genesis 17: 7,8; Exodus 20: 2; Deuteronomy 5: 2 f., 6; Jeremiah 24: 7; 30: 22; 31: 33; Ezekiel 11: 20; Zechariah 13: 9; Matthew 13: 17; Romans 4: 22; 2 Corinthians 6: 16. Now the fulfilment or realization of this glorious promise, as the parallel passages indicate, is clearly a matter not only of the future but also, at least in principle, of the present. God dwells even now in His Church through the Spirit. That divine indwelling will be perfected in the new heaven and earth after the judgment day.

The same is true with respect to several symbols that occur in this section. If anyone will take the trouble to look up the parallel passages in which they are rooted, he will immediately observe that the truths indicated and the promises made affect the entire span of time during which the Church has existed on earth. They belong, in a special sense, to this entire dispensation. New Jerusalem is constantly the opponent of Babylon. The bride should always be contrasted with the harlot. Yet the final and most complete reality is not attained until after the judgment day.

1. *The new heaven and the new earth* (21: 1–8)

The first heaven and the first earth have passed away. In our imagination let us try to see this new universe. The very foundations of the earth have been subjected to the purifying fire. Every stain of sin, every scar of wrong, every trace of death, has been removed. Out of the great conflagration a new universe has been born. The word used in the original implies that it was a 'new' but not an 'other' world.[1] It is the same heaven and earth, but gloriously rejuvenated, with no weeds, thorns or thistles, and so on. Nature comes into its own; all of its poten-

[1] The original has *kainos*, not *neos*.

tialities, dormant so long, are now fully realized. The 'old' order has vanished. The universe in which the dragon, the beast, the false prophet, and the harlot were carrying out their programme of iniquity has vanished. The sea, as we now know it, is no more. At present the sea is the emblem of unrest and conflict. The roaring, raging, agitated, tempest-tossed waters, the waves perpetually engaged in combat with one another, symbolize the nations of the world in their conflict and unrest (13: 1; 17: 15). It is the sea out of which the beast rises. But in the renewed universe—the new heaven and earth—all will be peace. The heaven and the earth and the sea as they now are shall vanish. The universe is going to be gloriously rejuvenated and transformed. 'And the city, the holy one, new Jerusalem, I saw coming down out of the heaven from God, having been made ready as a bride adorned for her husband.'

This Jerusalem is called 'new' in contradistinction to the earthly, Palestinian Jerusalem. It is called 'holy' because it is separate from sin and thoroughly consecrated to God. This new and holy Jerusalem is very clearly the Church of the Lord Jesus Christ, as is also plainly evident from the fact that it is here and elsewhere called the bride, the wife of the Lamb (Is. 54: 5; Eph. 5: 32; *etc.*). Even in the Old Testament the Church is represented under the symbolism of a city (Is. 26: 1; Ps. 48; *etc.*). A city calls to our mind the concepts of permanent residence, a great number of inhabitants, safety and security, fellowship and beauty. With respect to all of these characteristics the Church—in principle even today, in perfection by and by—is like a city. We read that John saw this Holy City coming down out of heaven from God. This, too, is true with respect to both the ideal Church of the present and the Church of the future. It is always born from above. It is always the result of the transforming work of the Holy Spirit (3: 12; 21: 9 ff.; *cf.* Gal. 4: 26; Heb. 11: 10,16; 12: 22). The words 'made ready as a bride adorned for her husband' find their commentary in Revelation 19: 7.[1]

John hears a great voice out of the throne, saying:

'Behold, the tabernacle of God is with men,
And he shall tabernacle with them.
And they themselves his people shall be,
And he himself, God, with them shall be.
And he shall wipe away every tear out of their eyes;

[1] See pp. 179 ff.

And the death shall be no more;
Neither mourning, nor crying, nor pain, any more;
The old order has passed away.'

Thus, beautifully, the everlasting marriage-feast of the Lamb, Christ, and of His bride, the Church, is pictured to us.[1] It is the climax of that entire process whereby God comes to His people. So close is this eternal communion between God and His elect that He, as it were, dwells with them in one tent—His tent, the glory of His attributes (Rev. 7: 15). The Lamb is their shepherd (7: 17). God wipes every tear out of their eyes (7: 17). They are constantly worshipping Him in His sanctuary (7: 15). They sit with Him on His throne: and He sups with them (3: 20 f.; *cf.* also Jn. 17: 23; 2 Cor. 6: 18). Thus, in striking symbols, the eternal fellowship between God and His people is set forth. Negatively speaking, death shall be no more (Rev. 20: 14; 1 Cor. 15: 26); neither mourning; nor crying (Is. 25: 8; 35: 10; 51: 11) nor pain (*cf.* also Rev. 7: 16). The order of the 'first things' has passed away (2 Cor. 5: 17; Heb. 12: 27).

The apostle now hears the voice of the One sitting upon the throne, that is, God in Christ (Rev. 4: 2; 22: 1) saying, 'Behold, new am I making all things.' Only God can make new. People may vainly imagine that by means of better education, a better environment, better legislation, and a more equitable distribution of wealth they are going to usher in a new era, a golden age, the Utopia of man's ardent desire. Their dream remains a dream! Neither economic nor disarmament conferences, neither better schools nor share-the-wealth programmes are going to bring about a really golden age, a new heaven and earth or a new order. It is only God who through His Spirit makes all things new.[2] He alone can restore and renew man and the universe. He does it now, though in a very restricted sense. He is going to do it by and by when Christ returns.

We can hardly imagine that the effects of sin can ever be removed. Yet they are going to be taken away so that all things shall actually be made 'new'. To strengthen us in our faith that He who promised will really do it, we read, 'Behold!'—an imperative indicating to John that he must take to heart what he has heard, and write it down for the comfort of others, for 'these words are faithful and genuine' (*cf.* Rev. 19: 9; 22: 6). So certain is the fulfilment of this promise that the voice speaks as if it were already fulfilled (*cf.* Rev. 16: 17). In fact, as far as

[1] For the full meaning of this wedding of the Lamb, see pp. 179ff.

[2] Babylon is 'great'; Jerusalem is 'new'. See chapter x, p. 131 note 1.

John's vision is concerned, these transformations had actually taken place. He sees the new heaven and the new earth.[1] The 'water of life' which is given freely refers to eternal life, which is salvation full and free. It is the realization of all these promises (Ps. 36: 8; Joel 3: 18; Zc. 14: 8; Jn. 4: 10; Rev. 7: 17; 22: 17). Remember that this 'water' is given now to the 'thirsty' one, and in eternity, in the new heaven and earth, it will be poured fresh and full into every living being. This water always proceeds from God, who is the Fountain. The conqueror shall receive these things. In him the covenant promise, 'I will be his God, and he shall be my son', attains realization.

In principle, that promise, which, as we have shown, runs through Scripture from beginning to end like a golden thread, is realized even in this life; in perfection it is fulfilled in the next, especially in the new heaven and earth. It is the great promise, for it includes all other promises.[2] Observe the terrible contrast in verse 8; those who show the characteristics of 'the harlot' are cast into the lake of fire and brimstone and endure the second death.

2. *The new Jerusalem* (21: 9–22: 5)

But over the ruins of the harlot-city of verse 8 there appears the splendid vision of the bride-city, the city of God, Holy Jerusalem coming down out of heaven from God. It is the ideal Church of the future foreshadowed by the ideal Church of the present.

One of the seven angels who had the seven bowls comes and converses with John (*cf.* Rev. 17: 1). 'Come hither, I will show thee the bride, the wife of the Lamb.'[3] Then the angel carries John away, not literally, but 'in the Spirit' (*cf.* Rev. 1: 10; 17: 3) to a mountain great and high (*cf.* Ezk. 40: 1,2). Only when we stand on the high mountain of faith are we able to see the Church as it exists ideally. The apostle now beholds a scene of transcendent beauty and splendour. He sees a city. The angel had promised to show him the bride. So the city is the bride; the two are identical. Both indicate the Church of God.

The description of the city, as found in Revelation 21: 9–22: 5, may be summarized as follows.

a. This is a city, the Holy City, Jerusalem (21: 10,16,18). As such it is the community of men who have fellowship with God. Nothing in the entire universe is as glorious as this fellowship

[1] On the expression 'I am the Alpha and the Omega', see pp. 54 f.
[2] See the author's *The Covenant of Grace.*
[3] On this designation, see pp. 179 ff.

with God, so that He tabernacles with us and we are His own. Moreover, as the symbol of the Holy City so clearly indicates, this communion is holy and lasting and it is enjoyed by a countless multitude. Thus, the transcendent splendour of the ideal Church is symbolized. Observe, moreover, that the entire conception is eschatological: the Church of the future is described here, and also the Church of the present, mainly as a shadow of what is to come. The city here described belongs to the realm of heaven: the city is constantly coming down out of heaven. It is the work of God's sovereign grace. It belongs to the future and has a constant future reference. It 'sojourns on earth'. It is 'the community of men who live according to God and have been predestined to reign with God eternally'.[1] Jerusalem is holy and new. Babylon is 'great' and 'old'.[2]

This city, moreover, is pure gold, similar to pure glass (*cf.* Rev. 4: 6; 15: 2). This symbolizes the pure, holy, gracious and radiant character of the fellowship between God and His people. In principle, we enjoy it here and now; in perfection we shall enjoy it by and by.

Finally, this city is a perfect cube—twelve thousand furlongs in every direction.

See the beauty of the symbol first of all. Here is a city extending fourteen hundred miles in each of its three dimensions—also fourteen hundred miles upward, and all of pure, transparent, smooth, shining gold. But what does it mean?

Twelve thousand is the product of three (for the Trinity) times four (for the universe) times ten times ten times ten (for reduplicated, ultimate completeness and perfection). Therefore this number expresses the complete and perfect result of the saving power of the triune God operating in the universe. That complete and perfect result is the Church of God enjoying fellowship with God in the new universe. That communion will be 'complete and perfect' in every direction. We enjoy a foretaste of it here and now. It was foreshadowed, moreover, by the Holy of holies in the Tabernacle and in the Temple of Solomon. That, too, was a perfect cube. Here the high priest entered into fellowship with God. But in the Holy City all believers are priests as well as kings. They all enjoy this fellowship.

[1] Augustine, *De Civitate Dei*, xv. 1; *cf.* xiv. 28; W. Walker, *Great Men of the Christian Church*, pp. 63 ff.

[2] The reading favoured by AV in 21: 10 is wrong. The term 'great city' never applies to the Holy Jerusalem—always to Babylon. See chapter x, p. 131, note 1.

b. This Holy City is the Bride, the wife of the Lamb (21: 9). The symbol is fully explained in Revelation 19: 7.[1] The fact that this fellowship between God and His children is both a most intimate and abiding love-relationship, and that it is the most gloriously beautiful thing in the universe, is symbolized by this figure (*cf.* Ps. 45).

c. The Holy City has a luminary, even the glory of God in the Lamb (21: 11,23; 22: 5). The luminary or light-bearer[2] is the glory of the One sitting upon the throne (*cf.* Rev. 4: 3). The brilliance of a diamond[3] is but a faint adumbration of the glory of God's attributes as revealed in the Church of the Lord Jesus Christ. Certainly, the lamp of the Church is the Lamb (*cf.* Jn. 1: 5; 8: 12). The lamp is the Lamb because He imparts to us the true and saving knowledge of God, abiding spiritual joy, and righteousness of state with a corresponding holiness of condition. Christ, the true Light, drives away the darkness of ignorance, misery, guilt, and moral pollution. In and through Him and His work the glory of God becomes manifest in the Church. Therefore, the Holy City needs neither natural nor artificial light, neither sunlight nor lamplight (*cf.* Is. 60: 1,3,5,19,20; Zc. 14: 7). There shall be no more night. All this is true in principle now but will be seen in perfection in the new universe of the future.

d. There is no sanctuary in this city, for the Lord God, the Almighty, and the Lamb are its sanctuary (21: 22). No longer need the inhabitants go to the Tabernacle or the Temple, somewhere in the camp or in the city, in order to have fellowship with God. The radiance of God's majesty and glory, in all its fullness, fills the entire city. It is not limited to any particular place in the city. It manifests itself everywhere. No sanctuary is needed, for the fellowship of believers with their God is direct and immediate. God tabernacles with His people; they are constantly in His immediate and loving and abiding presence (*cf.* Rev. 7: 15; 21: 3; Zc. 2: 5). The prophecy of Jeremiah 3: 16 (*cf.* Je. 31: 33 ff.) which attains its anticipatory fulfilment in the new dispensation in which we are now living (*cf.* Jn. 4: 23 f.; Heb. 8: 8 ff.), becomes fully realized in the new universe.

e. New Jerusalem has a wall, great and high (21: 12,17,18). A city has a wall for protection, for safety and for security. Here

[1] See pp. 179 ff.
[2] RV mg. is correct.
[3] See our comments on Rev. 4: 3, p. 85.

the meaning of the symbol is this: the Church remains secure in its possession of communion with God. The wall is great and high (*cf.* Zc. 2: 5). Moreover, to emphasize that it is a symbolical, not a literal, wall that is meant, we read that it measured 144 cubits (in height or thickness?). It is the wall of the Church of both old and new dispensations.[1] John 10: 28 furnishes a beautiful explanation of the symbol: 'no-one shall snatch them out of my hand'. The symbol applies now; it applies in an even more glorious sense to the security of God's people in the new universe. What is more glorious than this feeling of absolute safety?

f. The wall has twelve foundations (21: 14,19,20). On these twelve foundations appear the names of the twelve apostles. The meaning is easy to grasp. It was through the witness-bearing of the twelve apostles that men were and, by means of the writings of the apostles, are brought into the blessed condition of fellowship with God. (Eph. 2: 20; 1 Cor. 3: 9.) Of this foundation Christ Jesus is the chief corner-stone. The apostles are apostles 'of the Lamb'. They proclaim Him. By means of the preaching of the apostles the variety of the splendour and brilliance of all God's attributes shines forth. That is, in all probability, the meaning of the precious stones which adorn the twelve foundations (*cf.* Is. 54: 11). The manifold wisdom of God is revealed in the Church through the preaching of the Word whenever that Word is applied to the heart by the Holy Spirit (*cf.* Eph. 3: 10).

g. The city has twelve gates (21: 12,13,21,25,27; 22: 14,15; *cf.* Ezk. 43: 1; 48: 31–34; Rev. 22: 14). In other words, there is—from the standpoint of the new heaven and earth we should say there has been—abundant opportunity to enter into this glorious and wonderful fellowship with God. Open gates symbolize opportunities to enter. We enter into this glorious communion by means of God-given faith in God's promises. Every gate is a pearl. If we remember that a twenty-grain pearl is not quite as large as an ordinary marble, then these pearls which John saw in the vision must have been amazing both for size and beauty, and the child of God who, by means of faith in the promises, has entered into the city says, 'Indeed every gate is a pearl.' On the gates are written the names of the twelve tribes of Israel, for the city is the dwelling-place of the true Israel, the redeemed Church (*cf.* Rev. 7: 14). There are

[1] See our explanation of Rev. 7: 4.

three gates for each direction (*cf.* Gn. 28: 14; Is. 54: 3); the Church is gathered out of all the nations. At the gates are twelve angels. Therefore those who have the characteristics of the harlot[1] and her allies cannot enter. These unclean and abominable persons shall not enter the city. They remain outside. Only those whose names are written in the Lamb's book of life can enter (*cf.* Rev. 3: 5). But let no-one despair, for the gates are never shut. Shut gates symbolize not only darkness, night and danger but also lack of opportunity to enter. Now, throughout this entire age there is (and again from the standpoint of the new heaven and earth we should say there has been) abundant opportunity to enter by faith into the blessed fellowship with God.

h. The city has avenues of pure gold, transparent as glass (21: 21). Every gate is the door to an avenue, and the city is full of beautiful avenues, avenues of pure gold, for they symbolize a glorious truth. These avenues indicate that there is abundant opportunity for communication with the throne. There is ease of access to the rivers of life and to the trees of life.

i. The city has rivers of waters of life, bright as crystal, flowing from the throne of God and the Lamb (22: 1). Along the side of each avenue runs a river. The avenue and the river are separated only by a park (see section *j.* below). This river is the river of life for it symbolizes eternal life, salvation full and free, the gift of God's sovereign grace. And what is life but fellowship with God? (*Cf.* Jn. 17: 3; see also Ezk. 47: 1 ff.; Jn. 4: 10; 7: 38 and our explanation of Rev. 7: 17; 21: 6.) Observe that this river proceeds 'out of' the throne of God and of the Lamb. It does not flow 'by' the throne of God, as a beautiful popular hymn has it. Let us change the 'by' into 'from' and sing the hymn! This is not a point of minor importance, for the point of the symbolism hinges on this very question. When we say that the river of grace and life proceeds 'out of' or 'from' the throne of God and the Lamb, we emphasize the fact that our salvation was brought about by the sovereign will of God and was merited for us by the redemptive blood of Christ. To Him be all the glory. Observe the abundance and the holy character of this life: the river is full of water, and the water is crystal clear. Sin shall not mar our fellowship with God. This symbol, too, applies in principle here and now but in perfection there and then.

[1] For these characteristics of the harlot, see Rev. 17: 4–6; 18: 3,9; 19: 2.

j. Between the river and the avenue there is a paradise, a park or garden, full of trees of life (22: 1–3a). We translate this passage as follows: 'Between its avenue on this side and its river on that side was the tree of life bearing fruit twelve times, yielding its fruit every month; and the leaves of the tree were for the healing of the nations. And there shall be nothing accursed any more.'

First, let us take in the picture. The term 'tree of life' is collective, just like 'avenue' and 'river'. The idea is not that there is just one single tree. No, there is an entire park: whole rows of trees alongside the river, between the river and the avenue. This is true with respect to all the avenues of the city. The city is full of parks (*cf.* Rev. 2: 7). Appreciate, therefore, this wonderful truth: the city is full of rivers of life. It is also full of parks containing trees of life. These trees, moreover, are full of fruit. They bear fruit very regularly every month. Even the leaves of these trees are for healing. Taken together, all these items symbolize the superabundant character of our salvation, an absolutely full measure of most blessed and ever-abiding communion with God for all the inhabitants of the Holy City.

Surely, it is a very striking fact that according to this symbolism the park or garden is in the city. Reflect on this for a moment: the garden of abundance right in the heart of the city. The city, as has been indicated, symbolizes among other things, multitudes of people. Especially is this true with respect to New Jerusalem which extends for a distance of twelve thousand furlongs in every direction. The city, then, symbolizes a great crowd; it suggests many needs and desires and a great 'demand'. But where is the 'supply' going to come from? The garden symbolizes supply in abundance. But man has been driven out of the garden. Ever since that day the city, as it were, has been crying for the garden and the garden for the city. Finally, here in the New Jerusalem, the garden is inside the city. There is an abundance of eternal life and salvation for all the citizens. Return to Revelation 18: 22[1] and notice the contrast. Throughout this entire present age the leaves of the tree are—by and by we shall say 'have been'—for the healing of the nations. Eternal life heals the scars of sin and misery. The term 'tree' of life is really 'wood' of life. It is the term used to indicate the cross of Christ (Acts 5: 30; 10: 39; *etc.*). (*Cf.* Gal. 3: 13: 'Cursed is every one who hangs on a tree (wood).')

[1] See p. 177.

By means of the cross Christ merited eternal life for us, and in the New Jerusalem that tree of the cross is not accursed (*cf.* also Ezk. 47: 12; Rev. 2: 7). There is nothing accursed.

k. In this city is the throne of God and the Lamb (22: 3,4). In the Church of God His majesty and sovereignty is revealed. The 'throne' symbolizes sovereignty. Because of this the river proceeds out of the throne (see section *i.* above). Of course, that sovereignty of God is everywhere revealed, both inside and outside the city. But in the city it manifests itself as a sovereignty of love not of wrath. For the citizens joyfully obey God's will. His will is their desire. They see His face: they enjoy His favour (*cf.* Ps. 17: 15; 42: 2; Mt. 5: 8). They worship Him (*cf.* Rev. 7: 15). His name is on their foreheads,[1] for He openly acknowledges them as His very own, and they joyfully confess Him as their Lord. Thus, they reign for ever and ever in the new universe. All these symbols apply, in principle, to this present age; and in perfection to the new universe.

l. Who are the inhabitants of this city? (21: 7,12,24,27; 22: 3, 14). The citizens are the conquerors; the true Israel; the elect from every nation (*cf.* Rev. 7: 9), including even kings; those whose names are written in the Lamb's book of life (*cf.* Rev. 3: 5); those who worship Him; the sealed multitude (*cf.* Rev. 14: 1).

3. *Conclusion* (22: 6–21)

In these closing words there is little that requires special comment. For an explanation of the various symbols mentioned in this closing paragraph we refer the reader to all the preceding pages of this book.

First, the angel who showed John these visions attests the genuine character of the Apocalypse (*cf.* Rev. 1: 1; 19: 9; 21: 5). The book is, indeed, of divine origin. The God of the spirits of the prophets is the Author; the spirits of the prophets are under His constant guidance and control. For the expression 'the things which must shortly come to pass' see Revelation 1: 1; 4: 1.[2] The angel quotes Christ's own words: 'Behold, I come quickly' (see Rev. 1: 3,7).

Now John bears witness: 'And I, John, the one hearing and seeing these things'. Again the apostle is about to worship the angel, with the same result as in Revelation 19: 10.[3]

[1] *Cf.* our explanation of Rev. 14: 1, p. 151.
[2] P. 51, note 3; p. 82 and note 1.
[3] *Q.v.*, p. 181.

Continuing, the angel tells John not to seal up the words of the prophecy of this book; for the time is at hand. The prophecies begin to be fulfilled at once (see Rev. 1: 1). There follows a very serious warning. If we bear in mind that our English word 'let' may mean either one of two things, we shall have no difficulty in explaining verse 11. First of all, there is a 'let' of positive exhortation, for example, 'Let the wicked forsake his way'. Here the wicked is urged to forsake his evil way. This 'let' always comes first. But, suppose that in spite of all earnest pleadings, admonitions, invitations, and judgments, the wicked refuses to obey and to accept the water of life freely. What then? Then there is another 'let'. It is not the 'let' of positive exhortation, but the 'let' of withdrawal. God says, as it were 'let him be'.[1] It is this second 'let' that is meant here in verse 11. For the wicked it is a terrible 'let'. We can, therefore, paraphrase the verse as follows: 'Do not hinder the man who, in spite of all pleadings, admonitions, exhortations, *etc.*, has completely hardened himself in his wickedness: do not hinder him from continuing in his unrighteousness, neither hinder the filthy one from continuing in his filth. Similarly, do not hinder the righteous and holy person from continuing in the way of sanctification.' In this case, of course, the 'let' may even be taken in the sense of positive exhortation. The original actually allows the two-fold interpretation of 'let' which we have indicated (*cf.* Mt. 13: 20).

The angel again quotes Jesus: 'Behold, I come quickly; and my reward is with me.' This, in reality, is a tender admonition. It amounts to saying 'Do not become hardened in unbelief, but repent, for at my coming I will immediately reward all men.' Everyone then receives in accordance with his works (see Rev. 14: 14 ff.; 20: 11 ff.).[2] The promises and also the threats of Christ have eternal significance, for He is the Alpha and the Omega. That is the connection between verses 12 and 13.

We reach the seventh and final beatitude. Some translations have: 'Blessed are they that keep the commandments.' But the best reading is: 'Blessed are those washing their robes.' Every person carries about with him a robe. He is always weaving it, for his every thought, word, and deed enters into it. That robe is splashed, dirty and altogether filthy (*cf.* Zc. 3: 3). In the entire world, moreover, there is no power that can clean it.

[1] See 1 Jn. 5: 16 and our explanation of Rev. 15: 8, p. 160.

[2] For the meaning of verse 14 see pp. 54, 57 f., 64, 77.

As far as this robe is concerned, all earthly detergents are useless. They are of no avail. Read Jeremiah 2: 22, a very striking and beautiful passage. That robe is your character. God, however, has provided a remedy. It is He who says: 'Blessed are those washing their robes.' To wash your robe means to have recourse to the cleansing fountain of the blood of Jesus Christ. That blood not only removes all guilt, but also has merited for us the purifying and sanctifying Spirit and we must have recourse to it constantly.[1] The one who washes his robe in the cleansing fountain receives, by God's sovereign grace, the right to come to the tree of life (*cf.* 2: 7; 22: 2), and may enter by means of the gates into the city. Outside the city are all those who have the characteristics of the harlot (*cf.* Rev. 17: 2,4; *etc.*).

In this final section of the book there are three witnesses. The angel is the first witness and John is the second. The third witness is Jesus Himself who attests the genuine character of the book and its divine origin. 'I, Jesus, sent my angel to testify to you these things for the churches' (see Rev. 1: 1). The Apocalypse is intended for all the churches throughout all the centuries. Not John but Jesus Christ Himself is the Author of this book. He is the exalted One, being both the root of David, so that David owes his origin, fame and position to him, and the offspring of David[2] (*cf.* Ps. 110: 1; Mt. 22: 42–45; Is. 11: 1; 53: 2; *etc.*). He is the divine and human Saviour. This glorious, exalted Saviour is the Author of the book of Revelation. He is the bright star, the morning star.[3] This star is the symbol of royalty (*cf.* Nu. 24: 17).

Christ has promised to come quickly (*cf.* Rev. 22: 7,12) and the bride, that is, the Church, responds by saying, 'Be coming.' It is an ardent prayer to which the bride is moved by the Holy Spirit. Spirit and bride always work together (*cf.* Rom. 8: 16). They are constantly saying, 'Be coming.' This, be it noted, is a present imperative. It refers not only to the actual event, namely, the final coming of our Lord, but also the whole course of history that still precedes that event. It means, 'Carry out thy plan in history with a view to thy coming.' That divine plan includes the principles of moral government revealed under the symbolism of lampstands, seals, trumpets, conflict with the dragon and his allies, bowls of wrath, the

[1] *Cf.* p. 113.
[2] See p. 90.
[3] See pp. 72 f.

wedding of the Lamb, *etc*. In and through all these means and agencies cause Thy purpose to be realized and speed Thy coming! Whoever hears this prophecy when it is read in the Church—and whoever reads it—let him add his individual voice to the grand chorus of voices; let him say, 'Be coming.' Here let the reader pause for a moment. Let there be a moment of silence similar to that which precedes that glorious, final 'Hallelujah' in the Hallelujah Chorus of Handel's *Messiah*.

Then listen to the voice from the throne. It is the pleading voice of the Master, His tender, final invitation:

'And he that is athirst, let him come: he that will, let him take the water of life freely.'

The emphasis is on the word *freely*. Glorious sovereign grace! This is the love of God, so touching and tender, which is addressed here to all those who have been made conscious of the need of living water. Let them not hesitate. Let them come. Let them take. It costs *them* nothing. He paid the price. So let them come, take and drink.

Because this book of Revelation is so transcendently glorious, so divine, for God Himself is the Author, let no-one who hears or reads this book add or subtract a word. Let him not call this writing spurious. Let him not say that its meaningful passages are interpolations. Let him not deny its divinely inspired character. Let him not say that it is hardly worth studying. Let him not ridicule this book, filled with invitations and promises. If he refuses to heed this warning, the plagues written in this book shall be added to him. God shall take away his part from the tree of life and the Holy City.

Christ answers the ardent prayer of the Church for His coming by saying: 'Yea, I am coming quickly.' Let us, therefore, heed His warnings. John's heart is filled with rapture. His soul is consumed with longing. His eye attempts to pierce the clouds. In an ecstasy of love, he exclaims, 'Amen, come, Lord Jesus.'

BIBLIOGRAPHY

Abbott, E. A., *Johannine Grammar*, 1906.
Alford, H., *The Greek Testament*, IV, 1861.
Andrews, S. J., *Christianity and Anti-Christianity in their Final Conflict*, 1898.
Ante-Nicene Fathers, edited by the Rev. A. Roberts and J. Donaldsen, American edition arranged by A. C. Coxe, 1885.

Barnes, A., *Notes Explanatory and Practical on the Book of Revelation.*
Beckwith, I. T., *The Apocalypse of St. John*, 1919.
Benson, E. W., *The Apocalypse, An Introductory Study of the Revelation of St. John the Divine*, 1900.
Berkhof, L., *Reformed Dogmatics*, 1937 edn.
Vicarious Atonement Through Christ, 1936.
'Christ in the Light of Eschatology', in *Princeton Theological Review*, XXV, 1927.
New Testament Introduction, 1915.
Class Lectures on Rev. 2 and part of 3.
Class Lectures on Premillennialism.
Beyschlag, W., *New Testament Theology*, 1896 edn.
Blackstone, W. E., *Jesus is Coming*,[3] 1908.
Booth, A. E., *The Course of Time*, Key to chart.
Brookes, J. H., *Israel and the Church.* Also *Maranatha*, 1889.
Brown, C. E., *The Hope of His Coming*, 1908.
Brown, D., *Christ's Second Coming, Will It Be Premillennial?*, 1849.
The Structure of the Apocalypse, 1891.
Burton, A. H., *The Apocalypse Expounded.*
Burton, E. D., *Syntax of the Moods and Tenses in New Testament Greek*, 1898.

Calvin, J., *Institutes of The Christian Religion*, tr. John Allen, 1928 edn.
Charles, R. H., *Revelation* (*International Critical Commentary*), 2 vols., 1920.
Eschatology, Hebrew, Jewish, and Christian, 1899.
Clark, D. S., *The Message from Patmos.*
Cook, C. C., *God's Book Speaking for Itself*, 1890.
Cowles, H., *The Revelation of John*, 1890.
Crafer, T. W., 'The Revelation of St. John the Divine', in Gore's *New Commentary*, 1928.
Crosby, H., *The Seven Churches of Asia.*

Davidson, S., *The Doctrine of the Last Things*, 1882.
Dean, J. T., *The Book of Revelation*, 1915.
Deissman, A., *Light from the Ancient East*, 1923.
Driver, S. R., *The Book of Daniel.*

Eckman, S. P., *When Christ Comes Again*, 1918.
Edersheim, A., *The Life and Times of Jesus*, 1907.
The Temple.
Ellicott, C. J., *The Revelation* (*Handy Commentary*).

Elliott, E. B., *Horae Apocalipticae*, 1851 edn.
Erdman, C. R., *The Return of Christ*, 1922.

Fairweather, W., *The Background of the Gospels*, 1920.
From the Exile to the Advent, 1901.
Frost, H. W., *The Second Coming of Christ*, 1934.

Gaebelein, A. C., *The Harmony of the Prophetic Word*, 1907.
Gebhardt, H., *The Doctrine of the Apocalypse*, tr. S. Jefferson, 1865.
Godet, F., *Commentary on the Gospel of John*, 1883.
Goodspeed, E. J., 'The Book with Seven Seals', *Journal of Biblical Literature*, XXII, 1902–1905, pp. 70–74.
Gray, J., *Commentary on the Apocalypse* (*Christian Workers' Commentary*).
A Textbook on Prophecy, 1918.
Prophecy and the Lord's Return, 1917.

Haldeman, I. M., *The Kingdom of God*, 1931.
Harris, E. L., 'Some Ruined Cities of Asia-Minor', *The National Geographic Magazine*, Dec. 1908.
Hastings, J., *Encyclopaedia of Religion and Ethics*, 1913–1922.
Hengstenberg, E. W., *The Revelation of St. John*, 1851.
Hodge, C., *Systematic Theology*, 1893.
Hosford, B. F., 'Martyrdom in the Apocalypse', *Bibliotheca Sacra*, XXIII, pp. 309–333.

Ironside, H. A., *Lectures on The Revelation*, 1930.

Kellogg, S. H., *Are Premillennialists Right?*, 1903.

Lange, J. P., *The Revelation of John* (*Commentary of the Holy Scriptures*), X of the New Testament, 1874.
Larkin, C. D., *Dispensational Truth*, 1920.
Lenski, R. C. H., *Interpretation of St. John's Revelation*, 1935.

Mackie, G. M., *Bible Manners and Customs*, 1898.
Mains, G. P., *What Do the Prophets Say?*, 1920.
Masselink, W., *Why Thousand Years?*, 1930.
Mauro, P., *The Patmos Visions*, 1925; see also the revision of 1933.
The Gospel of the Kingdom, 1928.
The Number of Man, 1909.
McKnight, W. J., 'The Letter to the Laodiceans', *The Biblical Review*, XVI, 1931, pp. 519–535.
McKonkey, J. H., *Lectures on The Revelation*, 1928.
Milligan, E. M., *Is the Kingdom Age at Hand?*, 1924.
Milligan, W., *The Book of Revelation* (*Expositor's Bible*), 1889.
Discussions on the Apocalypse, 1893.
Moffatt, J., *The Revelation of St. John the Divine*.
The New Testament, A New Translation.
Introduction to the Literature of the New Testament.
Morris, L., 'The Book of Revelation', *The New Bible Dictionary*, 1962.
Morris, S. L., *The Drama of Christianity*, 1928.

Orr, J., *The Christian View of God and the World*, 1897.

Peake, A. S., *The Revelation of St. John*, 1920.
Pieters, A., *The Lamb, The Woman, and the Dragon*, 1937.
Plummer, A., *The Book of Revelation* (*Pulpit Commentary*).
Plumptre, E. H., *The Epistles to the Seven Churches*.

Ramsay, W., *The Letters to the Seven Churches of Asia*.
Robertson, A. T., *The Minister and His Greek New Testament*, 1923.
Syllabus for New Testament Study, 1923, esp. pp. 265 ff.
A Grammar of the Greek New Testament in the Light of Historical Research, 1923 edn.
An Introduction to the Textual Criticism of the New Testament, 1925.
Rutgers, W. H., *Premillennialism in America*, 1930.

Sadler, M. F., *The Revelation of St. John the Divine*, 1894.
Sanders, H. A., 'The Number of the Beast in Revelation', *Journal of Biblical Literature*, XXXVII, 1916–1918, pp. 95–99.
Savage, J. A., *The Voice of the Watchman*.
Sayce, A. H., *The Races of the Old Testament*, 1925.
Schaff, P., *History of the Church*, 1920–1923.
Schilder, K., *Christ in His Suffering*, 1938.
Christ on Trial, 1939.
Scofield, C. I., *What Do The Prophets Say?*, 1918.
Scofield Reference Bible.
Scott, C. A., *Revelation* (*The New Century Bible*).
Seiss, J., *Lectures on the Book of Revelation*, 1900.
Shedd, W. G. T., *Dogmatic Theology*, 1888 edn.
Silver, J. F., *The Lord's Return*, 1914.
Snowden, J. H., *The Coming of the Lord*, 1919.
Stevens, G. B., *The Theology of the New Testament*, 1925.
The Johannine Theology, 1894.
Stonehouse, N. B., *The Apocalypse in the Ancient Church*, 1929.
Stroh, G., *God's World Program*, 1924.
Stuart, M., *Commentary on the Apocalypse*, 1854.
'The Number of the Beast in the Apocalypse', *Bibliotheca Sacra*, O, pp. 332 ff.
'The White Stone of the Apocalypse', *Bibliotheca Sacra*, O, pp. 461 ff.
Swete, H. B., *The Apocalypse of St. John*, 1907.

Taylor, W. M., *Daniel the Beloved*.
Tenney, M. C., *New Testament Survey*, Revised edn., 1961.
Thayer, J. H., *A Greek–English Lexicon of the New Testament*, 1889.
Thompson, F. C., *The New Chain Reference Bible*, 1934 edn.
Trench, R. C., *Commentary on the Epistles to the Seven Churches in Asia*, 1861.
Synonyms of the New Testament, 1915 edn.
Turner, C. W. M., *Outline Studies in The Revelation*, 1917.

Vos, G., *The Teaching of Jesus Concerning the Kingdom of God and the Church*, 1903.
The Pauline Eschatology.
Outline Notes on New Testament Biblical Theology.
'Pauline Eschatology and Chiliasm', *The Princeton Theological Review*, 1911.

Waldegrave, S., *New Testament Millennarianism*, 1855.
Warfield, B. B., *Textual Criticism of the New Testament*, 1889.
Biblical Doctrines, XVI, 'The Millennium and the Apocalypse', 1929.
West, N., *The Thousand Years in Both Testaments*, 1880.
Westcott, B. F., and Hort, F. J. A., *The New Testament in the Original Greek*, 1921 edn.
Wimberly, C. F., *Behold the Morning*, 1916.
Wishart, C. F., *The Book of Day*, 1935.
Wijngaarden, M. J., *The Future of the Kingdom in Prophecy and Fulfilment*, 1934.

Young, R., *Analytical Concordance to the Bible*, Revised edn.

TOPICAL INDEX